DATE DUE

JUL 31			
JAN 26			
JUL 30			
GAYLORD			PRINTED IN U.S.A.

Notes on the LITERATURE of the PIANO

Da Capo Press Music Reprint Series

GENERAL EDITOR

FREDERICK FREEDMAN

VASSAR COLLEGE

Notes on the
LITERATURE
of the PIANO

By ALBERT LOCKWOOD

With a new Preface by
FREDERICK FREEDMAN
Vassar College

𝄞 DA CAPO PRESS · NEW YORK · 1968

A Da Capo Press Reprint Edition

Library of Congress Catalog Card Number 67-30400

PREFACE

The reappearance of this work may arouse the average musician's curiosity on at least two counts: first, he may not have heard of the work; second, he may not have heard of its author. Little wonder on either count, although extenuating circumstances explain both.

Notes on the Literature of the Piano was published posthumously by the University of Michigan Press at a time (1940) when university presses infrequently published works in the field of music. Perhaps more significant, the release of this work was overshadowed by the great depression and the approaching clouds of World War II. As a result, an extremely alert and comprehensive work became obscured, and musicians in general, and pianists in particular, were deprived of an important contribution by a man possessed of exceptional knowledge, experience, perception, and wit.

Albert Lockwood evidently was not widely known, if one is to use as a guide the small number of biographical citations in standard music reference works. Curiously, in works pertaining to piano music and pianists, he appears even less frequently. In spite of this limited recognition, however, other sources indicate that he was an excellent pianist and commanded much respect.

Music seems to have been a family tradition, as both Albert (1871-1933) and his brother, Samuel (1879–), began their music training early in their birthplace, Troy, New York, and in neighboring Albany. Like so many Americans of the last century, Albert went to Europe to further his training and commence a career. He studied at the Leipzig Conservatory for six years and graduated with a prize. He then spent three years in Vienna studying with Theodor Leschetizky, and six months in Florence with Giuseppe Buonamici, before making his debut in Paris in 1895. He performed in London and New York in 1896, and then went on to tour the United States, Canada, and Europe. From 1900 until his death at sixty-two, in 1933, he headed the piano department in the School of Music at the University of Michigan in Ann Arbor. His brother, Samuel, who prepared *Notes on the Literature of the Piano* for publication, headed the violin department at the same institution and, during most

v

of this time, directed the University orchestra as well. It must have been inter-esting, indeed, to witness the "brother act" when Samuel conducted while Albert executed one of the many piano concerti in his repertory.

Much of the material for the present volume undoubtedly was gathered while the author prepared his numerous "historical" concerts. During the first twenty-six years of his stay at the University of Michigan, he performed sev-eral hundred times, and a detailed count shows that he played more than three hundred different compositions. That the University was extremely proud to have so exceptional a musician on their faculty, is suggested by the following excerpt from the School of Music catalog:

> A catholicity of taste and interests, a phenomenal repertoire and a pianism of the first rank are combined in Mr. Lockwood to such a degree that the range of his attainments, both as player and teacher, is well-nigh unique. It is not too much to say that no interpreter was ever more fully in sym-pathy and conversant with every style, period, and composer; or more intuitive, sympathetic, and ingenious in solving the problems of every individual student.

In reading this volume, one must take into consideration that Lockwood did his final work on the manuscript some thirty-five years ago; in this con-text, the work divulges some rather fascinating viewpoints, ideas, and opin-ions. The author's views and remarks on a number of relatively obscure composers for the piano, for instance, would surprise more than one musicolo-gist today; for, despite his lack of scholarship in the modern musicological sense, he demonstrates considerable astuteness in evaluating the works of some eighteenth- and early nineteenth-century composers who have been overlooked by too many pianists of the post-World War II generation. Thus, his observations on the keyboard music of Charles-Henri Alkan (1813–1888), Karl Philipp Emanuel Bach (1714–1788), Muzio Clementi (1752–1832), Johann Ladislaus Dussek (1760–1812), Johann Nepomuk Hummel (1778–1837), Adolf Jensen (1837–1879), and Ignaz Moscheles (1794–1870), should prove rather enlightening even in this age of musical scholarship. Lockwood's comments and evaluations are of particular interest, since he never had the good fortune to know some of these composers' works in the well-edited and critical editions which are now so readily available to pianists.

Examination of the table of contents reveals a surprising number of little-known composers, as well as the unexpected omission of some "greats." In this apparent imbalance, however, Lockwood really performed an important service: he took the trouble to study the piano works of many of his contemporaries, primarily composers active from around 1860 to 1920, and has provided present-day pianists with at least one enlightened (not infrequently uncomplimentary!) opinion. This is not to say that one should trust Lockwood completely; but at least his remarks offer some guidance to pianists who wish to explore the possibilities offered by the works of these often-neglected composers, among whom are numbered Anton Arensky (1861–1906), Frank Bridge (1879–1941), Ferruccio Busoni (1866–1924), Ernst von Dohnányi (1877–1960), Alexander Glazunov (1865–1936), Benjamin Godard (1849–1895), Eugene Goossens (1893–1962), John Ireland (1879–1962), Anatol Liadov (1855–1914), Sergey Liapunov (1859–1924), Nikolai Medtner (1880–1951), Moritz Moszkowski (1854–1925), Selim Palmgren (1878–1951), Max Reger (1873–1916), Julius Röntgen (1855–1932), Florent Schmitt (1870–1958), Cyril Scott (1879–   ), and Christian Sinding (1856–1941).

Lockwood's opinions of these men are interesting and occasionally amusing. He remarks of Florent Schmitt:

> This voluminous composer of salon music is unnecessary to the happiness of pianists. The music is pallid and unconvincing.

He reminds us that Sinding found it

> . . . impossible . . . to escape from the nightmare grip in which the arpeggios and scales held him. He remains more or less unknown. His work displays good taste and invention, [yet] . . . he does not always succeed in avoiding respectable dullness.

Lockwood recognized Nikolai Medtner's talents earlier than many of his contemporaries:

> Medtner is primarily a man of ideas. . . . He is a direct descendant of the great tree of Bach, Beethoven, and Brahms . . . and one may well watch his career with interest.

History, as of the present time, has decided that Medtner was a Russian composer of German persuasion possessed of a strong flair for the romantic and post-romantic traditions; and in this context, he has been buried in the avalanche of twentieth-century composers whose works come closer to the Bartók, Hindemith, Schoenberg, or Stravinsky traditions. But the post-World War II generation has produced such a huge quantity of pallid, turgid, and "neo-classic" composition that it may very well be an appropriate moment to take a fresh look at Medtner!

Another composer whose cause Lockwood unhesitatingly championed was his direct contemporary, Alexander Scriabin:

> More than with any other composer of recent times the pianist has to concern himself with Scriabin. His figure looms too large and is still too close to be a subject for ripe judgment, but a man who wrote exclusively for the piano . . . and who imagined a new harmony and a new emotional outlook deserves profound study from the pianist who is deeply concerned with his art.

During the decades following his death in 1915, Scriabin was given considerable attention, but little has been written about him during the past quarter of a century. Indeed, were it not for the long-playing record, and especially the efforts of Vladimir Horowitz, Scriabin might be almost unknown today.

That certain composers receive special attention in *Notes on the Literature of the Piano* may surprise some readers, since their connection with pianism is not generally considered to be of substantial importance. This is especially true of Glazunov, who is better known as an orchestral and chamber music composer. Godard, the French composer, remains virtually unknown today, but his operas and chamber pieces are occasionally recalled. Sir Eugene Goossens, a leading conductor, also comes to mind as a composer of orchestral and chamber works. Liapunov is better remembered as a folk-song collector than as composer.

Had Lockwood lived another twenty-five years, it is quite likely that he would have been encouraged by the musicological activity that has developed, and particularly by the important new practical editions resulting from modern scholarly research. One is reminded of Ralph Kirkpatrick's reevaluation of Domenico Scarlatti; the discovery and publication of many keyboard works by Padre Antonio Soler, with editions prepared by Padre Samuel Rubio, Frederick Marvin, and others; the fresh and important new editions of works by K. P. E. Bach, J. Haydn, W. A. Mozart, and Chopin, to name but a few.

Were he writing in 1967, Lockwood undoubtedly would have given greater attention to such composers as Carlos Chávez, Aaron Copland, Henry Cowell, Roy Harris, Paul Hindemith, Charles Ives, Ernst Krenek, Darius Milhaud, Francis Poulenc, Arnold Schoenberg, Roger Sessions, Igor Stravinsky, and Ernst Toch; he also would have given space to composers who have been extremely active during the past three decades, including Samuel Barber, Elliott Carter, Alberto Ginastera, Aram Khatchaturian, Benjamin Lees, Vincent Persichetti, Walter Piston, Dmitri Shostakovitch; and his appraisal of Béla Bartók and Sergey Prokofiev might be very different.

Notes on the Literature of the Piano may dismay some pianists of the younger generation by the inclusion of certain oddities, fashions, and eccentricities which have disappeared in our time, among them the use of such phrases as "Bach's *Well-Tempered Clavichord,*" which now has become a gaucherie. Similarly, the innumerable listings of piano transcriptions and arrangements of non-piano music by such worthies as Charles-Henri Alkan, Ferruccio Busoni, Leopold Godowsky, Percy Grainger, and Franz Liszt, are clearly a vestige of the day when crystal sets and Edison cylinders were in vogue. The section (pp. 49–56) on *clavécinists* suffers from unscholarly traditions of the nineteenth century, and the student should be forewarned. It is also curious to see the name of the great Baroque Dutch organist spelled "Zweelinck" when one is accustomed to "Sweelinck."

These minor limitations notwithstanding, Lockwood's work should prove extremely worthwhile to the pianist and to the piano pedagogue as a source of information regarding both the standard piano literature and the more obscure repertory of the nineteenth century, a repertory which has not yet been explored by the present generation of musicians.

Vassar College
October 1967

Frederick Freedman

NOTES ON THE

LITERATURE of the PIANO

NOTES
ON THE
LITERATURE
of the PIANO

By ALBERT LOCKWOOD

ANN ARBOR: UNIVERSITY OF MICHIGAN PRESS
LONDON: HUMPHREY MILFORD, OXFORD UNIVERSITY PRESS
1940

PRINTED IN THE
UNITED STATES OF AMERICA
BY EVANS-WINTER-HEBB INC., DETROIT, MICHIGAN

NOTE

THE *Notes on the Literature of the Piano* is a posthumous work. My brother rewrote it several times, but in the end he left not only hundreds of items to be checked but a few composers to be evaluated and lists of their works to be completed. Among his memoranda I found, for example, such items as these: "Look up Zolotarev. Look up Fantasia for two pianos by N. Borezowsky. B. Wagenaar? De Kontski? Mention Sibelius, the two Scharwenkas. Coleridge Taylor forgotten in British list."

It seems to me that in view of the foregoing statement no contemporary composer can take offense at being omitted. Having done what I can to correct slips and to complete the statistics, without endeavoring to add any new material, I prefer to leave the book as it stands rather than to risk the introduction of comments based on a degree of background and vision necessarily inferior to those of the author.

SAMUEL P. LOCKWOOD

CONTENTS

CONTENTS

INTRODUCTION

THIS book is not intended as an encyclopedia of the piano literature, although it may be stated at the outset that I have endeavored to mention every piano work of importance, even if it no longer appeals to the taste of today. To the compositions of this class which have been overlooked I offer apology. My purpose has been to indicate more or less definitely the inexhaustible treasures, the key to which piano students are supposedly endeavoring to acquire through their technical studies.

The average student's ignorance of the extent of these treasures is perhaps not surprising. The literature is vast, and the player who does not read and readily assimilate hesitates before the serious step of exploration. He prefers to learn what he has heard played, since he thus knows beforehand whether he likes it or not.

Not only students, in the sense of pupils, but many teachers are guilty of a certain mental indolence and consequent lack of scholarship in the matter of becoming acquainted with the piano literature. If this book will guide taste and stimulate the spirit of adventure, the inclination to browse in strange pastures, and the aesthetic curiosity indispensable to artistic growth, it will achieve its aim.

The sources used in compiling the material were: Karl F. Weitzmann, *A History of Pianoforte Playing and Pianoforte Literature;* Oscar Bie, *Das Klavier und seine Meister;* Adolf Prosniz, *Handbuch der Klavierliteratur; Grove's Dictionary of Music and Musicians;* the catalogues of the publishing houses; and the experience of a lifetime devoted to the subject.

The books by Weitzmann and Bie complicate the study of the literature by occupying themselves with such matters as the lives of the composers and the virtuosi and the development of the instrument, all very interesting but for our purpose extraneous matter. There is too little comment in them on the music itself, and the compositions are listed in a casual way which gives the student little idea of their relative values. Prosniz is more single-minded than is Weitzmann, though he also gives short biographical sketches and includes all chamber music in which the piano takes part. He lists nearly nine hundred writers. His book, with which the thorough student must be familiar, is by far the best one on the subject, but it suffers from two disadvantages: it is too comprehensive for the average student, and it was published last in 1904, thus giving no account of the interesting movements since that year. It is in German, and I know of no translation. Of the small amount of modern music written up to that time it gives startlingly uncomprehending, not to say inimical, criticism. On the other hand the list of what one might call pre-first-period music is most valuable for those who want it.

Another great source is Hofmeister's monumental catalogue published yearly in Germany since 1844. This lists not merely piano music but all music published in Central Europe and is thus obviously only for the special student or research worker.

The lack of proportion in these books and the absence in them of any mention of modern music seem to leave room for this work. While it offers an evaluation of this music in a modest manner, it tries at the same time to avoid a course taken by some of the other books, which give a line to the Prélude, Choral, and Fugue" of César Franck and devote whole paragraphs to obviously unimportant pieces.

The question of the method of determining the importance of a piece is inevitably unanswerable. From whose point of view shall one judge? Good early-period, classic, salon, modern, dance, and atonal music (if that word can be adequately defined) exists, and there is also bad music of all the periods and styles. The question being subjective, each one must solve it for himself. Although I hope that no work of first-class value is omitted, I have included many pieces whose value is doubtful or whose appeal is small or personal.

In the much debated domain of American music I have begged the question and have contented myself with giving a list of what seems important, omitting comment. If someone would define "American," one might possibly say something about it.

Since there is no yardstick, logic, algebra, or litmus paper to gauge the quality of a work of art, I offer no apology on this score. As in poetry and prose we may also in music distinguish between journalism (good reading matter) and literature (of enduring greatness). In the greatest music, the true literature, one must have a feeling of inevitability and of the composer's ecstasy in composing, but one also demands a stern, unyielding intelligence. There are many kinds of ecstasy. Was not Bach a religious, Wagner a sensuous, Chopin a romantic, and dear old Czerny an industrious ecstatic? It would appear that even second-raters have their more puny ecstasies.

Conversely, the music that corresponds to good reading matter is not to be decried because it is not ecstatic. Were we to live exclusively on ecstasy we should weary of it, and a list which excluded the "good reading matter" would make this book far less extensive. These compositions occupy an important place in our lives, bridge gaps between ecstasies, depict our lesser emotions, and, for teaching purposes, save wear and tear on the great peaks of the literature.

Composers are usually the worst judges of music, for they inevitably have the strong personal bias and individuality indispensable to their self-expression. A few examples of the judgments of composers of the past bring out some amusing opinions. Rubinstein detested the great B♭ Concerto of Tchaikovsky. Tchaikovsky could see nothing in the music of Brahms. Chopin turned up his aristocratic nose at Schumann, who in turn was unfriendly toward Wagner. The only broad-minded critic of them all was the warm-hearted genius Liszt. How amusing it would have been to follow Mendelssohn, arising from the completion of a "Song without Words," to a concert at which works of Stravinski or Schönberg were to be performed. Is it possible that his tidy mind could react otherwise than antagonistically to such conceptions?

There are today people who apparently have said to themselves, "Look at the mistakes our forefathers made in judging new music. Let us hasten to admire all strange new works and thus pose as discerning connoisseurs." This attitude has brought about the "appreciation" of many a young composer of insufficient maturity and doubtful value.

How should one judge salon music? That music need not be recondite is amply demonstrated by the deathless "Blue Danube" waltz. Couperin is an example of a composer of classic salon music; but in his day, of course, any music not operatic or religious was necessarily salon. It is to be hoped that the world will not forget the pleasure to be derived from composers like Liadov, with his delicate miniatures, Arensky, with his genre pictures, or the brilliant and elegant Moszkowsky.

For some years after the World War anxiety was felt for the health of the classics; some diagnosticians predicted their early demise, and that they would be entirely superseded by the new music. This prognostication has proved incorrect, for at present the older music appears rather more firmly seated in the saddle than the new. Of course, some of the classics will be discarded; but an enormous quantity of as yet unprinted old music is being revived, both in its original form and in different guises, arrangements, and adaptations, and it comes refreshingly to our ears. Even such composers as Clementi, Dussek, Hummel, and Moscheles deserve an occasional hearing, if only to give better music a rest. There is much "good reading matter" in good salon music.

Works of art in painting, sculpture, and literature may be removed to museums or libraries where they are treasured and guarded as priceless objects, but music has no museums for the preservation of its outworn though still beautiful relics except the printed page. In this respect music, otherwise more direct and emotional in its appeal than are the other arts, is at a disadvantage, and its lovely as well as its dull pages are equally likely to be cast aside by a generation eager for the delights of a newer manner.

Students of the piano are generally not so much interested in the literature of the instrument as in the acquisition of a technique, although it is not clear what purpose this is to serve if not to play the works of the composers. Few students are so conversant with the literature as to have that contempt which familiarity is said to engender, so one must assume that the trouble arises either through ignorance or as a result of that stupid notion that the old is necessarily the tedious. The struggle of the old with the new is normal and healthy, and these pages have no intention of deprecating it. It is of advantage to both since both have to justify their existence.

There is another class of writers not noticed elsewhere in this book which, since they did so much for humanity, it seems unappreciative to ignore. One might first recall and thank Tekla Badarczewska, a Polish girl who, in her short span of twenty-four years, enriched musical life with "The Maiden's Prayer." The conception and execution of this masterpiece seem to have absorbed the entire energy of her life, and in giving birth to it she gave up the ghost. According to the test for great music solemnly laid down above—ecstasy subjected to calm judgment—"The Maiden's Prayer" should have been great music, but it is not.

A certain Mr. DeKontski also deserves gratitude for his Op. 115, "The Awakening of the Lion," and in a lesser degree for Op. 281, "The Falls of the Rhine." One wonders what Op. 282 could have been and whether genius was still burning, but not even Prosniz seems to know. Grandeur in its various manifestations was obviously his inspiration. Fortunately, his constitution seems to have been stronger than Miss Badarczewska's, and the labor of composition consequently less hazardous: he lived to be over eighty.

One Steibelt, a composing pianist, wrote a concerto for piano accompanied by two orchestras. This effort alone should have immortalized him, but he had another spirited idea—he wrote bacchanales for piano and tambourine, which he performed with his wife. A purist might question whether doing a bacchanale with one's wife is quite in keeping with the Greek spirit.

Hanon, the wonderful man who can make one a virtuoso with sixty exercises, stated that this same Steibelt could make his hearers shiver with his tremolo. A tremolo exercise was added to Hanon's collection in order that pupils should have practice in making people shiver. This exercise, however, is invariably unsuccessful, and one comes reluctantly to the conclusion that pianists have lost the power.

A debt to Lefébure-Wély for his "Monastery Bells" must be acknowledged. What *Weltschmerz* has this piece not been the means of exteriorizing in those who otherwise would never have found an emotional purgative! The same composer also wrote "The Hour of Prayer," perhaps with an eye to cutting into Miss Badarczewska's royalties; but although the piece ran through many editions it never attained the popularity or the immortality of its model. Alas, no one worships any more at these shrines, and the gods who presided over them are forgotten. We have lost in naïveté what we have gained in taste.

To return to the statement of aims and purposes conventionally required, let me state again that the aim of this book is to urge the student to diversify his taste and to hint at the pleasure of fishing in many waters. Some newspapers provide their readers with daily hints on what is called a balanced diet —the required number of calories or phosphates or vitamins or whatever it is translated into the more readily understood terms of fruits and vegetables. This book does not aspire to prescribe doses of this or that composer for what ails the student's taste. It hopes merely to stimulate curiosity and thus lead one away from a diet of meat and potatoes.

Adventures among the works of little-known writers and among the less-known works of celebrated writers provide one with a romantic occupation and with the unique pleasure of personal discovery. The hunt has fatigues to be sure (what real hunt has not?), but how richly is one rewarded! Even to those not endowed with a great technique it offers rich domains for exploration, and to the virtuoso it presents a field no one man can ever make entirely his own. The advantages of possessing a good musical library cannot be over-estimated. If more music is bought than is required at the moment, it will be on hand when one wants to explore. What can one not do with the "orchestra of the soul," as Huneker so happily calls the piano! I hope this book will help answer that question.

The remarks appended to the lists of compositions may seem sketchy, but I have purposely left them as they are, since the book is intended as a stimulus rather than an encyclopedia. I feel also that too extended analysis is as futile as too little. In only a few instances have I gone into detailed analysis of form, and then because the works might be found difficult of approach by the average student. The lists of books and articles (pp. 218-225) will furnish the reader with suggestions for further comments.

Concertos are listed, but chamber music is not. The word "modern" is avoided as having too relative a meaning. For composers who have used both the older and the newer manner of writing, I have employed the word "atonal" to designate a style of writing in which the harmony is difficult to define, or "bitonal," which, of course, is quite definite.

The use of the asterisk is misleading. This pet of Baedeker is placed beside a piece for various reasons, sometimes according to my own taste, sometimes according to the taste of critics of my acquaintance. Again, it is used to denote the best works of the writer in question or to signify that the piece was once upon a time immensely popular. The particular meaning is apparent through the context. The asterisk is usually omitted as meaningless for first-class composers.

The term "four hands" means four hands on one piano. The term "two pianos" means four hands on two pianos. Transcriptions—not mere arrangements—are listed only when intended for concert use. The publishers are usually named, but sometimes they are not, especially in connection with the classics, where the information is superfluous. For obscure editions one should turn to one or another of the great publishers, such as Schirmer, Breitkopf, Chester, Durand, Peters, and Universal. Chester is agent for many little-known Continental houses; Universal is agent for Hungarian and other houses. Publishing establishments are frequently taken over by other houses, and consequently it is difficult to keep up with the changes in their names.

Music publishers receive scant thanks or attention from the public, but what a debt do we not owe them! What high purpose and unfailing idealism have not been displayed by such houses as Breitkopf, Belaiev, Universal, and Schirmer! Anyone interested in editions per se is referred to Prosniz, who in his thorough way follows each piece through all its editions. Except for Bach, I have not discussed the relative merits of editions.

I have grouped many writers according to nationality. Of these a few works only are quoted. The pieces are considered representative of their composers. In these divisions I have also included some of the earlier writers who composed little for the piano, or who for one reason or another were not great enough for individual entry.

I decided on alphabetical rather than historical order, first, because the book is not a history, and, secondly, because I wished to emphasize the idea of the simultaneous existence of all composers—that Bach and Scriabin, Couperin and Debussy are equally alive.

In the lists of compositions the letter "m" added to a title means minor. No designation of mode means major.

The music of the early period is listed in a practical rather than in a thorough way. The difficulties of making a complete list without becoming bewildering are at present insuperable. Of nearly all of the clavecinists much yet remains to be printed, but complete editions are gradually being made. The printing presses have been humming with an output of Elizabethan music, which is becoming popular again.

At the end of the book will be found several lists which may be useful in selecting compositions of certain kinds: concertos, sonatas, works for two pianos, pieces for young people, concert études, volumes containing collections of all kinds of uses, and the programs played in 1885-86 by Anton Ru-

binstein in a series designed to show the development and scope of the literature of the piano. This series was the parent of all historical recitals, and it
seems appropriate to recall it in this place. It constitutes a landmark in piano
playing. Finally, there is a bibliography.

The following abbreviations are used extensively in the book:

Aug. . . . . Augener	R.M.V. (Russicher Musik Verlag).
B. and B. . . . . . Bote und Bock	
Breit. . . . . Breitkopf Publications	O.U.P. . . . . . . Oxford University Press
Chest. . . . . . . Chester	Ric. . . . . Ricordi
C.M.C. . . . . . . Century Music Co.	R.L. . . . . Rouart, Lerolle et Cie.
E.M.R. . . . . . . Édition musicale russe. In some of the older publications of this edition done in Germany, the abbreviation reads	Schirm. . . . . . . Schirmer
	Steingr. . . . . . . Steingräber
	U.E. . . . . Universal Edition
	U.M.E. . . . . . . Union musicale espagnole

ISAAC ALBÉNIZ
(1860-1909)

Iberia: Suite in Twelve Parts (Mutuelle).
  Evocación.
  El Puerto.
  Fête-Dieu à Séville.
  Rondeña.
  Almería.
  Triana.
  El Albaicín.
  El Polo.
  Lavapies.
  Malaga.
  Jerez.
  Eritaña.

Navarra (completed by De Sévérac and Granados).
  This supplementary, posthumous piece was to have been a part of *Iberia*.

Suite espagnole, seven pieces (U.E.).

Spanish Rhapsody, also with orchestra (U.M.E.).

Five sonatas.

About 250 pieces in the smaller forms, called chiefly by names of Spanish dances: La Vega, Zortzico, Tango, Azulejos, Seguidilla, Aragonaise, Menuet, Berceuse, Scherzino, Chant d'amour, Serenata espagnola, Canti d'Espagna, Preludi d'Espagna, Dansas espagnolas, Mazurkas de salon, Concerto.

A collection of ten pieces, including the Four Seasons, Aragonaise, Tango, Berceuse, Scherzino, Chant d'amour, is published by Leduc.

Publishers: U.M.E., Mutuelle, R.L., Leduc, Boston Music Co., Schirm., U.E.

In the chase after national expression, Albéniz sacrificed the broad field which his talent could have opened to him. Of the welter of tangos, habaneras, and seguidillas, which dripped too easily from his pen, the majority are trite and banal when stripped of the externally glittering rhythms and color. They lived a butterfly life.

The sonatas are salon sonatas in a larger form, but they are melodious and good. It is a pity that he could not have extended himself further since he had the ambition to attempt sonatas. The "Spanish Rhapsody" is worth playing and should be effective with orchestra. The most popular of these pieces in this country probably is the "Seguidilla" in F#.

Albéniz will live, however, by virtue of his great work *Iberia,* a masterpiece of virtuoso salon music, in which he extols his country in the grand manner. The work takes one and one-half hours to play, so that it is unwise to attempt all of it, though this feat has been performed by Iturbi. The pieces have so strong a family resemblance that they are heard to better advantage one or two at a time. Albéniz has in this work placed the Spanish musical atmosphere before us in a strikingly original and satisfactory manner, and he scales heights not attempted in his other works. Some of the numbers are spun out and would bear cutting, others contain damaging anticlimaxes, but taken as a whole it is a welcome and doubtless permanent addition to the literature. He has so absorbed the musical idiom of his country that he can give it out digested, idealized, and artistically conceived, in pieces worthy of the name of tone poems. The most individual are Nos. 2, 3, 6, 7, and 12. No. 13, as "Navarra" is sometimes listed, has an added interest, in that it displays the gifted hand of Granados.

CHARLES HENRI ALKAN
(1813-1888)

Op. 10. Concerto da camera, Am, with orchestra (Hofmeister).

Op. 12. Trois études de bravoure (improvisation).

Op. 13. Trois andantes romantiques.

Op. 14. Allelujah in F.

Op. 15. Trois morceaux dans le genre pathétique.
Aime-moi.
*Le Vent.
Morte (Hofmeister).

Op. 16. Trois études de bravoure, Scherzi (Costallat).

*Op. 16. Six morceaux caractéristiques.

Op. 17. Le Preux, étude de concert (Schirm.).

Op. 22. Premier nocturne, Bm.

*Op. 23. Saltarello, Em (Schott).

Op. 24. Gigue et air de ballet, style ancien.

Op. 26. Fantasietta alla moresca.

*Op. 27. Le Chemin de fer, étude (Schott).

Op. 29. Bourrée d'Auvergne (Schott).

*Op. 31. Twenty-five Preludes, in all keys (Schlesinger).

Op. 32. L'Amitié.

Op. 33. Sonata—First Part, at the Age of Twenty, Second at Thirty, Third at Forty, Fourth at Fifty (Joubert).

Op. 34. Scherzo, fuocoso.

Op. 35. Twelve études, in major keys (B. and B.).

Op. 37. Trois marches quasi de cavalleria.

Op. 38. Premier recueil de chants.
Assez vivement.
Sérénade.
Choeur.
L'Offrande.
Agitatissimo.
Barcarolle.
En choeur.

Op. 38b. Deuxième recueil de chants.
Hymne.
Allegretto.
Chant de guerre.
Procession.
Andantino.
Barcarolle en choeur.

*Op. 39. Douze études dans les tons mineurs (Costallat).
*1. Comme le vent.
*2. Rhythme molossique.
3. Scherzo diabolique.
Symphonie.
4. Allegro.
5. Marche funèbre.
6. Menuet.
7. Finale.
Concerto (a work of 122 pages).
8. Allegro assai.
9. Adagio.
*10. Allegro alla barbaresca.
11. Ouverture.
*12. Le Festin d'Esope (a set of variations).

Op. 40. Trois marches (four hands).

Op. 41. Trois petites fantasies.

Op. 42. (Op. 45) Salut, cendre du pauvre, paraphrase.

Op. 47. Saltarello, finale de la sonate pour piano et violon (four hands).

Op. 50. Capriccio alla soldatesco et Le Tambour bat aux champs.

Op. 51. Trois menuets.

Op. 52. Super flumina, Paraphrase of the One Hundred and Thirty-seventh Psalm.

Op. 52bis. Quasi caccia.

Op. 55. Une Fusée, introduction et impromptu.

Op. 57. Deux nocturnes (Nos. 2 and 3).

Op. 60. Deux petites pièces.
Ma chère liberté.
Ma chère servitude.

Op. 61. Esquisses (forty-eight motifs).

Op. 61bis. Le Grillon (fourth Nocturne).

Op. 64. Huit prières, for pedal pianos, transcribed by Da Motta.

Op. 65. Troisième recueil de chants.
Vivante.
Esprits folles.

En canon.
Tempo giusto.
Horace et Lydie.
Barcarolle.

Op. 67. Quatrième recueil de chants.
Niège et lave.
Chanson de la bonne vieille.
Bravement.
Doucement.
Appassionata.
Barcarolle.

Op. 70. Cinquième recueil de chants.
Duettino.
Andantinetto.
Allegro vivace.
La Voix de l'instrument.
Scherzo-coro.
Barcarolle.

Op. 74. Les Mois.
Nuit d'hiver, Carneval, La Retraite.
La Pâque, Sérénade, Promenade sur l'eau.
Nuit d'été, La Moissoneuse, L'Hallali.
Gros temps, *Le Mourant, L'Opéra.

Op. 75. Toccatina.

Op. 76. Trois grandes études.
Pour la main gauche seule.
Pour la main droite seule.
*Pour les mains réunies.

WORKS WITHOUT OPUS NUMBER

Jean qui rit et Jean qui pleut, due fughe da camera (Hofmeister).

Désir, fantasia.

Fantasticheria.

Chapeau bas.

Variations à la vieille.

Petite conte.

Bombardo-carrillon (four feet, pedal piano).

CONCERT TRANSCRIPTIONS

Bach . . . . Sonate (clavecin et flute).

Beethoven . . . . . Cavatine du quatuor, Op. 130.

Gluck . . . . Gavotte d'Orphée.

Handel . . . . Choeur des prêtres de Dagon.

Haydn . . . . Menuet du quatuor, Op. 76.
Finale du trentième.

Mozart . . . . Andante du huitième quatuor.
Ne pulvis et cinis (motette).
Menuet en sol mineur.

The Dm Concerto, with cadenza for piano solo (Cranz).

Weber . . . . Scherzo du trio, Op. 63.
Choeur-barcarolle d'Oberon.

Auteur inconnu. Rigaudons des petits violons de Louis Quatorze.

Beethoven . . . . . Première partie du concerto Op. 37, pour piano solo avec cadences (Cranz).

Publishers: Richault, Schlesinger, Costallat, Hofmeister, Joubert, Schott, B. and B., Schirm.

The works of this Berlioz of the piano loom grotesquely in the background of the literature, but it is unnecessary for the average student to concern himself with these fantastic and ponderous pieces, for they belong to a bygone day. They are important, however, in that Liszt was a friend of Alkan and is said to have been much influenced and even helped by him. Rubinstein and others of the great pianist-composers owed much to Alkan.

The pieces exhibit astonishing variety of technique, prodigious difficulty, great fluency, and length, but they lack a vital spark. The best ones are those in rapid tempo, for the interest is then in the technical difficulties and the aridity of thought is unnoticed. Op. 39 presents the most characteristic side of Alkan. In it he sums himself up and gives examples of all his tricks. Asterisks mark those pieces which for one reason or another are notable or at least partially suitable to the taste of today. The attention of armless pianists is called to the composition entitled "Bombardo-Carrillon" (for four feet on the pedal piano). It is safe to say that it is the only piece of its kind in existence.

MISCELLANEOUS AMERICAN COMPOSERS

GEORGE ANTHEIL
(1900—)

Concerto, with orchestra (U.E.).

FREDERIC AYRES
(1876-1926)

Op. 9. Two Fugues.
Op. 11. The Open Road.

Op. 12. Fugue—Moonlight.

EDWARD BALLANTINE
(1886—)

Variations on "Mary Had a Little Lamb"
  in the Style of Various Composers (A.
  P. Schmidt).

MORITZ BAUER
(1875—)

Piano Pieces (Cos Cob).

4

AMY (MRS. H. H. A.) BEACH
(1867—)

Prelude and Fugue, Am.
"De Profundis."
Concerto, C, with orchestra.

Les Rêves de Columbine.
Suite Founded on Irish Melodies, for two
  pianos.

JOHN J. BECKER
(1886—)

Concerto arabesque, with orchestra
  (New Music Ed.).

CARL M. BEECHER
(1883—)

Scherzo, "I Stood Tip-toe upon a Little
  Hill."

The Jester, for two pianos.
  (Both Ditson.)

ERNEST BLOCH
(1880—)

Five Sketches in Sepia.
In the Night.
Poems of the Sea—A Cycle of Three
  Pieces.
  (All Schirm.)

Enfantines, ten sketches (C. Fischer).
Concerto grosso, with strings.
  (C. C. Birchard.)

GEORGE F. BOYLE
(1886—)

Sonata (C. Fischer).

HOWARD A. BROCKWAY
(1870—)

Three American Folk Tunes.

Op. 21, 25, 26, 39. Piano Pieces.
  (All Schirm.)

CHARLES W. CADMAN
(1881—)

Op. 58. Sonata, A.
Idealized Indian Themes.

LOUIS CAMPBELL-TIPTON
(1877-1921)

Sonata (Schirm).
Op. 14. Legends.

Op. 15. Legends.
Op. 30. Étude in Octaves.

JOHN A. CARPENTER
(1876—)

Concertino, with orchestra.
Diversions.

Little Indian—Little Dancer.
Tango américain—Polonaise américaine.
(All Schirm.)

IGNACIO M. CERVANTES
(1847-1905)

Six Cuban Dances (Schirm.).

GEORGE W. CHADWICK
(1854-1931)

Five Pieces (Schirm).
  Danse joyeux.
  In the Canoe.

The Rill.
The Gloaming.
The Frogs.

ABRAM CHASINS
(1903—)

Twenty-four Preludes (Ditson).
Fairy Tale.
Keyboard Karikatures.
Rush Hour in Hong Kong.
A Chinese Flirtation.

A Shanghai Tragedy.
Étude appassionata.
  (All C. Fischer.)
Two Concertos.

CARLOS CHAVEZ
(1899—)

Sonata.
Unidad.

Piano Piece (New Music Ed.).

ROSSETTER G. COLE
(1866—)

King Robert of Sicily, with declamation.
Legend.
  (Both Schirm.)

EDWARD COLLINS
(1889—)

Passacaglia (Summy).
Waltzes.

Concert Piece, with orchestra.

AARON COPLAND
(1900—)

Concerto
Passacaglia.
   (Both Cos Cob.)

The Cat and the Mouse (Elkins and
   Vogel).

HENRY D. COWELL
(1897—)

Concerto (Senart).
Tiger (Russian State Ed.).
Whirling Dervish.
Advertisement.

Fabric.
Sinister Resonance.
   (All Associated Publishers.)

RUTH CRAWFORD
(1901—)

Piano Study in Mixed Accents (New Music Ed.).

BAINBRIDGE CRIST
(1883—)

Egyptian Impressions, four pieces.
Oriental Dances, four pieces.
   (Both C. Fischer.)

ROBERT N. DETT
(1882—)

In the Bottoms (contains the "Juba Dance").

FANNIE C. DILLON
(1881—)

Sonata.
Eight Descriptive Compositions (No. 2,
   "Birds at Dawn").

Six Preludes; Melodic Poems of the Mountains (Schirm.).

M. DVORSKY (JOSEF HOFMANN)
(1876—)

Trois impressions (Schirm).
    L'Orient.
    L'Occident.
    Penguins.

HERBERT ELWELL
(1898—)

Sonata.

BLAIR FAIRCHILD
(1877-1933)

Curios, ten pieces.
Indian Songs and Dances.
From a Balcony, four pieces.
Wind in the Cypresses.
The Harbour at Dusk.
The Unseen Singer.

The Village Fair (Schott).
En voyage, Suite (1923).
Été à Fontainebleau, nine short pieces (1925).
A Bel-Ébat, three pieces (1925. Durand).

ARTHUR FARWELL
(1872—)

Treasured Deeps.
The Flame-voiced Night.
Op. 8. Owasco Memories, five pieces.
Op. 11. Ten American Indian Melodies, with an Introduction.
The Domain of Hurakan.

Op. 12. Dawn.
Op. 16. Symbolistic Study.
Op. 20. From Mesa to Plain, five pieces.
Op. 21. Impressions of the Wa-wan Ceremonies of the Omahas (Schirm.).

ARTHUR W. FOOTE
(1853-1937)

Prelude, Nocturne, and Polonaise, for the left hand.
Op. 15 and Op. 30. Suites.

Op. 41. Five Poems from Omar Khayyam.
Op. 75. Silhouettes.

OSSIP GABRILOWITSCH
(1878-1936)

Caprice Burlesque (J. Church).
Op. 5. Melody.

Meditation (Roszavölgyi).
Intermezzo appassionata (Roszavölgyi).

RUDOLPH GANZ
(1877—)

Op. 15. Cadenza for Beethoven's Concerto (C.M.C.).
Op. 23. Four Pieces (Ries und Erler).
Op. 24. Four Pieces (Roszavölgyi).

Two Capricci (Schirm.).
Symphonic Variations on a Theme of Brahms.
Op. 29. Two Concert Pieces.

GEORGE GERSHWIN
(1898-1937)

Rhapsody in Blue, with special orchestra.
Concerto in F, with orchestra (Harms).

Three Preludes (New World Music Corp.).

PERCY GRAINGER
(1882—)

TRANSCRIPTIONS

Lullaby, from "Tribute to Foster."
Sea Chanty, "One More Day, My John."
Morris Dance, "Shepherds Hey."
Irish Tune, from "County Derry."
The Sussex Mummers' Christmas Carol.
"My Robin's to the Greenwood Gone."
Walking Tune.

Mock Morris.
Colonial Song.
"Blithe Bells," Ramble on an Aria of Bach, "Sheep May Graze in Safety," for two pianos.
Country Gardens (Schirm.).

CHARLES T. GRIFFES
(1884-1920)

Op. 5. Three Tone Poems.
    The Lake at Evening.
    Night Winds.
    The Vale of Dreams.
Op. 6. Barcarolle, Nocturne, Scherzo.

Four Roman Sketches.
    The White Peacock.
    Nightfall.
    The Fountains of the Acqua Paola.
    Clouds.
Sonata (posthumous), atonal.
    (All Schirm.)

ELLIOT GRIFFIS
(1893—)

Sonata, A♭ (C.M.C.).

LOUIS GRUENBERG
(1883—)

Op. 16. Polychromes.
Op. 25. Jazzberries.

Op. 30. Jazz Masks (Syncopated paraphrases of famous works. U.E.).

DAVID W. GUION
(1895—)

Concert Paraphrase on "Turkey in the Straw."

Pickaninny Dance.
Alley Tunes (Schirm.).

ROY HARRIS
(1898—)

Sonata.
Concerto for Piano, Clarinet, and Quartet.
   (Both Cos Cob).

EDWARD B. HILL
(1872—)

Jazz Study, for two pianos.
At the Grave of a Hero.
Country Idylls, six pieces.

Concertino, with orchestra.
   (All Schirm.)

JOSEF HOFMANN
(1876—)

Four Old Dutch Songs, arranged for piano
   (Schirm.).
   (See also under Dvorsky.)

HENRY H. HUSS
(1862—)

Concerto, with orchestra.
Ballade.
Minuet and Gavotte.
The Night.

Op. 17. Four Preludes in the Form of Études.
Op. 20. Three Pieces.
   (All Schirm.)

ERNEST HUTCHESON
(1871—)

Op. 10. Four Preludes (Schirm.).
Op. 11. Prelude and Caprice.
Op. 12. Three Pieces (C.M.C.).

TRANSCRIPTIONS
Wagner, "Ride of the Valkyries."
Mendelssohn, Scherzo from *Midsummer Night's Dream*.

CHARLES E. IVES
(1874—)

Concord Sonata.

J. ALBERT JEFFEREY
(1856-1929)

Barcarolle.
Gavotte of the Nineteenth Century.

Nocturne.
(All Breit.)

ERNEST R. KROEGER
(1862-1934)

Op. 17. Dance of the Elves (Kunkel Bros.,
St. Louis).
March of the Indian Phantoms (Presser).
Op. 33. Suite, Fm.
Op. 35. Egeria (Kunkel Bros.).
Op. 40. Sonata, Db.
Op. 41. Prelude and Fugue.

Op. 45. Scherzo, Ebm.
Op. 46. Three Mythological Scenes.
Op. 53. Ten American Character Sketches
(Shattinger Music Co., St. Louis).
Op. 54. Variations.
Op. 60. Twenty Moods.
(All Breit.)

EASTWOOD LANE
(1884—)

American Suite (J. Fischer).

CHARLES M. LOEFFLER
(1861-1935)

A Pagan Poem, with three obbligato trumpets, English horn, and orchestra
(Schirm.).

HARVEY W. LOOMIS
(1865-1930)

Lyrics of the Red-man, two books.
The Tragedy of Death.
(Both Schirm.)

ALEXANDER MACFADYEN
(1879-1937)

Sonata (Schirm.).

DANIEL G. MASON
(1873—)

Prelude and Fugue, with orchestra.
Three Silhouettes.

Country Pictures.
(Schirm.)

11

W. OTTO MIESSNER
(1880—)

Sonata, E (Amer. Mus. Co., Milwaukee).

LODEWIJK MORTELMANS
(1868—)

Old Flemish Songs (3 vols. C.M.C.).

ARTHUR NEVIN
(1871—)

From Edgworth Hill.
Southern Sketches, five pieces.
   (Both J. Church)

HORACE W. NICHOLL
(1848-1922)

Twelve Concert Preludes and Fugues.
   (Schirm.)

ARNE OLDBERG
(1874—)

Op. 17. Concerto.
Sonata.
Op. 26. A Legend.

Op. 32. Improvisation.
   (All Schirm.)

LEO ORNSTEIN
(1895—)

Pigmy Suite.
À la Mexicana.
Arabesque.
Four Sonatas.
Op. 44. Concerto.
Impressions of the Thames.
Sonatina.
Nine Miniatures.
Musings of a Piano.

Poems of 1917.
Burlesques.
Two Shadow Pieces.
Three Moods.
Eleven Short Pieces.
Six Short Pieces.
Three Preludes.
(Many other compositions.)

THORVALD OTTERSTRÖM
(1868—)

Preludes and Fugues.

Concert Studies (Peder Früs).

LEE PATTISON
(1890—)

Told in the Hills.
Op. 4. Seven Pieces (A. P. Schmid).
Two Florentine Sketches (Schirm.).

Transcriptions of "The Arkansas Traveler" (Schirm.).

ALFRED POCHON
(1878—)

Prelude (C. Fischer).

JOHN POWELL
(1882—)

At the Fair.
A Set of Genre Pictures.
Three Sonatas → Teutonica, Noble, Virginiaesque.

Rhapsodie nègre, with orchestra (Schirm.).
Suite sudiste.
Variations on a Theme of Hahr. (Both Mathot)

WALLINGFORD RIEGGER
(1885—)

Blue Voyage (Schirm.).

EDWARD ROYCE
(1886—)

Theme and Variations, Am.
A Set of Eight.
(Both Schirm.)

BERYL RUBINSTEIN
(1898—)

Sonatina, C♯m (O.U.P.).

LAZARE SAMINSKY
(1882—)

Ten Hebrew Folk-Songs and Folk-Dances.

ERNEST SCHELLING
(1876-1939)

Fatalisme.
Un Petit rien.
Au Château de Wiligrad.
Theme and Variations.

Romance.
(All Schirm.)
Episodes de la vie d'un artiste, with orchestra.
Suite fantastique, with orchestra (Rahter).

BORIS DE SCHLOEZER
(1884—)

Étude, A♭ (Schirm.).

ROGER SESSIONS
(1896—)

Sonata (Schott).

ARTHUR SHEPHERD
(1880—)

Two Sonatas.   Exotic Dance.

CHARLES S. SKILTON
(1868—)

Two Indian Dances.   Three Indian Sketches Based on Tribal
   Bear Dance.   Tunes Supplied by G. La Mere, a
   War Dance.   Winnebago Indian.
                                      (Both C. Fisher.)

NICOLAS SLONIMSKY
(1894—)

Studies in Black and White (New Music Ed.).

LEO SOWERBY
(1895—)

Ballade "King Estmere," for two pianos   Money Musk (Birchard).
   and orchestra.   Concerto (Boston Music Co.; and Birch-
From the Northland, five pieces.   ard).
Cantus Heroicus (Boston Music Co.).

ALBERT SPALDING
(1888—)

Op. 6. Four Piano Pieces. (C.M.C.).

TIMOTHY SPELMAN
(1891—)

Barbaresques (1922).   Five Whimsical Serenades (1923. Chest.).

WALTER W. STOCKHOFF
(1887—)

Sonata in Contemplation of the Nations at War (Breit.).

GEORGE T. STRONG
(1856—)

Op. 36. Four Poems.
Op. 44. In the Twilight.
Cortège rustique.
Au Moulin.

An der Nixenquelle, for two pianos.
In der Hexenhölle, for two pianos
(Breit.).

DEEMS TAYLOR
(1885—)

A Kiss in Xanadu, pantomine with piano.
Two Studies in Rhythm.
(Both J. Fischer)

L. VERSEL

Carillon de Bruges.

Boîte à musique (Schirm.).

ADOLPH WEISS
(1891—)

Sonata.
Six Preludes (*New Music,* Vol. II, No. 3,
1929).

MARK WESSEL
(1894—)

Concerto, for piano, horn, and orchestra.
Symmetrical Toccata.

Green River.
Isle of Death (Schirm.).

EMERSON WHITHORNE
(1884—)

La Nuit.
The Rain.
Hototogiau (Schirm.).

New York Days and Nights.
Poem, with orchestra (C. Fischer).
The Aeroplane (C.M.C.).

KARL ZEISS

Transcriptions of the "German Dances"
and the "Country Dances" of Beethoven (Schirm.).

Within the last forty years there has been an immense stir made about American music—what it ought to be and what it ought not to be. Nature was not to be allowed time to develop an idiom. Something had to happen at once; consequently, a vast amount of nonsense was talked. It was necessary to settle the meaning of the term American. This, of course, was a Gordian knot. How long must a foreigner live in the atmosphere of this country before he becomes imbued with its style? This and other questions proved to be unanswerable. Finally, jazz was hailed as truly American; it was to be the savior of the situation. Unfortunately, it transpired that jazz meant merely an enormous rhythmical technique and that it entirely lacked ideas. Several composers who worked at Indian and Negro themes endeavored to create "American" music in that way.

The efforts of those who devote themselves to a preconceived notion of any manner of work are foredoomed to produce an effect of self-consciousness and pedantry. There is a substitution of inventiveness for inspiration. This attitude seems to question the adequacy of existing musical art as an expression of the spirit of today, and to indicate that these composers are groping along various lines.

While the search for a so-called "American" idiom proceeds, the music of the present day seems to me to become more and more international. It is no longer possible to label a work Russian, Italian, French, or German. The introduction of the objective mechanistic ideals of the present into music tends to eliminate the national quality of a work.

It is impossible to suppress a feeling of pity for the composer of today, living as he undoubtedly does in a period of transition. If he lives long enough, however, he may achieve the rank of a Bach, a Beethoven, or a Wagner.

ANTON ARENSKY
(1861-1906)

Op. 1. Six Pieces in Canon Form.
Op. 2. Concerto in F (Rahter).
Op. 5. Six Pieces (Jurgenson).
  Nocturne.
  Intermezzo.
  Romance.
  Valse.
  *Basso ostinato.
  Étude.

*Op. 8. Scherzo in A (Schirm.).
*Op. 15. Suite, for two pianos (Schirm.).
  Romance.
  Valse.
  Polonaise.
Op. 19. Three Pieces.
  Étude, Bm.
  Prelude.
  Mazurka, A♭.

16

Op. 20. Bigarrures, F, Dm, B.

*Op. 23. Silhouettes, for two pianos.
  Le Savant.
  La Coquette.
  Polichinelle.
  Le Rêveur.
  La Danseuse.

*Op. 24. Three Sketches, F, A♭, Fm.

Op. 25. Impromptu, Rêverie, Étude, Scherzino.

*Op. 28. Sketches on Forgotten Rhythms Found in the Poetry of the Greeks, Romans, and Other Peoples.
  Logaèdes.
  Péons.
  Ioniques.
  Säri.
  Strophe alcéenne.
  Strophe sapphique (Fritsch; Hug; etc.).

Op. 30. Four Pieces.

*Op. 33. Third Suite, for two pianos, nine numbers (Jurgenson).

*Op. 34. Six pièces enfantines (four hands), including Valse, *Le Coucou, and Les Larmes (Jurgenson).

Op. 36. Twenty-four Pieces, in all keys (No. 13 is the well-known étude in F♯).

*Op. 41. Four Études, E♭, F♯, E♭, Am (Jurgenson. Melodious, and not difficult).

*Op. 42. Three Pieces (Rahter).

Op. 43. Six Caprices, Am, A, C, G, D, B (Jurgenson).

*Op. 46. At the Spring . . . . (Jurgenson).

Op. 48. Fantaisie russe, with orchestra.

*Op. 52. Près de la mer (Schirm.).

Op. 53. Six Pieces.

Op. 62. Fourth Suite, for two pianos.

Op. 63. Twelve Preludes.

Op. 65. Fifth Suite, Eight Canons for Young People (four hands).

Op. 66. Twelve Pieces (four hands).

Op. 67. Arabesques.

*Op. 74. Twelve Études.

Fughetta (Boston Music Co.).

Valse, A♭.

Publishers: Jurgenson, Rahter, Schott, Breit., Schirm., Bosworth, Hug, Fritsch.

Arensky, orderly, conservative, and smooth as he is, furnishes one with excellent material of a lighter sort. The two-piano suites are indispensable for "two-pianists." "Près de la mer," "At the Spring," the Étude in F♯, the Basso ostinato, some of the études, and other pieces indicated above will be found worth playing. The "Sketches on Forgotten Rhythms" are individual and unusual and are recommended. The pieces with orchestra are rather uninteresting, but they are melodious and not very difficult.

JOHANN SEBASTIAN BACH

(1685-1750)

It is probable that everything of J. S. Bach is now published and is to be had in the edition of the Bach Gesellschaft (Breit.). This music is published in more or less detail by all the great publishing houses, and one's choice should depend on what is asked of an edition. The following list, numbering, and sequence is made from Peters.

Vol.			Vol.		
	1.	Well-tempered Clavichord (Vol. I).	212	15.	Fantasia, Cm.
	2.	Well-tempered Clavichord (Vol. II). (In two editions, by Czerny and Kroll)			Fugues in Dm, Dm, A, Em, Am.
200	3.	Twelve Little Preludes and Fugues for Beginners.			Fragment of a Suite in Fm. Fugue, Cm. Prelude and Fugue on B-A-C-H.

Vol.

1. Well-tempered Clavichord (Vol. I).
2. Well-tempered Clavichord (Vol. II). (In two editions, by Czerny and Kroll)
200 3. Twelve Little Preludes and Fugues for Beginners.
   Six Little Preludes and Fugues for Beginners.
   A Little Two-part Fugue.
   Fugue in C.
   Prelude and Fughetta, Bm.
   Prelude and Fughetta, Em.
   Prelude and Fugue, Am.
201 4. Two- and Three-part Inventions.
202 5. French Suites.
203 6. English Suites (Vol. I, 1-3).
204 7. English Suites (Vol. 88, 4-6).
205 8. Partitas (Vol. I, 1-3).
206 9. Partitas (Vol. II, 4-6).
207 10. Italian Concerto.
   Chromatic Fantasia and Fugue.
   Prelude and Fugue, Am.
208 11. French Overture.
   Fantasia and Fugue.
   Capriccio on the Departure of a Beloved Brother.
   Four Duets.
209 12. Thirty Variations (the "Goldberg" Variations).
210 13. Four Toccatas, F♯, Cm, Dm, D.
211 14. Toccata, Gm.
   Prelude and Fugue, Am.
   Fantasia and Fugue, D.

Vol.

212 15. Fantasia, Cm.
   Fugues in Dm, Dm, A, Em, Am.
   Fragment of a Suite in Fm.
   Fugue, Cm.
   Prelude and Fugue on B-A-C-H.
   Fantasia and Fughetta, Bb.
   Fantasia and Fughetta, D.
213 16. Three Sonatas in Am, C, Dm.
214 17. Prelude and Fugue, for lute or piano.
   Fugue, Bm.
   Three Suites, Am, Ebm, Em.
   Two Preludes and Fugues in F and G.
   Prelude, G.
215 18. Fantasia, Am.
   Aria variata, Am.
   Toccata, G.
   Ouverture, F.
   Fantasia, Gm.
216 19. Capriccio, E.
   Fantasia, B.
   Sonata, D.
   Fugue, A.
   Fugue, A.
   Three Minuets.
217 20. Sixteen Concertos after Vivaldi and others.
218 21. The Art of Fugue.
219 22. Das musicalische Opfer.
220 23. Favorite Preludes (a collection).
221 24. Favorite Pieces (a collection).
   25. A supplement of hitherto unpublished pieces.

CONCERTOS WITH ACCOMPANIMENT

248–54 Seven volumes of concertos with orchestral accompaniment.
255 and 265 Two volumes of concertos for three pianos with accompaniment of violin and flute.
256–57 Two volumes of concertos for two pianos.
258–59 Two volumes of concertos for three pianos.
260 Concerto for four pianos, after Vivaldi.

THE CHIEF TRANSCRIPTIONS OF
BACH'S COMPOSITIONS

Albert, E. d'....Passacaglia, Cm, organ.
Prelude and Fugue, D, organ.

Bauer, H......The first Partita, B♭ (Schirm.).
Concerto for Three Harpsichords, C, arranged for two pianos (Schirm.).

Borwick, L.....Sarabande, f r o m cello suite.
Erbarme dich.
O, Lamm Gottes unschuldig.
Herz und Mund und That und Leben.
(All O.U.P.)

Brahms, J.....Studies for Piano, Nos. 3, 4, 5.
3. Presto.
4. Presto.
5. Chaconne for the Left Hand Alone.

Busoni, F.....Busoni's list is a large one. See under his name.

Cohen, H.....Beloved Jesu, We Are Here (O.U.P.).

Cooper, G. M...Four Choral Preludes (O.U.P.).

Craxton, H.....Largo, from Fm Concerto (O.U.P.).

Friedman, I....Two Choralvorspiele (U. E.).

Godowsky, L...Three violin sonatas and three cello suites (C. Fischer).

Heinze, S......A volume of pieces chosen from the smaller works for various instruments, easily and attractively arranged (Schirm.).

Henseler, R....Siciliano, from sonata for piano and flute.

Hess, M.......Jesu, Joy of Man's Desiring (O.U.P.).

Labunski, W...Prelude in E (B. and B.).

Liszt, F.......Fantasia and Fugue, Gm, organ.
Six Preludes and Fugues, organ, Am, C, Cm, C, Em, Bm.

Philipp, I......Twelve transcriptions for two pianos (Ric., Paris branch).
Toccata, F.
Prelude and Fugue, Gm.
Prelude and Fugue, G.
Toccata, Dm, in the Dorian Mode.
Prelude and Fugue, Dm.
Sonata No. 2, Cm.
Toccata, Adagio, and Fugue.
Prelude and Fugue, Em.
Prelude and Fugue, A.
Prelude and Fugue, Fm.
Fugue, Gm.
Chorale, "Allein Gott in der Höh' sei Ehr'."

Reger, M......Arrangements of, and studies based on, the Choralvorspiele (Aibl; Aug.; U.E.).
Preludes and Fugues in Em, E♭, D.
Toccata and Fugue, Dm.
(Both Schott)

Rheinberger, J..Goldberg Variations, for two pianos, revised by Reger (Kistner).

Rummel, W....Adaptations from J. S. Bach.
Series I. Seven Choral Preludes.
Series II. Seven Extracts from the Cantatas.
Series III. Three Extracts from the Cantatas.

Saint-Saëns, C. . Six Fragments from Bach's Works (Rieter-Biedermann).
(These pieces with six more are published by Durand.)

Stradal, A. . . . . . Preludes and Fugues, Em, G (Kahnt).
Second organ concerto, Am.
Passacaglia, Cm.
Preludes and Fugues, organ, Fm, Gm, Dm, E♭, G, C, D.
Sonata, Cm, organ.
Toccata, Dm, organ.
Toccatas and Fugues, organ, F, C.
(All Schuberth)

Szántó, T. . . . . . Prelude and Fugue, organ, "The Greater Gm."
Prelude and Fugue, organ, "The Lesser Gm."
(Both Kahnt)
Prelude and Fugue, Am (U.E.).

Tausig, C. . . . . . Toccata and Fugue, Dm.

Whittaker, W. . . We All Believe in God the Father (O.U.P.).

Zadora, M. V. . Aria from St. Matthew Passion (B. and B.).

It should be recalled here that the works of J. S. Bach supply the foundation for all music after him and must ever be reverently studied. The proverb about apples might be paraphrased: "A fugue a day keeps bad taste away." No one for whom the music of Bach has meaning and beauty needs to distrust his taste in other composers.

It will probably suffice to indicate those pieces with which every pianist should be familiar. The Busoni edition is advised for those who need an intelligent guide. Busoni maintains that a student can and should develop his technique by means of Bach and certain transcriptions and studies in octaves, thirds, and sixths. His scheme is elaborately worked out in his edition of the *Well-tempered Clavichord*. Even if one does not follow it out in all its ramifications, it is none the less enlightening. The edition of the Bach Gesellschaft (Breit.) clears away the accumulations of previous editors and is welcome for that as well as for other reasons, but inexperienced and even many advanced students will want the Busoni version.

A LIST ALL STUDENTS SHOULD KNOW

The Fifteen Two-part and the Fifteen Three-part Inventions.
The Well-tempered Clavichord (at least Vol. I).

The Chromatic Fantasia and Fugue.
The Italian Concerto.
Selections from the English and French Suites.

Selections from the Partitas (possibly substituting Bauer's transcription of the first one for the original text).

The Dm Concerto.

The Toccatas, especially those in A, Dm, F♯.

The great Prelude and Fugue in Am (with the short prelude and the running fugue theme).

The transcriptions by Liszt, Tausig, Busoni, Bauer, and Godowsky.

The student is strongly advised to study the concertos for one, two, or three pianos. They offer the most stimulating and satisfactory music, and they can be performed either without accompaniment or with a very small accompanying group. The student should also try some of the less well-known pieces such as, in volume 215 of the Peters list, the Fantasia and the "Aria variata" (one of Bach's rare variation sets); volume 209; the "Goldberg Variations" (which no one should try to play entire—this advice is undoubtedly needless!); volume 216 for the Sonata in D, with its amusing cock-crowing fugue subject (the whole thing is unique in Bach); volume 210 for the D minor Toccata; volume 207 complete (as mentioned above).

CARL PHILIPP EMANUEL BACH

(1714-1788)

Up to 1900 only about two hundred and fifty of his works had been published. According to Prosniz there are:

420 works in all, 250 of which are printed.
52 concertos, 9 of which are printed.
146 sonatas, 99 of which are printed.

170 miscellaneous works, 125 of which are printed.

75 of the 420 works are for piano in combination with other instruments.

AVAILABLE AT PRESENT

Concertos in C, Cm, G, D, D (No. 2) (Breit.; Steingr.).

*Concertos for two pianos, E♭, F, Dm (Steingr.).

*Six Sonatas, ed. by Bülow (Peters; Ric.).

Rondos, in Dm, E, G (Breit.).

*Rondo, Bm.

*Allegro, Fm.

Rondo D.
   (Anthologie classique; Schlesinger.)

Fantasie, C (Forberg).

Three "Württemberg" sonatas (Senart).

Rondos in A♭ and E (Senart).

Solfegietto (numerous publishers).

Two volumes of compositions (U.E.).

Other works may be found in the anthologies. See under "Clavecinists." "Alte Klaviermusik" (various houses). Eighteenth Century Music (Chest.). Popular Pieces of C. P. E. Bach (Aug.). Alte Meister (Breit.).

What is given above would undoubtedly be sufficient for any but the special researcher, who should apply to Breitkopf for the latest information.

One of C. P. E. Bach's titles to fame, his aid in the fixation of the sonata form, is only alluded to here; but another one, sensing the difference between the harpsichord and the piano style, is really of importance to us, for it means that he is the real father of the literature of the piano.

One should recall in this connection that he wrote a short book called *Die wahre Art das Klavier zu spielen,* in which he urged the superiority of the intellectual-emotional over the purely technical manner. The enormous and ever increasing shadow of his father has hitherto obscured Carl Philipp Emanuel, but it is time he stood forth in the light, for his style is not a repetition of that of his father. It presents the first true sensing of the powers of the new instrument. It is unfortunate that so few of his works are available, but undoubtedly more will be published.

JOHANN CHRISTIAN BACH

(1735-1782)

Two Concertos (Peters).
Op. 7. No. 5. Concerto, Eb, with accompaniment of two violins and cello.
Op. 13. No. 4. Concerto, Bb, with accompaniment of two violins, cello, bass, two oboes, two horns (also in an arrangement for two pianos).
Eighteenth Century Music (Chest.) contains more of his music.

Like most of the "concertos" of this period, these are what today are called chamber music and form attractive pieces to play in one's home. Some adaptation generally improves these works.

WILHELM FRIEDEMANN BACH

(1710-1784)

According to Prosniz (1900) there are, in all, the following compositions: ten concertos, ten fugues, ten sonatas, one suite, seven larger and four smaller fantasias, thirty polonaises, and a few other odd pieces. Probably not more than half of his works have as yet been printed or are available. The following list gives what is now to be had.

Five Concertos with orchestra. The orchestral part is arranged and printed underneath the solo part. Edited by Riemann. They are in Eb, Em, D, Am, F (Steingr.). As in all of Riemann's editing the pages are so filled with superfluous phrasing marks and the symbols are so curiously subdivided that the eye can scarcely take in the poor little notes the composer modestly placed there. Such pedantry merely confuses.

Concerto, organ, transcribed by Zadora (Simrock).

Concerto, Dm, organ, transcribed by Stradal with an added cadenza (Breit.). This work created a sensation on its publication in 1906. It was later definitely accredited to Vivaldi. Prosniz notes that the original manuscript was in the handwriting of J. S. Bach.

Twelve Polonaises (Peters; Ric.).

Concerto for two pianos, Eb (Steingr.—new edition by Bruno Hinze-Reinhold).

Sonata, F, for two pianos (Peters).

An Album containing Suite, four Fantasias, Capriccio, March (Steingr.).

Some of his music is in the anthologies, as follows:

Eighteenth Century Music (Chest.).

"Alte Meister" and "Alte Klaviermusik" (various houses; see under "Clavecinists").

Perles musicales (Breit.).

The best work of this composer manqué appears to have been done by Vivaldi, who is now considered to have written the concerto transcribed by Stradal. The mistaken attribution was probably the result of J. S. Bach's failure to affix the name of the composer when he copied out the manuscript. The concerto in question is none the less effective and worth while. It achieved a prominent place among transcriptions of the first rank in a short time. Since it is still published under the name of W. F. Bach, it is listed here. The unquestioned compositions which he wrote contain less of interest than his great talent would lead one to expect, but the two-piano Concerto is said to be good; the D minor Capriccio is poetic, and some of the polonaises are fair. The sonatas and fugues have little worth.

MILI BALAKIREV

(1837-1910)

Two Valse caprices (transcription by Taneiev).

Seven Waltzes.

Seven Mazurkas (Gutheil).

*Complainte—Doumka (Zimmermann).

Three Scherzos (No. 1 Zimmermann; others Gutheil).

Gondola Song (Zimmermann).

*Islamey (Schirm.).

Chant du pêcheur (Zimmermann).

*Nocturne (Gutheil).

Sonata Bm (Zimmermann).

La Fileuse.

Humoresque (Zimmermann).

Rêverie (Zimmermann).

*Au jardin (Ed. by Lhevinne, Schirm.).

Tyrolienne.

*The Lark of Glinka, transcribed (Schirm.).

Fantasia on Russian Airs of Glinka (Gutheil).

Many other pieces.

Publishers: Zimmerman, Gutheil, Schirm.

"Islamey," that extraordinarily strange, exotic, and colorful inspiration, thoroughly chastened by years of study and testing, is the one piece of Balakirev which one must not miss. Contained in its surging, writhing, kaleidoscopic harmonies, and in its snaky melody is all the mad ecstasy of the whirling dervishes. The piece is unique in the literature and is an excellent example of what was suggested in the Introduction to this book as required of the greatest music, be it fugue, fantasia, sonata, or simple prelude. The form of the composition develops so satisfactorily out of the thematic material that one gets a feeling of inevitability.

Balakirev has written no other work which one may put in the same class with "Islamey." The Sonata, a crabbed work, comes nearest (the last two movements are the best), but does not equal it. "The Lark of Glinka," well known and loved, and "Au jardin" are next choice, but one might also find pleasure and profit in studying some of the waltzes, the mazurkas, and the Nocturne.

BÉLA BARTÓK

(1881—)

Op. 1. Rhapsody, with orchestra (1910).
Op. 6. Fourteen Bagatelles.
Op. 8a. Two Roumanian Dances.
Op. 8b. Two Elegies.
Op. 8c. Three Burlesques.

Op. 9. Sketches.
Op. 14. Suite; Allegretto, Scherzo, Allegro.
Op. 18. Études.
Op. 20. Improvisations.

WITHOUT OPUS NUMBERS

Allegro barbaro.
Four Nenies ("Threnodies").
Roumanian Folk Dances.
Roumanian Christmas Songs.
Sonatina.
Three Popular Hungarian Peasant Songs.
Fifteen Hungarian Peasant Songs.

Eighty-five Little Pieces for Children.
Ten Easy Pieces.
A Gyermekeknek, forty-two pieces for children.
Concerto, with orchestra.

Publishers: Roszavölgyi, Rosznyai (but all pieces are to be had through U. E.).

Bartók devotes himself to the revival of the ancient Hungarian music and to the presentation of it to a world accustomed to think of the Rhapsodies of Liszt and the Hungarian Dances of Brahms as typically Magyar. The Liszt pieces are based on gypsy melodies—Hungarian only in that certain gypsies live in Hungary—and the Dances are by known composers and are not traditional, Brahms merely transcribed them.

The old airs and melodies with which Bartók busies himself have nothing in common with these, but resemble the old church modes, especially the Doric (see remarks on Op. 29 of Dohnányi). It will be seen that Bartók has a field of his own, and an interesting one, whose beginnings date back one thousand years, and, in the oldest examples, bear traces of Asiatic origin in their pentatonic scale.

Fortunately for those not possessing a virtuoso technique, many of the pieces are not difficult. The following are not beyond the powers of a player of medium attainments: Op. 6, 9, the Sonatina, the "Ten Easy Pieces," both sets of the charming and original pieces for children, both sets of the Hungarian pieces, and the "Roumanian Folk Dances."

For those who are advanced and not afraid of bold harmonies, Op. 8a, 8b, 8c, 18, and 20 offer the best material. These pieces are nearly all for one's own edification, since little effort has been made to render them structurally interesting, and they are not long enough for concert use. The music is strong and primitive, and the arrangements for piano (one cannot call them transcriptions) have retained largely an original wild and vigorous character.

The more developed pieces include the Études, Suite, Op. 14, Improvisations, Op. 20, Allegro barbaro, Elegies, Op. 8b, and "Two Roumanian Dances." The music in general seems like a sketchbook in which were set down ideas to be worked out later, germs of pieces, a fount of inspirations for a dull day, when one can stop collecting and amuse oneself by making pieces out of elemental tunes.

One may confidently expect greater works of art from this gifted man when he has completed his routine work of gathering the songs of his fatherland. In any event he has rescued these ancient melodies from an oblivion which might easily have overtaken them.

ARNOLD BAX

(1883—)

Symphonic Fantasia.
Valse de concert.

Mask.
Toccata.

The Happy Forest.
Passacaglia.
Mediterranean.
A Hill Tune.
Ceremonial Dance.
On a May Morning.
Romance.
First Sonata, F♯m (1910, revised 1922).
Second Sonata, Gm.
Third Sonata (recent).
Serpent Dance.
Water Music.
Lullaby (1920).
Country Tune.
Burlesque (1920).
    (All Murdoch and Murdoch)
May Night in the Ukraine (1913).
The Maiden with the Daffodil (1913).
Gopak (1913).
    (Joseph Williams)

In a Vodka Shop.
Apple Blossom Time.
The Princess' Rosegarden.
Sleepyhead.
    (Aug.)
Dream in Exile (1918).
Nereid (1916).
Winter Waters, Tragic Landscape.
A Mountain Mood (variations).
Whirligig (1919).
Moy Mell ("The Happy Plain"), An Irish Tone Poem, for two pianos (Chest.).
What the Minstrel Told Us.
The Slave Girl (both 1920).
The Devil Tempted St. Anthony, for two pianos.
The Poisoned Fountain (O.U.P.).

Publishers: Murdoch and Murdoch, Williams, Chest., Aug., O.U.P.

Arnold Bax has devoted more attention to the piano than has any other British composer of today except Cyril Scott. He has the true Celtic note in his music, the twilight mystery, the dreaminess and melancholy of his race. Although his works are new and original, they have the weakness as well as the strength of the Celtic temperament. The sentimental and moody characteristics of the Celts account for the poetic strain in their temperament. All the pieces except the sonatas have programs. The music, like that of Liszt, seems a record of outside impressions. The imagination of Bax is roused more by external stimuli than by pure tonal thinking. He has, however, added many valuable works to the repertory of the pianist.

One of the foremost, and certainly one of the most original and Celtic of his pieces, is the poetic and melancholy "Moy Mell," for two pianos. It has qualities never before exploited for that combination. It is not easy to interpret, but it offers absorbing delights to the persistent, but advanced, student.

The humor of Bax is displayed most delightfully in the "Burlesque." This piece might be described as a gavotte done in the "Charleston" manner. Humor of this sort is all too rare in music. His merry side is shown again in the "Whirligig," a kind of finger exercise which suddenly finds itself in a "real piece."

The "Slave Girl," an Oriental picture, is musically and pianistically attractive; "Mediterranean" is a great favorite; "What the Minstrel Told Us" is a long ballade-like composition of power and dramatic strength; "Dream in Exile," a study in homesickness, lapses at times into rank sentimentality.

As he shows in his three fine sonatas, Bax can maintain interest in works of longer form. He has the "long breath" and sustained eloquence necessary for success in larger compositions. These works should appear oftener on the programs of pianists. The first and second are from the early twenties; the third is of fairly recent date.

His visits to Russia have inspired a few pieces, notably "Gopak" and "May Night in the Ukraine." "Country Tune" has also a strong Muscovite flavor. "In a Vodka Shop" is another of this period.

Bax's music is eminently personal and in a sense feminine, and it is not easy for everyone to interpret, since it requires practice until one begins to acquire the style. Every piece is instinct with feeling and differs greatly from the general manner of composing of today. It is a pleasure to find melodies again.

LUDWIG VAN BEETHOVEN

(1770-1827)

Op. 2. No. 1. Sonata, Fm.
    No. 2. Sonata, A.
    No. 3. Sonata, C.
Op. 6. Sonata, D (four hands).
Op. 7. Sonata, Eb.
Op. 10. No. 1. Sonata, Cm.
    No. 2. Sonata, F.
    No. 3. Sonata, D.
Op. 13. Sonata pathétique, Cm.
Op. 14. No. 1. Sonata, E.
    No. 2. Sonata, G.
Op. 15. Concerto, C.
Op. 19. Concerto, Bb.
Op. 26. Sonata, Ab.

Op. 27. No. 1. Sonata quasi fantasia, Eb.
    No. 2. Sonata quasi fantasia, C♯m ("Moonlight").
Op. 28. Sonata, D ("Pastorale").
Op. 31. No. 1. Sonata, G.
    No. 2. Sonata, Dm.
    No. 3. Sonata, Eb.
Op. 33. Seven Bagatelles.
Op. 34. Six Variations on an Original Theme.
Op. 35. Fifteen Variations on a Theme from the *Eroica Symphony*.
Op. 37. Concerto, Cm.
Op. 39. Two Preludes.

Op. 45. Three Marches (four hands).

Op. 49. No. 1. Sonata, Gm.

No. 2. Sonata, G.

Op. 51. No. 1. Rondo, C.

No. 2. Rondo, G.

Op. 53. Sonata, C ("Waldstein").

Op. 54. Sonata, F.

Op. 56. Triple Concerto, for piano, violin, and cello.

Op. 57. Sonata, Fm ("Appassionata").

Op. 58. Concerto, G.

Op. 73. Concerto, E♭ ("Emperor").

Op. 76. Six Variations on an Original Theme.

Op. 77. Fantasia, Gm.

Op. 78. Sonata, F♯.

Op. 80. Fantasia, for piano, chorus, and orchestra.

Op. 81a. Sonata, E♭ ("Lebewohl").

Op. 89. Polonaise, C.

Op. 90. Sonata, Em.

Op. 101. Sonata, A.

Op. 105. Six Themes and Variations ("Scotch").

Op. 106. Sonata, B♭ ("Hammerklavier").

Op. 107. Ten Themes and Variations ("Scotch").

Op. 109. Sonata, E.

Op. 110. Sonata, A♭.

Op. 111. Sonata, Cm.

Op. 119. Eleven Bagatelles.

Op. 120. Thirty-three Variations on a Waltz of Diabelli.

Op. 126. Six Bagatelles.

Op. 129. Rondo capriccioso ("The Rage over the Lost Groschen").

WORKS WITHOUT OPUS NUMBERS

IN VARIATION FORM

Nine variations on a waltz by Dressler (very early work).

Nine variations in A on "Quant' è più bello."

Six variations in G on "Nel cor più non mi sento."

Twelve variations in C on Menuet à la Vigane.

Twelve variations in A on a Russian dance, "Das Waldmädchen."

Eight variations in C on "Une Fièvre brûlante."

Ten variations in B♭ on "La Stessa, la stessissima."

Seven variations in F on "Kind, willst du ruhig schlafen."

Eight variations in F on "Tändeln und scherzen."

Fifteen variations in A on "Es war einmal ein alter Mann."

Six variations in G (easy).

Six variations in F on a Swiss song.

Twenty-four variations in D on "Vieni amore."

Seven variations in C on "God Save the King."

Five variations in D on "Rule Brittania."

Eight variations in B♭ on "Ich hab' ein kleines Hüttchen nur."

Thirty-two variations in Cm.

Nine variations in A on a theme from "La Molinara."

Six variations in G on a theme from "La Molinara."

For Four Hands

Variations in C on a theme of Count Waldstein.

Variations in D on "Ich denke dein."

IN OTHER FORMS

Rondo in A.

Andante in F.

Bagatelle, "Für Elise" (the authenticity of this piece was formerly questioned, but it is now considered genuine).

Ecossaises (edited by Reinecke and later by Busoni).

Dreizehn Ländler.

Prelude, Fm.

28

Gavotte (for four hands; published first by Schirm. in 1910).

Cadenzas for the first four concertos, ten in all.

Rondo in B♭, with orchestra (posthumous and unfinished. It was completed by Czerny and published in 1829).

CADENZAS FOR THE FIRST FOUR CONCERTOS

Albert .... for No. 4 (B. and B.).

Beethoven .... see above.

Brahms .... for No. 4 (Breit.).

Bülow .... for No. 4 (Leuckart).

Busoni .... for No. 4 (Rahter).

Beach .... for No. 4.

Czerny .... for No. 1 (Haslinger).

Dohnányi .... for No. 4 (Doblinger).

Dreyschock ...... for No. 3.

Ganz .... for No. 1 (C. M. C.).

Godowsky .... for No. 4 (C. Fischer).

Henselt .... for No. 2 (Schlesinger).

Jadassohn .... for No. 4 (Breit.).

Medtner .... for No. 4 (E. M. R.).

Moscheles .... for Nos. 1, 2, 3, 4 (Senff).

Reinecke .... for Nos. 1, 2, 3, 4 (Breit.).

Röntgen .... for Nos. 1, 2, 4 (Alsbach).

Rubinstein ...... for Nos. 1, 2, 3, 4 (Schott).

Schumann, C. .... for Nos. 3, 4 (Rieter-Biedermann).

Saint-Saëns ...... for No. 4 (Durand).

A fine transcription of the "German Dances" and the "Country Dances" by Zeiss is published by Schirmer.

Liszt has transcribed some of the songs, among which the "Penitential Song" stands out as especially good (Schirm.).

This Olympian personage has established himself so completely that remarks here are all but out of place. His music represents the noblest thought of his era and will always remain one of its most surprising products. He did some inferior writing from the tonal standpoint as well as some poor orchestration, but there is very little poor thought. There are many things that would benefit tonally by transcription (who shall aspire to do it?); but it is rare to find anything stupid or silly, though Op. 80 is almost that, and certainly some of the sonata movements are dull.

It is illuminating to recall that during the World War Parisian audiences fell off so much at orchestral concerts at which only "Allied" music was played that Beethoven had to be reinstated in order to attract attendance again. This, as much as anything, indicates the universality of his music. The sturdy peasant-Jupiter will doubtless continue to fling his thunderbolts with effect for another century.

There are a dozen sonatas which are good from beginning to end and adapted to concert performance. These are Op. 13, the "Pathétique" (perhaps a trifle too well known), Op. 26, 27, Nos. 1 and 2 (also too familiar), 28, 31, No. 2, Op. 53, 57, 90, 101, and 111.

Another group of sonatas contains movements of unequal merit. Some have one or two movements of great beauty and a tiresome one. These sonatas are not adapted for public playing, but may be enjoyed in private if one skips the dull parts: Op. 7 (*second and third movements), 10, No. 2 (*second and third), 10, No. 3 (*second and third), 14, No. 1 (*second), 14, No. 2 (*second), 31, No. 3 (*second and third), 78 (*first).

Several sonatas are quite unattractive—Op. 22, 31, No. 1, and 54 have very little to commend them. Op. 28 is effective and not too frequently played. Its pastoral character in the first and last movements, its finely tempered slow movement, and its humorous scherzo offer charming pictures. The dramatic and picturesque Op. 31, No. 2, is magnificent from beginning to end. Op. 53 and 57 are, of course, among the most memorable. Op. 90 displays marvelous artistry and skill in writing and remarkable economy of means. There is hardly another sonata in which the great voice of Beethoven speaks as directly and as simply as here. Op. 101, with its Madonna-and-lilies first movement, its contrasting march, its short adagio where float foreshadowings of *Tristan*, and its good-humored finale, is too rarely played. Because of its Gargantuan fugue, which, however, Busoni champions, Op. 106, the "Hammerklavier," can never be genuinely successful. This fugue taxes the power of the piano too severely and cannot give the effect obviously intended, though one is lost in admiration for the pianist who arrives safely at the end. The other movements are wonderfully beautiful and not too difficult. The adagio is so long (it takes about ten minutes to play it) that it could be introduced on a program without the other movements. Op. 109 is a lovely work of fine quality and good contrasting parts: the finale loses itself in the true ecstasy of Beethoven. Op. 110 begins with a movement containing dull technical devices, but it improves in interest as the contrapuntal parts and the aria-like sections begin. The sonata unexpectedly emerges from the introspective quality which has pervaded it to end brilliantly. Op. 111 is altogether perfect and glorious; the movements contrast admirably, and the work ends on a highly spiritual and ethereal note. It is amusing to recall that a friend of Beethoven, on hearing him play the sonata, asked why he did not add a brilliant third movement. Beethoven, sizing him up, answered that it was because he had no time to write it.

There are few occasions when the early bagatelles are desirable. Their moods are fleeting and obvious. The later bagatelles, Op. 119 and 126, are mildly pleasing. The Prelude in F would be a satisfactory novelty on a program, but the other preludes, Op. 39, which ramble vacuously through every key in turn, have only a special interest. Among the frankly tedious pieces are the Polonaise, Op. 89, the Fantasy, Op. 77, and the Fantasy, Op. 80, though the latter has attractive spots and a superb elemental theme which recalls the great melody from the last movement of the Ninth Symphony.

Of the variation sets Op. 120 takes first place undoubtedly, but more as a macrocosm of Beethoven's genius than as a piece for a program, for it is of endless length. The Beethoven student, however, must know it; Beethoven intended it as a summing up of his art. If Op. 120 is the macrocosm, the Thirty-two Variations in C minor are the microcosm. The strong, simple theme of eight measures with its strict adherence to the harmonic scheme suggests a passacaglia. It is of admirable proportions, dignified and entertaining. Many of the other sets are so charming that it is a pity they are neglected. How pleasant it would be to hear "Nel cor piu" played with exquisite finish on a program once in a while! May the human race never become too sophisticated to enjoy its childlike naïveté. Many other pleasures will be revealed to the one who browses among the many sets.

The concertos enjoy continued vogue, and even Op. 15, formerly neglected by virtuosi, has been brought out of obscurity. The orchestration of Op. 73 is very poor. The work could be made far more beautiful and effective with a good one. Why does no one try his hand at it? The orchestrations of Op. 37 and 58 are much better, and new ones are less needful. If anyone wants a novelty by Beethoven, he should play the posthumous Rondo in B♭ with orchestra. The Triple Concerto is another little-played work, but it is very curious and interesting. Though it bears the opus number 56, the next one to that of the "Appassionata," it might be taken in part to be a work by Mozart, though many of the passages could never have occurred to him. The use of the three instruments is also reactionary—in the manner of the old concerto grosso.

Attention is called to the Rondo, "The Rage over the Lost Groschen." It is a charmingly comic rage, musically very interesting and a certain success for a pianist with good fingers. Another long forgotten piece worth remembering is the "Fifteen Variations" on a theme from the *Eroica Symphony*. The charmingly frivolous "Ecossaises," the little *Albumblatt* "Für Elise," and the transcriptions by Zeiss are not to be forgotten.

31

JOHANNES BRAHMS

(1833-1897)

Op. 1. Sonata, C.

Op. 2. Sonata, F♯m.

Op. 4. Scherzo, E♭m.

Op. 5. Sonata, Fm.

Op. 9. Variations on a Theme of Schumann.

Op. 10. Four Ballades (No. 1, "Edward").

Op. 15. Concerto, Dm, with orchestra.

Op. 21. No. 1. Variations on an Original Theme.

No. 2. Variations on a Hungarian Theme.

Op. 23. Variations on a Theme of Schumann (four hands).

Op. 24. Variations and Fugue on a Theme of Handel.

Op. 35. Variations on a Theme of Paganini, two books.

Op. 39. Waltzes (four hands; also to be had for two hands).

Op. 52. Liebeslieder Waltzes (for four hands and vocal quartet).

Op. 56b. Variations on a Theme of Haydn, for two pianos.

Op. 65. Neue Liebeslieder (for four hands and vocal quartet).

Op. 76. Piano Pieces (Clavierstücke).
Capriccio, F♯m.
Capriccio, Bm.
Intermezzo, A♭.
Intermezzo, B♭.
Capriccio, C♯m.
Intermezzo, A.
Intermezzo, Am.
Capriccio, C.

Op. 79. Two Rhapsodies, Bm, Gm.

Op. 83. Concerto, B♭, with orchestra.

Op. 116. Fantasias.
Capriccio, Dm.
Intermezzo, Am.
Capriccio, Gm.
Intermezzo, E.
Intermezzo, Em.
Intermezzo, E.
Capriccio, Dm.

Op. 117. Intermezzi.
E♭ ("Cradle Song").
B♭m.
C♯m.

Op. 118. Piano Pieces.
Intermezzo, C.
Intermezzo, A.
Ballade, Gm.
Intermezzo, Fm.
Romance, F.
Intermezzo, E♭m.

Op. 119. Piano Pieces.
Intermezzo, Bm.
Intermezzo, E.
Intermezzo, C.
Rhapsody, E♭.

WORKS WITHOUT OPUS NUMBERS

Twenty Hungarian Dances.

Gavotte of Gluck for Clara Schumann.

Studies for Piano (transcriptions).
Étude after Chopin's Op. 25, No. 2.
Rondo after Weber's "Perpetual Motion."
Presto after Bach (first arrangement).
Presto after Bach (second arrangement).
Chaconne (Bach) for the Left Hand Alone.

Impromptu for the Left Hand Alone after Schubert.

Two Gigues and Sarabandes after Bach.

Theme and Variations after the Second Movement of the Sextet, Op. 18.

Sonata, for Two Pianos, after the Piano Quintet.

Cadenzas to the Bach Dm Concerto.

Cadenzas to Mozart concertos in Dm, G, Cm.

Fifty-One Exercises.

Presser publishes a Brahms album.
Schirmer publishes an album of pieces chosen by Joseffy (*Musician's Library*).

TRANSCRIPTIONS

Klengel ....
    Choralvorspiel and Fugue, "O Trau-
    rigkeit, O, Herzeleid" (Siegel).

Busoni ....
    Choralvorspiele, Op. 122 (2 vols.
    Simrock).

Kirchner ....
    Album of Songs and Lieder (Sim-
    rock).

Behr ....
    Fugue, Ab (Simrock).

Breitkopf publishes the complete works in a definitive edition.

Brahms was formerly considered unpianistic because those who had confined their keyboard experiences to the classics and Chopin and Liszt found difficulty in mastering his different idiom. But, since nothing is considered unpianistic today, he must be called a technical innovator. He developed a type of playing which one may call, somewhat clumsily, virtuoso musicianship, or better perhaps, musical virtuosity. Those who know his "Fifty-one Exercises" (as opposed to those of Czerny and Chopin) will understand what is meant. This type of exercise lacks the Czerny fluency and the Chopin, Bach, and Beethoven manner. It demands an independence of the fingers gained by much contrapuntal work as a basis, with less study of the development of speed as such. With all Brahms's interest in the piano it must be regretfully admitted that his piano works as a class are not the equal in interest of his orchestral works, chamber music, or songs.

Most of his piano compositions, however, are worthy of study, and some few achieve equality with those of Bach, Beethoven, and Chopin. His first three may be considered to have been written before he had developed his own manner. They recall previous composers and are obviously patterned on them. Certain movements of the first two sonatas are fine. The slow movement of Op. 1, the theme of which is based on a folk song, "Verstohlen geht der Mond auf," preserves the *volkstümlich* quality throughout and is worth playing alone. The entire sonata is good, even if not original. In the second sonata the best parts are the slow movement and the scherzo, although the last part of the scherzo contains some poor writing. The rest of the sonata is full of the ghosts of Mendelssohn and Beethoven. The Scherzo, Op. 4, is brilliant and pleasing in an old-fashioned way. The Variations, Op. 9, are for self-communion and are lovely for that purpose. They lack brilliance and variety, but are sincere and appealing music. The theme is from the *Albumblätter,* and he uses another of these for his ninth variation. The Sonata, Op. 5, is the only one heard much in concerts, and though magnificent in its general effect, it has a badly written finale. It has one technical passage which a pianist cannot do without either counterfeiting or slowing down, for it is physically impossible to play it. The form of the finale is also unconvincing, and the last page requires more *ff* than the given notes allow without forcing the tone. For those who lack the power for the heavier movements there is the lovely andante with its ecstatic close. The first Ballade, "Edward," and the second one, unnamed, should be known to all pianists. The third is less interesting, and the fourth is arid.

The variation sets, Op. 21, seem to have been forgotten, but pianists of the future may exploit them. Virtuosi of the present have not been able to wear out either the Handel or the Paganini sets of variations. Although the Handel set is difficult to play really well, it is not beyond the powers of an ordinarily good pianist; the Paganini sets are locked and sealed with seven seals.

One of the waltzes, in Ab, has achieved fame, but the other fifteen are just as good, and many of them are much more interesting. They are not very suitable for concert use, for they are merely arrangements for two hands and not transcriptions; but they are perfect to play for oneself.

Brahms at one time deserted the piano except as an adjunct to chamber music and songs, and it was not till Op. 76 that he returned to his own instrument. This work is one of the high points of piano music, and no pianist should omit to study some of the pieces of which it is composed. In the days when Brahms was considered unpianistic the first edition of *Grove's Dictionary* had the following to say of the opus in question: "Some of the Intermezzos, simple and touching, contrast pleasantly with Capriccios which offer almost insurmountable difficulties to the most skillful virtuoso." This opinion of 1889 need deter no pianist of today from enjoying these eight remarkable pieces.

No. 1 of this group is a picture of gloom lightened later by a plaintive melody; No. 2 is the much played and loved B minor; No. 3 is a delicate serenade; No. 4 is a simple lied; No. 5, a piece of great rhythmic interest, contains in its short span a lifetime of emotion; No. 6 is a pastoral; No. 7 has a "King of Thule" atmosphere; No. 8, with no set melody, contrives to appear endlessly melodic. The Two Rhapsodies are very well known.

After this work there is another interim in Brahms's activity in writing for the piano. It seems strange that in the last decades of the nineteenth century

34

the adjective "austere" was indiscriminately applied to most of his compositions; we have since learned that there are actually few works to which that
epithet justly applies. Brahms never approaches the sentimental, yet he is far
from the bleak region of austerity. The first and third pieces of Op. 116 might
possibly be described as austere, for there is little lusciousness about them; but
these alone out of the whole Brahms literature deserve the epithet. And after
all, why should he not depict "austerity" along with other moods? What wistful loneliness there is in No. 2! Huneker has called No. 4 the most beautiful
piece in the world. If one considers a sense of otherworldliness a quality out-
ranking every other, then the piece may well be worthy of such praise. No. 5
presents a riddle which no one should miss; its strange dissonances foreshadow
the more modest of the curious harmonies of today and resemble nothing else
in the piano music of Brahms. No. 6 is supernal in its calmness; No. 7, agitated
and rugged. On the whole Op. 116 is less attractive than any of the other
works.

Op. 117, No. 1, is the celebrated "Cradle Song," one of his most lovely
compositions. Its middle section, if played *ppp,* is like the vagueness of sleep
when the song drifts away. It is fully equaled in beauty by No. 2. One must
not be deterred by its unpromising look. Brahms often confuses the eye by
writing uncompromising-looking, large, black notes, which must sound like
small white ones, if the phrase be allowed. This piece should be played with
Chopinesque delicacy of touch and an infinity of nuance. Chopin would have
written the piece so that it expressed itself better to the eye. Brahms does not
bother, with the result that it has taken him much longer to make his way.

The depths of Op. 118 are on the whole easy to plumb, for the moods of
the six pieces are fairly obvious. With what exhilaration the first piece
launches itself! Like a parachute it descends, rapidly at first then more slowly.
The second, a tender andantino, is easily understood, though not so easily
played. The third is the rugged Ballade; the fourth, truly Brahmsian, turns
and twists with an inner urge; the fifth, a charming romance, contains little
flutelike runs and tiny cadenzas; the sixth, his grandest short piece, in the
heavy key of E♭ minor, is a lament, a dirge, a threnody, but Brahms called it
merely "Intermezzo," so little did he care for the labels of his pieces.

Op. 119 ends with the brilliant Rhapsody in E♭, of which it is unnecessary
to speak, since it is now very frequently played. The other intermezzi are gen-

35

erally interesting and melodious, especially No. 3 in C, with the clear and joyous atmosphere of a June day. No. 1 has less charm and gives the impression of having been done with the head alone. No. 2 of this opus deserves attention not only because of its beauty but because of its compact structure and a certain manipulation of the theme, which easily escapes the casual player. The piece contains apparently two themes, but closer study reveals the fact that they are one and the same, but so modified rhythmically and modally that it seems impossible that the melody should be identical. Brahms accomplished this feat twice in these later pieces (the other example is in Op. 117, No. 2), both times without a trace of pedantry.

The transcriptions, with the exception of the ineffably lovely one of the Gavotte of Gluck, are not successful, although the transcription of the Chaconne of Bach may be of use in providing good music for training the left hand. Busoni's version is very much finer, if one is not bent on doing it with one hand alone. The idea of putting Chopin's Étude Op. 25, No. 2, into sixths would appear to indicate that Brahms had little feeling for Chopin's quality. The same may be said of his treatment of the "Hungarian Dances." They are good solid pieces, but they do not retain the lightness and temperament of the originals. They differ widely from those of Liszt (compare also remarks on Bartók and Dohnányi), who was undoubtedly in closer sympathy with the feeling of the music. It is not generally known that these pieces were written by known composers, many of whom were still alive when Brahms took their property. They had good reason to be highly indignant when not a whisper about them appeared on the title page of the transcriptions.*

The two concertos are equally magnificent, but they possess distinct characteristics. In recent years they have been almost the most popular concertos, since the present trend gives the piano a part in a symphony—and that is what these concertos really are—rather than effective pianistic passages with the orchestra for a background. The piano part is very difficult, but the musical delights derived from playing, even very imperfectly, these gigantic works are unexcelled. Endlessly melodic, they flow on and on in great rivers of sound. Brahms wrote nothing for piano more inspired than these two concertos.

*If anyone wishes to see the originals of these melodies one can find them in Volume 327 of the Steingräber edition. The volume is entitled *Ungarische, türkische, und slavische Tänze und Märsche.*

FRANK BRIDGE
(1879—)

Four Characteristic Pieces (1917).
  Water Nymphs.
  Fragrance.
  Bittersweet.
  Fireflies.

Three Improvisations for the Left Hand (1918).
  At Dawn.
  A Vigil.
  A Revel.

Three Sketches (1915).
  April.
  Rosemary.
  Valse capricieuse.

Sally in Our Alley, and Cherry Ripe (four hands).

Miniature Pastorals (two sets, easy).
  (All Rogers)

A Fairy Tale, in four parts.
  The Princess.
  The Ogre.
  The Spell.
  The Prince.

Arabesque, a Sea Idyll (1905).

Two Capriccios, Columbine, Minuet, Romance.

Three Poems.
  Solitude.
  Ecstasy.
  Sunset.

The Hour-glass (1920).
  Dusk.
  The Dew Fairy.
  The Midnight Tide.

Three Lyrics.
  Heart's Ease.
  Dainty Rogue.
  The Hedgerow.

In Autumn.
  Retrospect.
  Through the Leaves.

Sonata (1926).
  (All Aug.)

Lament (Curwen).

Publishers: Aug., Winthrop Rogers, Curwen, Schirm.

With the exception of the sonata all the piano music of Bridge is minor poetry. Lovers of miniatures will enjoy his works. For the left hand alone the "Three Improvisations" may be used, or they may be played with both hands. They are not difficult and thus may fill a place. The sonata was introduced in 1926 without much success.

MISCELLANEOUS BRITISH COMPOSERS

Older Writers

W. STERNDALE BENNETT
(1816-1875)

Op. 10. Three Musical Sketches.
Op. 46. Maid of Orleans Sonata.

Four Concertos (*No. 3. The celebrated Barcarolle is in No. 4).

JOHN FIELD
(1782-1837)

Eighteen Nocturnes.

Newer Writers

WILLIAM BAINES
(1899-1922)

Paradise Gardens.
Milestones.

Seven Preludes (Elkins).

GRANVILLE BANTOCK
(1868—)

Scotch Scenes (Swan).
English Scenes.
Russian Scenes (Bosworth).

Arabian Nights (Swan).
Tales and Dances from Lalla Rookh (Swan).
Numerous pieces in the smaller forms.

ARTHUR BENJAMIN
(1893—)

Piano Suite (O.U.P.).

LORD BERNERS (GERALD TYRWHITT)
(1883—)

Fragments psychologiques.
   Hatred.
   Laughter.
   A Sigh.
Le Poisson d'or.

Three Little Funeral Marches.
   For a Statesman.
   For a Canary.
   For a Rich Aunt.

ARTHUR BLISS
(1891—)

Masks (Curwen).

YORK BOWEN
(1884—)

Concert Polonaise.
Sonata.
Ballade.

Hans Andersen's Fairy Tales (*Nos. 4 and 6. Ascherberg).
Second Suite.

BENJAMIN DALE
(1885—)

Sonata, Dm (1906. Novello).

FREDERICK DELIUS
(1863-1934)

Three Preludes (O.U.P.).
Dance for the Harpsichord (1922).
Concerto, Cm (1907).

Five Pieces.
  (All U. E.)

H. BALFOUR GARDINER
(1877—)

Five Pieces (easy).
Michaelschurch.
Humoresque.
Mere.
Prelude: De Profundis (Forsyth).
Shepherd Fennel's Dance—after Hardy.

Shenandoah (*Nos. 2 and 4. Schirm.).
Jesmond.
Malcombe.
A Sailor's Piece.
(All Schirm.)

ARTHUR HINTON
(1869—)

A Summer Pilgrim to the White Mountains.

Op. 24. Concerto, Dm.
(J. Fischer)

JOSEPH HOLBROOKE
(1878—)

Op. 4. Ten Pieces (No. 1 is Valse Caprice on "Three Blind Mice").
Op. 18. No. 1. Kleine Suite (*Scherzo).
Op. 42. Ten Rhapsody Études (1907. Larway).

Op. 52. Poem Concerto "Gwyn-ap-Nudd" (Chest.).
Op. 59. Four Futurist Dances (Chest.).
Impressions of a Tour, ten pieces (Ric.).

GUSTAV HOLST
(1874-1934)

*Toccata (Curwen).
*Chrissemas Day in the Morning.
Two Folk Song Fragments (O.U.P.).

HERBERT HOWELLS
(1892—)

Snapshots (1918).
The Street Dance.
The Polar Bear.
Wee Willie Winkie.

*Op. 14. No. 3. The Procession (Ascherberg).
Concerto (1925. Curwen).

GORDON JACOB
(1895—)

Concerto, for piano and strings.

CONSTANT LAMBERT
(1905—)

Sonata.

LEO LIVENS
(1896—)

Impressions (1915).
The Moorlands, five pieces (W. Rogers).

Three Studies (1916. O.U.P.).
Naiades.
Heat Waves.
Hailstorms.

JOHN B. MCEWEN
(1868—)

Vignettes (1913).
Sonata, Em.

ALEXANDER MACKENZIE
(1847-1935)

Scottish Concerto, with orchestra.
Concerto, with orchestra (Schott).

MORFYDD OWEN
(1892-1918)

Volumes of collected writing (O.U.P.).

FLORIAN PASCAL (JOSEPH WILLIAMS)
(1888—)

Five Sketches in Irish Style (J. Williams).

KAIKHOSRU SORABJI
(1896—)

Two Concertos.
Three Sonatas.
Prelude, Interlude, and Fugue.

Other compositions, all atonal.
(Curwen)

WILLIAM WALTON
(1902—)

Sinfonia concertante.

The situation of the British composer today is unusual. After having made a good beginning and produced Purcell, the country came under Continental influence, especially the German, and the composers remained slaves to it until recently when they suddenly took the bit in their teeth, bolted Handel, Mendelssohn, and Wagner, and went gaily about their own business scrapping all the old inhibitions, traditions, and complexes.

Elgar, though he started the movement many years ago, worked on traditional lines, but he did advance the music of England from the Mendelssohn period to the Wagnerian. Later composers easily fell in line with the desire for a newer music. The chief field of their endeavors is still vocal music—since that has ever been the national manner of musical self-expression—and, to a lesser degree, orchestral; but certain composers like Bax and Ireland and, in a smaller way, Scott and Goossens have added considerably to the literature of the piano. Some of this music, as in Bax and Ireland, puts down roots deep in British soil, whereas other writers turn to the Continent for inspiration. A Hindu has discovered atonality and counterpoint and has wedded these seemingly antagonistic elements into gigantic freaks. Bowen, Holbrooke, Scott, Coleridge-Taylor, and Bantock have been very prolific, and their works suffer in consequence. Probably not much of their music will survive.

Interest among the English in their traditional music and in their earliest writers is strong, and great numbers of editions of early works are appearing. For these early writers see under "Clavecinists."

Among the composers on the present list (it must be recalled that the most prominent writers are given elsewhere in full) Field occupies an important position as one of Chopin's chief inspirations. He really need be remembered solely for this reason, for his imperfect mastery of form, except in the Bb Nocturne, kills the nocturnes, though they contain good ideas. Bennett with his Mendelssohnian compositions need not detain us long either; but the first edition of Grove indicates the enormous seriousness with which he was taken. The pieces listed here were considered important at his time. Op. 10 was famous in its day.

The jolly transcriptions of Stanford's "Four Irish Dances" by Grainger are not to be missed by those looking for the humorous in music. York Bowen's work is all in the older manner and does not offer strong fare. His is a practiced hand, and his pieces are well made. "Masks" by Arthur Bliss is an effective series, brilliant, entertaining, free harmonically, and with good ideas. Coleridge-Taylor endeavors to develop the Negro note in his writing, but it is all rather light and tenuous. Delius, however important he may be in other fields, is not successful in his piano compositions. Dale wrote a sonata in the older German romantic style, melodious and playable. The humorous "Futurist Dances" of Holbrooke are perhaps his most original and entertaining work.

The fresh Toccata on a Northumbrian tune by Holst whets the appetite for more original and personal pieces like it. The folk tune lends itself admirably to the toccata style. The dissonances of the close recall the wheezy noises of the street organ. Here again is humor. A few years ago he published one or two more pieces which present other old tunes in a new light with excellent effect. Morfydd Owen was a Welsh writer of great promise; his works have been collected in a memorial edition. In these simple pieces is to be found a quality closely related to the old folk tunes, simple, full of deep, almost religious feeling, voicing the thoughts of inarticulate people. As a pianistic expression of the Welsh musical genius it is interesting. Florian Pascal's "Five Sketches in Irish Style" do for the Irish what Owen did for the Welsh, though as music they are more developed and as pieces they are better.

Other writers are R. E. Agnew, Hugo Anson, E. L. Bainton, George Garratt, Ernest Moeran, Colin Taylor, Dorothy Howell, Martin Shaw, Norman Peterkin, Sir Arthur Somervell, Gordon Slater, H. E. Randerson, Felix Swinstead, Felix White, and John Williams.

FERRUCIO BUSONI

(1866-1924)

ORIGINAL COMPOSITIONS

Op. 3. Five Pieces for Piano (Cranz).

Op. 4. Piano Piece (Doblinger).

Op. 5. Piano Piece (Doblinger).

Op. 6. First Ballet Scene.

Op. 8. Sonata (fragment).

Op. 9. Una Festa di villagio, six pieces.

Op. 11. Danze antiche.

Op. 12. Macchiette medioevale.

Op. 13. Danza notturna.

Op. 14. Menuetto.

Op. 16. Six Études (Breit.).

Op. 17. Étude in Form of Variations (Gutmann).

Op. 19. Tre pezzi nello stilo antico.

Op. 20. Second Ballet Suite (Breit.).

Op. 22. Variations and Fugue on Chopin's Cm Prelude (Breit.).

Op. 27. Finnish Folk Melodies (four hands; Peters).

Op. 30. Two Dance Pieces
War Dance.
Peace Dance (Rahter).

Op. 31a. Third Ballet Scene (Breit.).

Op. 31b. Konzertstück, with orchestra (Breit.).

Op. 33a. Fourth Ballet Scene—Waltz and Galop (Breit.).

Op. 33b. Six Pieces, in two books (Peters).
I. Schwermut.
Frohsinn.
Scherzino.
II. Fantasia in modo antico.
Finnish Ballade.
Exeunt omnes.

Op. 36. Prelude and Fugue.

Op. 37. Twenty-four Preludes.

Op. 39. Concerto, with orchestra and male chorus, in five parts (Breit.).

Op. 44. Indian Fantasia, with orchestra (based on American Indian themes; Breit.).

Op. 53. Tanzwalzer. In Memoriam Strauss (Breit.).

Op. 54. Romance and Scherzo (two more movements to be added to Op. 31b; Breit.).

Op. 61. Menuetto capriccioso (Cranz).

Op. 70. Gavotte (Cranz.).

WITHOUT OPUS NUMBERS

Die Klavierübung (Breit.).
First part . . . Six Etudes (exercises) and Preludes.
Second part . . . Three Études (exercises) and Preludes.
Third part . . . Lo Staccato.
Fourth part . . . Eight Études of Cramer.
Fifth part . . . Variations on the Cm Prelude of Chopin.
Perpetuum mobile and scales.

Elegies, Six Pieces (Breit.).
1. Nach der Wendung ("Recueillement").
2. All'Italia ("In modo italiano").
3. Meine Seele bangt zu dir.
4. Turandot's Frauengemach ("Intermezzo").
5. Die Nächtlichen.
6. Erscheinung ("Notturno").

Three Albumblätter (Breit.).

Kultaselle Variations on a Finnish Melody.

Nuit de Nöel.

Berceuse.

Indian Diary, four studies on American Indian motifs (Breit.).

Five Short Pieces for the Development of Polyphonic Playing (Breit.).

An die Jugend (Breit.).
Preludietta, Fughetta ed Esercizio.
Prelude, Fugue, and Fuga figurata (after Bach).
Giga, Bolero e Variazioni (after Mozart).
Introduzione e Capriccio (Paganinesco), Epilogo.

Sonatina.

Sonatina secunda.

Sonata in Diem nativitatis Christi MCMXVII.

Sonatina brevis "In Signe Joanni Sebastiani Magni."

Sonatina super Carmen, Kammerfantasia.

Toccata (Prelude, Fantasia, Ciacona).
(All Breit.)

ARRANGEMENTS, TRANSCRIPTIONS, STUDIES, AND IMITATIONS
(NACHDICHTUNGEN) INSPIRED BY BACH

Vol. I. Arrangements I.
Dedication.
Twelve Little Preludes.
Six Little Preludes and a Fughetta.
Fifteen Two-part and Fifteen Three-part Inventions.
Four Duets.
Prelude and Fugue, and Allegro, Eb.

Vol. II. Arrangements II.
Masterpieces. Chromatic Fantasia and Fugue.
Concerto, Dm.
Aria with Thirty Variations.

Vol. III. Transcriptions.
Prelude and Fugue.
Prelude and Fugue Eb.

Organ Toccato, Dm.
Organ Toccata, C.
Ten Choralvorspiele.
Chaconne.

Vol. IV. Compositions and Imitations ("Nachdichtungen").
Fantasia on the Death of My Father.
Preludio, Fuga, and Fuga figurata.
Capriccio on the Departure of a Beloved Brother.
Fantasia, Adagio, and Fugue.
Choralvorspiel and Fugue on a Bach Fragment (the short edition of the Fantasia contrappuntistica).
Fantasia contrappuntistica.

Vol. V. The Well-tempered Clavichord.
  First Part, with Appendix and an Analysis
    of the Fugue from Beethoven's Sonata,
    Op. 106.
Vol. VI. The Well-tempered Clavichord.
  Second Part.
Vol. VII. Toccata and Fugue, E♭.
  Two Toccatas.

Improvisation on a Bach Chorallied, two
  pianos.
Two Counterpoint Studies.
Fantasia and Fugue, Am.
Canonical Variations on a Theme from
  Bach's "Das musicalische Opfer."
Chromatic Fantasia and Fugue, arranged
  for piano and cello.
Versuch einer organischer Notenschrift.

ARRANGEMENTS, TRANSCRIPTIONS, AND STUDIES OF COMPOSERS
OTHER THAN BACH

Beethoven . . Ecossaises.

  Two Cadenzas for the Con-
    certo in G (Rahter).

Brahms . . . Choralvorspiele, Op. 122
    (Simrock).

Cornelius . . Fantasia on motifs from *The
    Barber of Bagdad*
    (Kahnt).

Goldmark . Piano score of *Merlin,* and
    a Fantasia on the same
    (Kahnt).

Liszt . . . . . . Fantasia and Fugue on a
    Choral of Meyerbeer "Ad
    nos ad salutarem undam"
    (Breit.).

  Polonaise, E, with a closing
    cadenza (Simrock).

  Spanish Rhapsody, arranged
    for piano and orchestra
    (Siegel).

  Figaro Fantasia (completed
    from an unfinished man-
    uscript; Breit.).

  Six Paganini Études (Breit.).

  Heroic March in the Hun-
    garian Style (Schle-
    singer).

  Mephisto Waltz (Schuberth).

  Instructive Edition of the
    Fantasia on "Don Juan"
    and the Paganini Études
    (Breit.).

Hungarian Rhapsody, No. 19.

Andantino capriccioso
  (Breit.).

Mozart . . . Cadenzas for concertos, Dm,
    E♭, C, Cm, E♭ (see under
    Mozart).

  Fantasia für eine Orgelwalze,
    two pianos.

  Overture to *Don Giovanni.*

  Overture to *Die Entführung
    aus dem Serail.*

  Overture to *Die Zauberflöte,*
    for pianola.

  Andantino from the Ninth
    Concerto, with cadenza.

  Duettino concertante on the
    E♭ Concerto, for two
    pianos.

Novaček . . Scherzo from First String
    Quartet.

Schubert . . Five "Deutsche Tänze," with
    Coda and Seven Trios.

  Five Minuets with Six Trios.

  "Der Teufel als Hydrauliker."

  Overtures in B, D, D, E.

  Overture in the Italian Style,
    C.

  Overture in the Italian Style,
    D.

  (All Breit.)

J. S. BACH'S WORKS IN THE BUSONI EDITION

I, II . . . . . . Well-tempered Clavichord.
III . . . . Small Preludes.
IV . . . . Two-part Inventions.
V . . . . Three-part Inventions.
VI . . . . French Suites.
VII . . . . . . English Suites.
VIII . . . . English Suites.
IX . . . . . . Partitas.
X . . . . Partitas.
XI, XII . . . Concertos after Benedetto Marcello.
XIII . . . . . Italian concerto, etc.
XIV . . . . . Chromatic Fantasia.
XV . . . . . . Aria with Thirty Variations ("Goldberg").
XVI . . . . . Fantasia and Fugue, Dm.
XVII . . . . . Toccatas.
XVIII . . . . Toccatas, Fantasia, and Fugue.

XIX . . . . . Preludes and Fugues.
XX . . . . . . Preludes, Fughettas, and Fugues.
XXI . . . . Fugues.
XXII . . . . Fantasias and Fugues.
XXIII . . . . Suites.
XXIV . . . . Suites and Sonatas.
XXV . . . . Sonatas, Cm Concerto, Fugues, etc.

(All Schirm.).

This edition, which almost occupies the position of an original work, is highly recommended to students. It gives a sympathetic introduction to Bach, especially to those for whom he is not easy of access.

Publishers: Breit., Zimmerman, Siegel, Schlesinger, Schuberth, Simrock, Kahnt, Cranz, Gutmann, Peters, Doblinger.

To make a just estimate of this Janus-faced musician is not easy. His music is experimental, intellectual, and often cold. He loves mystery hardly less than counterpoint, energy no less than vagueness. He is as absorbed with the invention of a new aesthetic of music as he is with Bach. To understand this imposing figure these things must be remembered. His music falls therefore into three types: the first is for the virtuoso, the second gives a backward look toward Bach, and the third looks forward toward a possible new ideal.

Busoni has undoubtedly enlarged the outlook of pianists by the nobility and grandeur of his treatment of Bach. His words "I want the unknown" explain him perhaps as well as anything, and they give the reason for his restlessness as well as for the continual alteration of his three styles, for they coexisted practically during his whole life. His ideals for the education of a pianist-musician were of such a dizzy altitude (they are set forth in the first volume of the *Clavichord*) that few will attain them; but they serve as a criterion. It should be added that Busoni practiced what he preached.

His preoccupation with Bach, his love of playing with the themes of other writers and of developing them after his own ideas, and his search for the unknown form the key to the understanding of his greatness. It is natural to suppose that granted such premises, a sort of theoretic music might result, a music to be read and not heard, and that the end of it all would be a species of mathematics. As a matter of fact much of the harmonically advanced type as well as the *Fantasia contrappuntistica* is better read than heard, at least to our, possibly deaf, ears.

One of Busoni's greatest services to pianists is his edition of Bach, a work illuminating and inspiring to an extraordinary degree, and one of the greatest "interpretations" ever compassed. If the *Well-tempered Clavichord* is regarded as the pianist's Bible, then this edition may very properly be looked upon as the "translation." No pianist can afford to remain ignorant of it. In no other way can the budding musician receive such an introduction to the great heart of Bach.

Perhaps the most important and beautiful of all his transcriptions of Bach is the Chaconne. This much transcribed piece emerges from his hands with its character intact and reinforced in a way to enhance its astonishing vigor and feeling. Transcribing transcription seems like painting the lily, but some virtuosi prefer the manner in which Busoni presents Liszt's transcriptions of the Paganini Études to Liszt's own version. (See remarks on this subject under Liszt.)

Those who wish to acquaint themselves with the three sides of Busoni's character may find perhaps the best examples in the following pieces:

Virtuoso Style (Youthful)
Variations on the Cm Prelude of Chopin (1885).
Fourth Ballet Scene, in the form of a concert waltz (1894, mature).
Completion of Liszt's unfinished Fantasia on Mozart's "Figaro's Wedding" (1912).
Transcriptions of Liszt's Paganini Études (1914).
Classical Style
Ciacona (from the Toccata, and not to be confused with his transcription of Bach's Chaconne).
Six Études.

"Searching-for-the-unknown" Style
Elegies, six pieces.
No. 1. "Nach der Wendung" ("After the Turning") represents the actual beginning with the experiments in the "new" style. The other five are in the nature of improvisations on themes from his own compositions.
Sonatina secunda.

The Concerto should also be mentioned. This is his only symphonic work. It is in five movements and uses a male chorus in the finale. The style is neither classical nor Lisztian, but develops a form of its own. He offers in it the results of his musical maturity, a blending of the older and the newer types. It is enormously long and, so far, has not been successful in making its way on the concert stage. This may be on account of the difficulties of adequate presentation, or it may be that, like so many of his compositions, it lacks the vital spark. It is a pity that a man of such remarkable intellectual powers, erudition, and breadth of sympathy, such will to compose and such capability for hard work should lack that something without which it all goes for nothing. Of course, it is possible that to another generation his compositions will appear quite different and that they are merely quiescent for the time.

FRÉDÉRIC FRANÇOIS CHOPIN

(1809-1849)

Op. 1. Rondo, Cm.

Op. 2. Variations on "La ci darem," with orchestra.

Op. 4. Sonata, Cm.

Op. 5. Rondo à la Mazur.

Op. 6. Four Mazurkas, F♯m, C♯m, E, E♭m.

Op. 7. Five Mazurkas, B♭, Am, Fm, A♭, C.

Op. 9. Three Nocturnes, B♭m, E♭, Bm.

Op. 10. Twelve Études.

Op. 11. Concerto, Em (reorchestrated by Tausig).

Op. 12. Brilliant Variations, B♭.

Op. 13. Phantasie on Polish Airs, with orchestra.

Op. 14. Krakoviak, with orchestra.

Op. 15. Three Nocturnes, F, F♯, Gm.

Op. 16. Rondo, E♭.

Op. 17. Four Mazurkas, B, Em, A♭, Am.

Op. 18. Valse, E♭.

Op. 19. Bolero.

Op. 20. Scherzo, Bm.

Op. 21. Concerto, Fm (re-orchestrated by Klindworth).

Op. 22. Andante spianato and Polonaise, with orchestra.

Op. 23. Ballade, Gm.

Op. 24. Four Mazurkas, Gm, C, A♭, Bm.

Op. 25. Twelve Études.

Op. 26. Two Polonaises.

Op. 28. Twenty-four Preludes.

Op. 29. Impromptu, A♭.

Op. 30. Four Mazurkas, Cm, Bm, D♭, C♯.

Op. 31. Scherzo, B♭.

Op. 32. Two Nocturnes, B, A♭.

Op. 33. Four Mazurkas, G♯, D, C, Bm.

Op. 34. Three Waltzes.

Op. 35. Sonata, B♭m.

Op. 36. Impromptu, F♯.

Op. 37. Two Nocturnes, Gm, G.

Op. 38. Ballade, F.

Op. 39. Scherzo, C♯m.

Op. 40. Two Polonaises, A, Cm.

Op. 41. Four Mazurkas, C♯, Em, E, A♭.

Op. 42. Valse, A♭.

Op. 43. Tarantella.

Op. 44. Polonaise, F♯m.

Op. 45. Prelude, C♯m.

Op. 46. Concert Allegro, arranged with orchestra by Nicodé (Aug.).

Op. 47. Ballade, A♭.

Op. 48. Two Nocturnes, Cm. F♯.
Op. 49. Fantasia, Fm.
Op. 50. Three Mazurkas, G, A♭, C♯m.
Op. 51. Impromptu, G♭.
Op. 52. Ballade, Fm.
Op. 53. Polonaise, A♭.
Op. 54. Scherzo, E.
Op. 55. Two Nocturnes, Fm, E♭.
Op. 56. Three Mazurkas, B, C, Cm.

Op. 57. Berceuse.
Op. 58. Sonata, Bm.
Op. 59. Three Mazurkas, Am, A♭, F♯m.
Op. 60. Barcarolle, F♯.
Op. 61. Polonaise-phantasie, A♭.
Op. 62. Two Nocturnes, B, E.
Op. 63. Three Mazurkas, B, Fm, C♯m.
Op. 64. Three Waltzes.

POSTHUMOUS WORKS

(In some editions assigned high opus numbers)

Fourteen Mazurkas.
Five Polonaises.
Three Ecossaises.
Fantasie-Impromptu, C♯m.
Variations, E.
Fugue, Am.
Two Waltzes and a Mazurka, in possession
of Joseph Elsner (Breit.).

Nocturne, Em.
Seven Waltzes.
One Variation for the Hexameron.
Funeral March, Cm.
Rondo, C, for two pianos.
À feuille d'album (Gebetner und Wolff,
available through Breit.).

The works of Chopin form, historically, the third great massif in the mountain range of piano literature—the first being Bach's, the second Beethoven's compositions. For pure piano music Chopin is the greatest of the three. Every student of Chopin is advised to study Huneker's book, *Chopin, the Man and the Musician*. No critic has ever analyzed musical works with greater acumen or sympathy or with better literary style. He leaves the subject exhausted. He describes with extraordinary keenness and beauty of language every one of Chopin's compositions. As a book of reference it is essential to the student, for no other writer has done so much for this composer.

In his feeling for the keyboard Chopin far surpassed Bach and Beethoven. His fecundity of invention of passage work was not in any way approached by them, as was, of course, natural; and in his dazzling harmonic scheme, his endless variety of melody, his charm of rhythm, his immaculate sense of form, he is fully their equal.

The only works the student can afford to overlook are the following opus numbers: 1, 2, 4, 5, 12, 13, 14, 16, 19, 46, and some of the posthumous waltzes and mazurkas. Even in these early works there is much good material for pleasure and profit (Op. 1 and 12 might be examined), but on the whole

there is so much first-class music from his pen that only after becoming familiar with it need one embark on the few second-class pieces he left. It is well
to remember that the posthumous pieces are all early, youthful, and imma-
ture works which he himself never would have published.

Attention is called to several little-played works which deserve greater
favor. The "Tarantelle," though not conceived with the abandon of a Liszt, is
nevertheless beautiful as music. The Prelude, Op. 45, is a mystic threnody
whose harmonies melt with the true Chopin magic. The Eb Nocturne, Op. 55,
has a novel form; conceived as a lied, it possesses no middle section. The Polonaise-Phantasie, Op. 61, is another little-known piece. It will probably never
be popular, for its brooding self-communion is too long for a concert audience,
and it retains the identical mood for so long a time that the listener is either
hypnotized or bored, according to his mood and the manner of the performance. For personal edification or for a friend or two it is unrivaled. The Barcarolle, Op. 60, is also not overplayed. It is a gorgeous boat song.

The pianistic world without Chopin is inconceivable. A piano recital
without some of his compositions is rare. One cannot learn to play the piano
without his works. The more one ponders on his value and his position in the
musical world, the more miraculous he seems. With the passage of the years
his star only shines the brighter.

THE CLAVECINISTS

Clavecin Composers Other Than the Bach Family and Scarlatti to Whom the Publishers Devote Entire Volumes

Arne, T. A. (1710-1778) . . Suite for Clavicembalo (Ric.).
   Eight Sonatas (Aug.).
Blow, J. (1648-1708) . . . . . Ten Pieces (Aug.).
Bull, J. (1563-1628) . . . . . . Ten Pieces (Aug.).
   Three Dances, ed. by Granville-Bantock (Novello).
Byrd, W. (1543-1623) . . . . Collection (Aug.).
   Dances Grave and Gay (W. Rogers).
   Twelve Selected Works (Novello).
   Collection of Twenty-One Pieces (Reeves).
Cimarosa, D. (1749-1801) . Thirty-two Sonatas, in three books (Eschig).
Couperin, F. (1668-1733) . . Complete Works, ed. by Brahms (Aug.).
   Complete Works, ed. by Diemer (Durand).
   Album (Breit.).

49

Durante, F. (1684-1755)..Sei divertimenti (Ric.).

Farnaby, G. (*ca.* 1565)....Album of works selected from the FitzWilliam Virginal book, ed. by Granville-Bantock.

> Contains notes on the composer and compositions and lists all his compositions.

Frescobaldi, G.

(1583-1643) ....Venticinque canzoni (Boghen).

Cinque partite.

Corrente.

Toccata and Fugue, transcribed by Brugnoli, in four parts.

Transcriptions, by Respighi.

(All Ric.)

Transcriptions, by Stradal (Schuberth).

Twelve Toccatas, in six parts (Breit.).

> Some of the above were taken from "Toccate e partite d'intavolatura di cimbalo," ed. by Borboni in Rome in 1614.

Frohberger, J.

(*ca.* 1605-1667) .....Suites and Toccatas (Breit.). A selection.

Vol. I of the *Meisterwerke deutscher Tonkunst* (Breit.).

Frohbergiana (Simrock).

> A selection made by Walter Niemann.

Galuppi, B. (1706-1785)..Two Sonatas (Breit.).

Gibbons, O. (1583-1625)..Collection (Aug.).

Grazioli, G. (1770-1820)..Sonata in G (Breit.).

Hässler, J. (1747-1822)...Gigue (Breit.).

Hasse, J. A. (1699-1783)..Collection of pieces (Breit.).

Krebs, J. L. (1713-1780)..Transcriptions, by Stradal (Schuberth).

Kuhnau, J. (1660-1722)...Sieben Partien, Frische Clavier-Früchte oder Sieben Sonaten, biblische Historien nebst Auslegung in sechs Sonaten. (These are among the earliest examples of program music.)

Clavierübung aus vierzehn Partien bestehend (a collection of dance tunes).

Selected Works, Vol. II, *Meisterwerke deutscher Tonkunst* (Breit.).

"David and Goliath" (transcribed by Harold Bauer), Sonata in eight parts.

> (See also in anthologies of Breitkopf and Senff.)

Marcello, B. (1686-1739)..Toccata con variazioni (Ric.).

Muffat, G. (1690-1770)...Compositions, Vol. III, *Meisterwerke deutscher Tonkunst* (Breit.).

Paganelli, G. A. (1710-?)..Sonata in F (Breit.).

Paradisi, P. (1712-1795)...Four Sonatas, published separately (Breit.).

Pasquini, B. (1637-1710)..Partite diverse di follia (Ric.).

Pescetti, P. (1704-1766)...Sonata (Breit.).

Poglietti, A. (d. 1683).....Collection, Vol. IV, *Meisterwerke deutscher Tonkunst* (Breit.).

Purcell, H. (1658-1695)...Three Albums (Aug.).
Suites, Toccatas, Lessons. Pieces for the Harpsichord (4 vols. Chest.).

Purcell-Arne ....Album of Sixteen Pieces (W. Rogers).

Rameau, J. (1683-1764)...Complete Works, ed. by Saint-Saëns (Durand).
Complete Works (Breit.).
Five Concertos, Cm, G, A, B, Dm (Steingr.).

Rolle, J. H. (1718-1785)..Sonata, E♭ (Breit.).

Rossi, L. de' (1598-?).....Six Sonatas (Ric.).

Rossi, M. A. (*ca.* 1600)...Toccata, in the original version and also transcribed by A. Toni.
It may be had in another version for piano and small string orchestra (Ric.).

Rutini, G. (1730-1797)...Sonatas in C, A, C (Breit.).

Sacchini, A. M. G.
(1734-1786) ....Sonata, F (Breit.).

Scarlatti, A. (1659-1725)..Compositions (Ric.).

Scheidt, S. (1587-1654)...Collection, Vol. V, *Meisterwerke deutscher Tonkunst* (Breit.).

Turini, F. (1749-1812)...Sonata (Presto), D♭ (Breit.).

Wagenseil, G. (1715-1777).Sonata, F (Breit.).

Zipoli, D. (1675-?).......Suite, of four pieces (Ric.).

Zweelinck, J. P.
(1540-1621) ....Piano Works, *Fantasia No. 27, "Mein junges Leben hat ein End'" (Alsbach).

Many pieces in the preceding list are also found in the following collections. Nearly all the great anthologies contain works by every one of these composers; generally there is a difference in choice of selection.

Albums, Anthologies, Collections, and Transcriptions of the Early Clavecinists

It should be noted in regard to the following list that, although it deals chiefly with the composers listed on previous pages, many of the anthologies, albums, and collections, especially the first nine and the *Golden Treasury*, contain many pieces by such composers as Couperin and Rameau and also by the Bachs and Scarlatti.

Alte Klaviermusik (3 vols. Peters).

Alte Klaviermusik (3 vols. Senff).

Alte Klaviermusik (3 vols. Simrock).

Altmeister des Klavierspiels, ed. by Riemann (2 vols. Steingr.).

Alte Meister (6 vols. Breit.).

> Selected Pieces from the FitzWilliam Virginal Book, ed. by Fuller-Maitland and Barclay Squire.
> Old English Melodies (2 vols.), Ballads and Dances from the Sixteenth Century, ed. by Grimshaw.
> Musica antica italiana. Six pieces, ed. by B. Cesi.
> Corelli, A. (1653-1713). Twenty-four Selected Compositions.
> Couperin, F. (1668-1733). Selected Works.
> Frohberger, J. J. (*ca* 1605-1667). A collection from the suites and sonatas.
> Gavottes—A collection of celebrated French, German, and Italian gavottes (E. Pauer).
> Grétry, A. E. M. (1747-1822). Danses villageoises.
> Hässler, J. W. (1747-1822). Grand Gigue, Dm.
> Hasse, J. A. (1669-1783). Selected Works, arranged for piano by Otto Schmied.
> Haydn, Michael (1736-1806). Selections, by Schmied.
> Keiser, R. (1674-1739). Suite of Dance Pieces (Zelle).
> Kuhnau, J. (1660-1722). Selected Compositions, and Sonata in B♭.
> Muffat, G. (1690-1770). Selected Compositions.
> Poglietti, Allessandro. Aria with Variations, ed. by Hinze-Reinhold.
> Rameau, J. P. (1683-1764). Gavotte and Variations (E. Pauer).
> Rococo—Gavottes, Rigaudons, Bourrées, Passepieds, Minuets, Sarabands, fourteen dance compositions by Christian Foerster, G. Phil. Telemann, J. J. Fux, and J. F. G. Fasch.
> Scarlatti, D. (1685-1757). Three Sonatas, transcribed by Tausig.
> Scheidt, S. (1587-1654). Selected Compositions.
> Tuma, F. (1704-1774). Album, selected by Schmied.

Alte Tänze (Breit.).

Anthologie classique (Schlesinger).

Anthology of Early French Piano Music (Ditson).

Anthology of Early Italian Piano Music (Ditson).

Anthology of Early German Piano Music (Ditson).

Antichi danze e arie, transcribed by Respighi (Ric.).

Antichi maestri italiani (Ric.).

> Toccatas.
> Fugues.
> Compositions.
> Eighteen Sonatas.
> Partitas.
> Courantes.

Antologia di musica antica e moderna, ed. by Tagliapietra (18 vols. Ric.).

At the Court of Queen Anne, twenty-one easy pieces by English court composers and others, ed. Fuller-Maitland (Chest.).

Biblioteca di rarità musicale. (This is a collection of facsimiles of various unusual ancient manuscripts, ed. by Vitali; Ric.).

Classiker, Der junge, (4 vols. Breit.).

Clavecinistes belges, Les.

Clavecinistes espagnoles, Les, twelve sonatas, ed. by J. Nin.

Clavecinistes français, Les, ed. Diemer (4 vols. Durand).

Clavicembalisti italiani (2 vols. Ric.).

Contemporaries of Purcell (7 vols.).

> Vols. I and II. John Blow.
> Vols. III and IV. William Croft.
> Vol. V. Jeremiah Clarke.

Vol. VI. Benjamin Rogers, Mark Coleman, Gerhard Diesner, Robert King, Daniel Purcell, John Eccles.

Vol. VII. Francis Pigott, William Turner, John Barrett.

Cosyn, B. Virginal Book, ed. by Barclay Squire and Fuller-Maitland (Chest.).

Early English Harpsichord Music, ed. by Rowley (6 vols. W. Rogers).

Contains works by Jeremiah Clarke, James Hook, Anthony Young, Samuel Arnold, W. Richardson, Charles Dibdin, James Nares, Peter Lee, Samuel Wise, and John Burton.

Early English Sonatinas, ed. Rowley (W. Rogers).

Works by Duncombe, G. T. Attwood, C. H. Wilson, James Hook, M. Camidge, and J. Jones.

École de piano du Conservatoire Royal de Bruxelles, in forty parts (Breit.).

The first three have bearing on this epoch.

Elizabethan Virginal Composers (to be completed in 25 vols.).

FitzWilliam Virginal Book, ed. by Fuller-Maitland and Barclay Squire (Curwen and Chest.).

Twenty-five pieces for keyed instruments, by John Bull, William Byrd, Benjamin Cosyn, Orlando Gibbons, and an unknown composer.

Friedmann, I. Transcriptions of Twelve Ancient Pieces (U.E.).

Godowsky's Transcriptions (see under Godowsky).

Golden Treasury of Music (Schirm.).

Several volumes treat of this epoch.

Herscher, J. Transcriptions (E. Demets).

Bach, J. S.	Chorals in G and Dm.
	Fugue in Cm.
	Prelude and Fugue in C.
Couperin, F.	"Dominie Deus."
	Allegretto in Am.
	Agnus Dei in F.
Daquin, C.	Four Noëls, Dm, G, Dm, D.
Marchand, L.	Dialogue.
	Basse de trompette.
	Fond d'orgue.
Clérambault, N.	Basse et dessus de trompette.
	Dialogue.
Roberday, F.	Fugue et caprice, Dm.
	Caprice, F.

Maîtres classiques de la musique, Les, ed. by D'Indy (Roudanez).

Musik am sächsischen Hofe (10 vols. Breit.).

A collection of unusual ancient music, some of it being transcriptions of old fanfares, etc.

Old Composers Series (4 vols. Aug.).

English.
French.
German.
Italian.

Old English Worthies (W. Rogers).

Pieces by Babell, Hook, Richardson, Lee Clarke, Barratt, Camidge, Worgan, Young, Stanley.

Piano Music of Old Times, ed. by E. Pauer (Simrock).

Pièces de clavecin de l'école française, Les plus belles, ed. by G. Grovlez (2 vols. Chest.).

Compositions by Chambonnières, Le Bégue, Marchand, Couperin, Dandrieu, D'Anglebert, Daquin, Dornel, Clérambault, Dagincourt, Rameau, Duphluy, Corrette.

53

Respighi, O. Antiche danze ed arie per liuto (sixteenth and seventeenth century), **seven** pieces (Ric.).
> Transcriptions by Molinaro, Galilei, Roncalli, and three unknown composers.

Rimbault, E. F. History of the Pianoforte.
> The second half of the book contains a quantity of music of this period by Blitheman, Byrd, Bull, Frescobaldi, Dumont, Chambonnières, Lully, Purcell, Mürschhauser, Kuhnau, Mattheson, Scarlatti, Couperin, J. S. Bach, Handel, Muffat, C. P. E. Bach, as well as a sketch of these composers and also a collection of specimens showing the progress of music for keystring instruments.

Tunes from the Eighteenth Century, five transcriptions by Harold Bauer (Schirm.).

Weitzman, C. F. A History of Pianoforte Playing and Pianoforte Literature.
> At the end of the book are fifty pages of music of this period.

Most of these writers are to be had only in collections and anthologies, and for this reason they are treated as a group. The arrangement will be found practical, but it may be annoying to the student who desires very detailed information to have the collections and anthologies listed without an index of their contents. Since such students are few and the catalogues of the contents would enlarge this book to undesirable proportions, the present plan seems best.

Much of this music retains its pristine charm, but some is of archaic interest only. It is emerging more and more both in its original form and in the guise of transcriptions and is proving to be a mine of gold to those who understand how to modernize without burying it either under a blanket of counterpoint or in a fog of incompatible harmonies. The music of this period is pre-eminently adapted to the confines of a room and loses when heard under unfavorable conditions. All of it is well suited to the needs of the amateur transcriber who can arrange it for any appropriate group of instruments.

With William Byrd begins the literature of the predecessors of the piano, and it was with his "The Carman's Whistle" that Rubinstein began his celebrated historical series of piano music. Byrd's "Sellenger's Round" and "The Lord of Salisbury, His Pavin" are still noted. These pieces date from the close of the sixteenth century. John Bull and Orlando Gibbons wrote at approximately the same time. A "Fantazia in Foure Parts" is an early fugue of Gibbons. These three writers published for the virginal what is probably the first "album" ever collected. It was called *Parthenia*. Frescobaldi was their most important contemporary, and he wrote the first fully developed fugues. Kuhnau, though much later than the four just noted, was the greatest German pre-Bach composer.

The most noted composers of this whole period, aside from Bach and Scarlatti, are Couperin and Rameau, though there are a dozen more or less unknown ones, especially Italians, who have written music which is fresher and more spontaneous. Couperin's music is heavily embellished, but the excrescences may be omitted or modified, thus enhancing the beauty and simplicity, and the music will appear more crystalline and suave. He may be regarded as the premier French composer of his day of the "salon" type. Rameau, on the other hand, has more depth and emotion and offers better fare. It may be noted here that Prosniz holds exactly the opposite opinion in regard to these two composers.

The names chosen by French composers of this period for their pieces strike modern ears strangely; they were obviously chosen at random, much as were the names of old hymns. They are no more ridiculous than such names as "Old Hundred," and "Duke Street," though they are certainly more worldly—"La Ténébreuse," "L'Auguste," "La Lugubre," "La Milordine," and "Les Barricades mysterieuses." The following pieces of Couperin are recommended to those who for the moment have no choice: 'Le Bavolet flottant," "Le Carillon de Cythère," Les Petits moulins à vent," "Soeur Monique," "Les Rozeaux," "L'Engageante," "La Fleurie ou la tendre Nanette," "La Bersan," "L'Ausonienne," and "Les Charmes." Couperin's pieces were first published under the name *Pièces de clavecin* in four volumes, in 1713.

Those who feel as I do in regard to the relative values of Rameau and Couperin will derive more pleasure from Rameau. The following list is suggested for a beginning: "Gigue en rondeau" (this has been transcribed by Godowsky, combined with another gigue, and called "Élégie" in his "Twenty-four Renaissance Pieces"), "Le Tambourin" (also done, and perhaps overdone, by Godowsky), "Les Tendres plaintes," "Les Niais de Sologne," "Les Soupirs," "Les Tourbillons" (Godowsky), "Le Livri," "L'Agaçante," "La Timide," "Les Trois mains," "Fanfarinette," "La Triomphante," "L'Indifférante," "L'Entretien des muses," "La Poule," "Gavotte," and "Variations" in A minor. These pieces were first published in 1730.

Many of the following composers' works are at present "music of the future," since they are buried in anthologies and collections, but it can hardly be doubted that much will return in time: Frohberger, Kerll, D'Anglebert, Rossi, Lully, Buxtehude, Pasquini, Blow, Pachelbel, Kuhnau, Mürschhauser,

Mattheson, Purcell, Zipoli, Marcello, Wagenseil, Muffat, Hasse, Laganelli, Galuppi, Graun, Pescetti, Arne, Paradisi, Marpurg, Rolle, Turini, Benda, Kirnberger, Krebs, Sarti, Schobert, Rutini, Sacchini, Hässler, Martinez, Grazioli, Cherubini, Méhul, Matielli. These men may be studied in the anthologies and collections listed here.

MUZIO CLEMENTI

(1752-1832)

Sixty-four Sonatas, of which the following are considered the best:

No. 1. C.
No. 6. Gm.
No. 16. Eb.
No. 19. Fm.
No. 20. La Chasse.
No. 30. A.
No. 31. F#m.
No. 57. Bm.
No. 63. Dm.
No. 64. G (Didone abbandonata).
Breit. and Litolff publish the sonatas complete in 3 vols.

Seven duet sonatas (four hands).
Gradus ad Parnassum.
Two duets, for two pianos.
Preludes and Exercises.

Waltzes with Tambourine and Triangle.
Op. 49. Monferrinas (dances).
Caprice in 5/4 time (published in some editions as Op. 47, No. 2).
The opus numbers are often duplicated in works for piano with some other instrument, so that no reliance can be placed upon them. They run only to fifty. No. 61 is the sonata Clementi played before Joseph II in the presence of Mozart and from which Mozart took the well-known tune used in *The Magic Flute*. No. 64, "Didone abbandonata," is considered by some critics his greatest sonata.

Clementi is at present indifferently appreciated. He was a man of high mentality and great intellectual curiosity, a manufacturer of pianos, a publisher, one not to be overcome by adversity, a traveler, the friend of Haydn and Beethoven, the greatest piano teacher who had lived up to his time, and a practical business man. Such a personality offers material of lasting interest to humanity.

He is known today solely as the composer of a few sonatinas and of the "Gradus ad Parnassum," as he conceived it a colossal work which occupied him off and on many years and which presents among its one hundred pieces many of real musical interest and beauty, and worthy (if furbished up a bit and baptized with attractive names) of appearing on concert programs. Tausig conceived the idea that Parnassus could be climbed by means of a short cut and reduced the work by one-half. It is generally known today in its abbreviated form. There is so little demand for Clementi's music nowadays that my efforts to purchase "Didone abbandonata" in the chief music store in Rome, his birthplace, were unavailing.

One should not forget that the spirit of Scarlatti, that gay, indomitable genius, survives, though necessarily transmuted, in Clementi, and that he thus becomes practically the last representative of the greatest period of Italian piano writing. In him one discovers an Italian Mozart, and one will find, as Mozart did, that his compositions deserve looking into.

MISCELLANEOUS CZECH COMPOSERS

Older Writers*

ANTONÍN DVOŘÁK
(1841-1904)

Op. 3. Silhouettes.
Op. 33. Concerto (Hainauer).
Op. 85. Poetische Stimmungsbilder, ten pieces.

Op. 101. Humoresques.
Slavic Dances (four hands).
Legends (four hands).
(All Simrock)

ZDĚNEK FIBICH
(1850-1900)

Stimmungen, Eindrücke und Erinnerungen, 372 pieces.

EDWARD NAPRAVNIK
(1839-1915)

Op. 27. Concert symphonique, with orchestra.

Fantaisie russe (Russian themes including the "Volga Boat Song"), with orchestra.
(Both Rahter)

OTTOKAR NOVAČEK
(1866-1900)

Op. 8. Concerto eroico (Hauser).
Twelve Short Pieces, in two books (Schirm.).

Two Concert Pieces (Hauser).
Prelude.
Toccata.
Four Concert Pieces (Schirm.).

*Dussek and Smetana are listed separately.

VÍTĚZSLAV NOVÁK
(1870—)

Op. 9. Serenades.
Op. 10. Barcarolles.
Op. 11. Eclogues.
Op. 13. In der Dämmerung.
Op. 14. Bohemian Dances.
Op. 24. Sonata eroica.
Op. 30. Winternachtsgesänge.

Op. 32. Slovak Suite.
  (All Simrock)
Six Sonatinas.
Op. 43. Pan—A Tone Poem, in five parts
  (U.E.).
Op. 55. Jeunesse, for children.
  (All Hudebni Matice)

Recent Writers

ALOIS HABA
(1893—)

*Op. 1*b*. Variations on a Schumann
  Canon.
Op. 3. Sonata.
Op. 6. Six Pieces.

Op. 8. Concert symphonique, with or-
  chestra.
  (All Hudebni Matice)
Scherzo and Intermezzo.
Suite No. 3, for quarter-tone piano.
Op. 19. Fantasia, for quarter-tone piano.
  (All U. E.)

KAREL B. JIRÁK
(1891—)

Suite en style ancien, in six parts
  (*Gavotte. Hudebni Matice).

ERNST KŘENEK
(1900—)

Op. 2. Sonata, Eb.
Op. 13. Toccata and Chaconne.
Op. 18. Concerto.
Op. 26. Two Suites.

Op. 59. Sonata.
Completion of an unfinished sonata of
  Schubert.

JAROSLAV KŘIČKA
(1882—)

Op. 11. Caprices, five short descriptive
  pieces.
Suite lyrique, in five parts (*Serenata).
  (All Hudebni Matice)

Op. 13. Merry Pieces (Simrock).
Op. 17. Intimate Pieces.
*Op. 45. Puppet Dances, for children.

FELIX PETYREK
(1892—)

Suite—Eleven Little Children's Pieces.
Variations and Fugue, C.
Choral, Variations, and Sonatina.
Eight Concert Studies after Cramer.

Twenty-four Ukrainian Folk Songs.
Six Grotesque Piano Pieces.
Six Greek Rhapsodies.
  (All U. E.)

OTAKAR ŠÍN
(1881—)

Op. 6. Chanson du printemps, three pieces (*No. 1).
De l'aube au crépuscule, ten pieces for children.

Les Vacances, ten pieces for children.
  (All Hudebni Matice.)

BOLESLAV VOMÁČKA
(1887—)

*Op. 4. Hledani (Recherches), four pieces.

Op. 6. Intermezzi.
*Op. 7. Sonata.

LADISLAV VYCPÁLEK
(1882—)

En passant, six short compositions (Schott).

Publishers: Simrock, U.E., Rahter, Hudebni (to be had through Chester or U.E.).

Of the older compositions those by Novák are possibly the most desirable, although nothing in the whole list rises above the level of good salon music. The Dvořák compositions are in the main cold and lifeless, though the four-hand pieces offer some good entertainment. The "Fantaisie russe" of Napravnik is an excellent effective piece in the older, familiar manner, and it is not very difficult. The now rather hackneyed "Volga Boat Song" is the theme of the opening section. Fibich is an out-and-out *Vielschreiber*. No other human being ever put so many pieces in one opus number, except possibly Czerny. He is scarcely rewarding.

Novaček was a far more gifted composer whose promising work was cut short by death. His ideas are good, but he had not yet achieved the freedom of movement and taste in development to make the most of them.

Haba has chosen the curious field of quarter tones for playground. I am unfamiliar with this type of music. It is at least original for keyed instruments, though one has occasionally heard stringed instruments indulge in it. His "Variations on a Schumann Canon" are good, but the sonata seems labored.

Křenek makes an occasional excursion into the newer harmonies, of which his "Toccata and Chaconne" is an example. There seems no good reason for the "Completion of an Unfinished Sonata by Schubert" when there are already so many that no one plays. Křenek is variously judged by critics and seems to hold out promise of things as yet unfulfilled.

Křička, one of the most popular of the younger men, was long under Russian influence. His talent is lyrical, and his songs are noted in his native land. Petyrek is a seeker after the new, but not a despiser of the old, as his Cramer transcriptions show. It is pleasant to find this recognition of the old études. They have musical value. This opus tries to make them appropriate for concert use.

Šín is a composer of pleasant music for children. Pieces by a composer of this name ought to enlarge their horizons and offer ideas for new kinds of deviltry. Vomáčka and Vycpálek are among the most important of the newer men, but they have not done their best work for the piano.

CLAUDE DEBUSSY

(1862-1918)

1888   Deux arabesques.
      Fantaisie, with orchestra (published in 1911).

1890   Ballade.
      Danse.
      Mazurka.
      Rêverie.
      Valse romantique.
      Nocturne.
      Suite bergamasque (published in 1905).
        Prélude.
        Menuet.
        Clair de lune.
        Passepied.

1891   Marche écossaise.
      Pour le piano.
        Prélude.
        Sarabande.
        Toccata.

1903   D'un cahier d'esquisses.
      Estampes.
        Pagodes.
        La Soirée dans Grenade.
        Jardins sous la pluie.

1904   Masques.
      L'Isle joyeuse.
      Danse sacrée et danse profane, with string orchestra accompaniment.

1905 Images (first book).
    Reflets dans l'eau.
    Hommage à Rameau.
    Mouvement.

1907 Images (second book).
    Cloches à travers les feuilles.
    Et la lune descend sur le temple qui fût.
    Poissons d'or.

1908 Children's Corner.
    Dr. Gradus ad Parnassum.
    Jumbo's Lullaby.
    Serenade of the Doll.
    The Snow is Dancing.
    The Little Shepherd.
    The Golliwog's Cake-walk.

1909 Hommage à Haydn.

1910 La Plus que lente.
    Préludes (first book).
    Danseuses de Delphe.
    Voiles.
    Le Vent dans la plaine.
    "Les Sons et les parfums tournent dans l'air du soir."
    Les Collines d'Anacapri.
    Des pas sur la neige.
    Ce qu'a vu le vent d'ouest.
    La Fille au cheveux de lin.
    La Sérénade interrompue.
    La Cathédrale engloutie.
    La Danse de Puck.
    Minstrels.
    Préludes (second book).
    Brouillards.
    Feuilles mortes.
    La Puerto del vino.
    "Les Fées sont des exquises danseuses."
    Bruyères.

    Général Lavine—eccentric.
    La Terrace des audiences.
    Ondine.
    Hommage à S. Pickwick, Esq.
    Canope.
    Les Tierces altérnées.
    Feux d'artifices.

1913 La Boîte à joujoux.

1914 Berceuse héroïque.

1915-16
    Douze Études (published in two books).
    Pour les "cinq doigts," after Czerny.
    Pour les tierces.
    Pour les quartes.
    Pour les sixtes.
    Pour les octaves.
    Pour les huit doigts.
    Pour les degrées chromatiques.
    Pour les agréments.
    Pour les notes répétées.
    Pour les sonorités opposées.
    Pour les arpèges composées.
    Pour les accords.

1915 Six épigraphes antiques (four hands).
    Pour invoquer Pan, dieu du vent d'été.
    Pour un tombeau sans nom.
    Pour que la nuit soit propice.
    Pour la danseuse aux crotales.
    Pour l'Égyptienne.
    Pour remercier la pluie au matin.
    En blanc et noir.
    Qui reste à sa place.
    Prince, porté soit des serfs Éolus.
    Yver, vous n'êtes qu'un vilain.

Publishers: Durand, Fromont, Schirm., Boston Music Co., etc.

Nothing makes one realize the speed of recent musical development more keenly than a glance at the sudden appearance of Debussy, his rapid rise to fame, and his quick assimilation by the public. At the beginning of the century he was known as a writer of graceful salon music of a good type. Then, suddenly, he burst on the world, astonished everyone by his gospel, finished his work, was weighed, measured, catalogued, and now for a long time has not seemed "queer." It is, of course, idle to say that he has been correctly adjudged for all time—only posterity can do that, and posterity is never on hand when one wants its opinion. But he already seems curiously easy to "place."

Anxious to escape the overpowering Wagnerian influence, Debussy betook himself to the whole-tone scales. These two stepsisters of the scale family seem at first glance to possess that glamorous strangeness which is a necessary or at least a desirable quality of beauty; but one finds on living with them that the strangeness soon wears off and that familiarity, true to the old saying, does breed a bit of contempt. From the scales to research among overtones was but a step. In turning his great and well-trained genius into these paths Debussy gave enormous impulse to music, released French composers from German influence, stimulated individuality, and, best of all, wrote a series of extremely idiomatic works which, fortunately, include some for the piano. He was an excellent tonal architect and employed all of the old devices for development except canon and fugue. He was not a builder of cathedrals, like Franck, but we find in his "castles in Spain" such solid materials as organ points, transpositions, sequences, rhythmical modifications of themes, amplifications, contractions, and so forth, used as logically as by Bach or Chopin, granted the different premises.

His weakness lies in his slightness of texture and in his emotional side. There is something pallid, though not unwholesome, about his music, which he himself deplored, regretting that it was the only kind of music he could write. It is, however, most entertaining to wander in his twilight world. In these virgin forests one may at any moment encounter a griffin or a unicorn, and one may well enjoy the excursion into Debussy's kingdom even if one does not want to remain there eating lotus for very long at a time.

The music of Debussy is excellent for pianists who have forgotten that it is discriminative to play pianissimo occasionally. He did the instrument good service in pointing out what is so often forgotten—that it should not emulate the orchestra. Toward the end of the last century the piano was in danger of suffering the fate of the frog who thought he was as large and important as the ox.

There is little of interest in his pieces that date before 1890. They survive merely because their author later became justly famous, although they are good salon music and appeal to many people. The "Fantaisie" with orchestra, which was not published for so many years, might possibly be "featured" some day. The piece is in three movements, and the piano is used in the symphonic rather than in the virtuoso manner. It was first performed in 1919.

The suite "Pour le piano" is an attractive set, especially the prelude, which displays astonishing vigor. The Toccata is often heard in recital programs. From this point on his style is fully matured, and the pieces of the next few years are his best. All those pieces in the collections entitled "Estampes" and "Images" are works of real inspiration, pictures painted in a style hitherto unknown.

Of the two pieces dating from 1904, "L'Isle joyeuse" is the better. It is a virtuoso piece full of interest and loveliness and has a brilliant end. It is longer than most of the pieces. "Masques," a good carnival picture, is also worth studying for its rhythmic interest and tonal effects. The "Children's Corner" needs no remark except possibly to say that it contains humor, which is rare with Debussy. The two books of Préludes contain glimpses and flashes of the composer's best art, and some of them have become household words. They are the last compositions, chronologically, to have made their way. The first book is, in general, the better.

"La Boîte à joujoux" is a puppet play which one might with a little trouble perform in one's home. The negligible "Berceuse héroïque," was written during the war and is dedicated to the late King Albert.

The "Twelve Études" in time may become important. These are probably the first études to have been written with the more recent harmonies in mind. The new music requires to a certain extent a new technique, and these études endeavor to supply it. Most composers have written their "Douze Études" or their "Zwölf Etüden"—twelve is the conventional number—but most of them since Chopin have been elaborate tone poems, especially if intended for concert performance. Debussy obviously intended these for genuine exercises (see titles), though doubtless many of them would make welcome concert pieces. They are in the sophisticated, highly polished, somewhat cold and calculating French style. They display remarkable invention and are interesting in that they only faintly resemble his "Images" period. They stress dynamics and also give new viewpoints on sixths. It is hard to recall a previous étude dealing with fourths or with the fingers, without the thumbs. He handles even octaves in a more or less original way.

The pieces after 1915 add nothing to his stature.

ERNST VON DOHNÁNYI

(1877—)

Op. 2. Four Pieces.
  Scherzo.
  Intermezzo.
  Intermezzo.
  Capriccio.
Op. 3. Waltzes (four hands).
Op. 4. Variations and Fugue.
Op. 5. Concerto, Em, with orchestra.
*Op. 6. Passacaglia.
  (All Doblinger)
*Op. 11. Four Rhapsodies.
  Gm, F#m, C, Ebm (U.E.).
Op. 13. Winterreigen, Ten Bagatelles.
  Dedication.
  March.
  To Ada.
  Friend Victor's Mazurka.
  Music of the Spheres.
  Valse aimable.
  At Midnight.
  A Mad Party.

  Dawn.
  Postlude.
*Op. 17. Humoresques (U.E.).
  March.
  Toccata.
  Pavane and Variations (sixteenth-century
    "Gaudeamus Igitur").
  Pastorale.
  Introduction and Fugue.
Op. 23. Aria, Valse Impromptu, Capriccio.
Op. 24. Suite in the Old Style.
*Op. 25. Variations on a Children's Song,
  with orchestra.
*Op. 28. Six Concert Études.
  Am, Db, Eb, Bm, *E, *Fm Capriccio.
*Op. 29. Variations on a Hungarian
  Theme (Roszavölgyi).
Op. 32a. Ruralia Hungarica, seven
  pieces (Roszavölgyi).

WITHOUT OPUS NUMBER

Cadenzas for Beethoven's Concerto in G.
Cadenza for Mozart's Concerto in G
  (K453).
Gavotte and Musette (Doblinger).

*Waltz from Delibes' "Naila" for Concert
  Use (Roszavölgyi).

Publishers: Doblinger, Roszavölgyi, Simrock,
U.E.

Dohnányi has contributed many valuable pieces to the literature, and they are achieving more and more frequent performance. A conservative, he is nevertheless able to give a novel and individual turn to his work without resorting to fantastic methods. His music is the offspring of a genuinely musical temperament under perfect intellectual control.

Among his earlier compositions the Passacaglia stands out, a work of magnificent proportions, tonally well balanced, solid and musicianly in the older style. It is worth playing even if one does not intend to learn it. The rhapsodies are pieces of a type differing greatly from Liszt's pieces of the same name. The second and the third are the most played, but the fourth, based on the granitic old tune "Dies irae" in the gloomy key of Eb minor, is very fine; it reproduces the feeling of the "Dance of Death" in an excellent manner. The first three of these pieces, being Hungarian rhapsodies, may be compared with those of Liszt, and the fourth one may be compared with Liszt's "Todtentanz," which is also based on the "Dies irae" theme. Some of the humoresques are gaining in popularity, especially the March.

Of his later work, Op. 29 stands out as a piece of unique value. Hungarian melodies can be divided into three categories: gypsy music, the genuine Hungarian music, and the curious and very ancient songs based on the pentatonic scale which date back a thousand years and seem to connect the Hungarian with his Asiatic origin, since the pentatonic scale is still found in China. It is melody of the second category which Dohnányi has used, studied, and developed. These melodies resemble the old church modes, especially the Doric, and the importance of this composition is thus seen to consist in being genuine Hungarian folk music developed, probably for the first time, by a highly cultivated Hungarian musician and therefore in a serious manner.

The very delightful "Variations on a Children's Song" on "Ah vous dirais-je maman" (an old tune used by Mozart in K265) is another important contribution to the not very large literature of first-class pieces for piano and orchestra. The piano is used as an obbligato instrument rather than in the virtuoso fashion. The work is brilliant, varied, and, even better, humorous.

The remarkable études should not be forgotten, for they present unusual and important problems to the virtuoso. His "Ruralia Hungarica" gives another example of a musician's use of genuine Hungarian (as opposed to gypsy) music. It is very long, but Nos. 4, 5, and 7 would make an unusually attractive group for a concert.

JAN LADISLAW DUSSEK

(1761-1812)

(The confusion in the opus numbers is caused by misunderstanding between publishers.)

Op. 1. Three Concertos, with quartet.
Op. 3. Concerto, Eb, with orchestra.
Op. 6. Six Airs variées.
Op. 9. Three Sonatas, Bb, C, D (Schirm.).

*Op. 10. Three Sonatas, *A, Gm, E (U.E.).
Op. 13. Rondo militaire.
Op. 14. Concerto, F, with orchestra.
Op. 15. Concerto, Eb, with orchestra.

*Op. 16. Twelve Progressive Lessons.

Op. 17. Concerto, F, with orchestra.

*Op. 20. Six Sonatinas.

Op. 22. Concerto, B♭, with orchestra.

Op. 23. The Sufferings of the Queen of France.

*Op. 23. Sonata, B♭: Three Airs variées (Aug.).

Op. 26. Concerto, E♭.

Op. 29.
 or 30. Concerto for Piano or Harp, with orchestra.

Op. 32. Grand Sonata, C (four hands).

Op. 33. Il Rivocato.

*Op. 35. Three Sonatas, B♭, *G, *Cm.

Op. 38. Sonata, E♭, for two pianos.

*Op. 39. Three Sonatas, G, C, B♭.

Op. 40. Concerto militaire.

Op. 43. Sonata, A.

*Op. 44. Sonata, E♭, ("The Farewell," dedicated to Clementi).

*Op. 45. Three Sonatas, *B♭, G, D.

Op. 47. Two Sonatas, D, G.

Op. 48. Grand Sonata (four hands).

Op. 49
 or 50. Concerto, Gm, with orchestra.

*Op. 50
 or 55. Fantasia and Fugue, Fm (dedicated to Cramer).

*Op. 61. Élégie harmonique sur la mort du Prince Louis Ferdinand de Prusse, F♯m.

Op. 62. La Consolation, B♭ (Schirm.).

Op. 63. Concerto, for two pianos and orchestra.

Op. 64. Fugues à la camera.

Op. 66. Concerto, F, with orchestra.

Op. 67. Three Progressive Sonatas, C, F, B♭.

Op. 70. Concerto, E♭, with orchestra.

*Op. 70. Sonata, A♭ ("Le Retour à Paris." U.E.; Peters).

Op. 71. Plus Ultra Sonata, A♭.

Op. 71. Airs connus variées.

Op. 72. Grand Sonata (four hands).

Op. 73. Sonata, F (four hands).

Op. 75. Sonata, E♭ (four hands).

Op. 76. Fantasia, F.

*Op. 77. Sonata, Fm—L'Invocation (U.E.; Peters).

Many sonatas, waltzes, rondos, and duos were published without opus numbers. All the sonatas are published separately by Breitkopf.

Aside from a few great names, late eighteenth century music has vanished more completely than seventeenth century, perhaps for the same reason that the just outworn fashions always seem more hopelessly antiquated than those of our great-grandfathers—the latter take on picturesqueness across the mellowing distance of time. To exhume Dussek may seem irreverent or futile. It is worth persisting in this body-snatching mood, however, to discover whether or not he still has something for the listener and player of this century.

If one selects wisely one will discover that some of his sonatas reflect quite charmingly the somewhat faded style of his day. Lest this seem damning and not worth the labor of grave-robbing, it should be added that the music really presents something intrinsically good. Those to whom his music is unfamiliar will be surprised at its generous and abundant flow. It seems to come from a rich source and bubbles on somewhat in the manner of Schubert. The first surprise is that of his astonishing ease and fluency of modulation. His harmonic scheme is far more varied than one would expect. Does one see correctly, and is it possible that a movement ostensibly in A♭ begins in F♯ minor? One had supposed that such freedom originated in more recent times, but there it is in the minuet movement of Op. 70.

Another point which is interesting is that Dussek begins by composing somewhat in the manner of the younger Bachs and ends by writing in the style which immediately preceded Chopin. If one turns to an early sonata like the G minor from Op. 10 one finds a two-movement work (grave, adagio; vivace con spirito) somewhat in the Italian manner. This was his background, but by the time he wrote his last sonata, and as a matter of fact much earlier, he was writing in a well-developed romantic style.

In his works there is sometimes the frivolity of Weber, but oftener, it must be confessed, that sort of frivolity which contains nothing gay, and which in consequence is extremely depressing. This mood pervades the concertos which were written to catch the applause of unmusical audiences and which it would be stupid to try to bring back. Liszt, later on, had to write fantasias on operatic airs with startling technical extravagances, and Dussek had to do something of the same kind. The discouragements under which he labored may be appreciated by recalling that his public vastly preferred his concerts on some kind of mouth organ, on which he also performed, to his piano recitals. (In those days the public was still valiantly fighting against the piano recital—how ingloriously it lost the battle is apparent to concertgoers today.)

By connoisseurs of the next century Dussek may possibly be revived and again become fashionable, even as the seventeenth-century composers are now. Probably the most that the ordinary taster will require is Volume No. 274a in the Peters edition. It contains three sonatas and gives one an early, a middle, and a late composition. They are also published as a group by Breitkopf and by Ricordi.

CÉSAR FRANCK

(1822-1890)

Op. 3. Eclogue (Schuberth).

Op. 4. Duo for Four Hands on "God Save the King" (Litolff).

Op. 7. Souvenir d'Aix-la-Chapelle (Schuberth).

Danse lente.

Les Plaintes d'une poupée.

Prélude, Chorale, and Fugue.

Prélude, Aria, and Finale.

Variations symphoniques, with orchestra.

Les Djinns, with orchestra.

Schirmer publishes the last six. A collection of some of his pieces has been published by Ditson.

Publishers: Hamelle, Litolff, Peters, Schuberth, U.E., Enoch, Schirm.

The great and lasting works of César Franck were all composed in the later years of his life. They are of such a serious nature, so profound, idiomatic, and unworldly, architecturally so intricate and harmonically so individual, their sweep so elemental, and, it may be added, their interpretation so difficult, that it is not to be wondered at that they took a long time to establish themselves. They have arrived, however, and taken their seats beside the recognized works of the Olympians. The student is referred to D'Indy's book on Franck for further information. I shall content myself by pointing out a few of the essential underlying ideas in detail for those who do not wish to go deeper into the subject.

Structurally, Franck was an innovator of the first rank. In his two great solo piano pieces, "Prélude, Chorale, and Fugue" and "Prélude, Aria, and Finale," he gives his ideas on a possible destiny of the fugue and sonata forms respectively. One discovers in these two great works that his aim was to unify the movements of the sonata and of the prelude and fugue by means of identical themes and motifs throughout the entire course of the composition. D'Indy maintains that this idea, which he calls "cyclical," was Franck's own, since the idea of the *idée fixe* or leitmotif was already in the air. This, however, is not important, since all the composers who worked out this plan achieved different results. Franck's are all masterpieces, and that is all one can ask.

His themes appear sometimes in fragmentary, sometimes in fully developed form, and the "technique" is always a result of the clash of harmonies and themes, never a cosmetic applied to such themes to beautify them in an extrinsic manner. Scales, trills, bravura octaves, and the paraphernalia of

68

the keyboard virtuoso scarcely exist for Franck. His nature is grave but not dull; it is simple but not empty, religious but not fanatical. He achieves brilliance at times, but it is the brilliance of the ruby, not of the diamond. One's novitiate is likely to be long, however, because it is not merely a question of "learning a piece" but of entering a high place, of gradual initiation through growth in insight. But the task is infinitely worth while, and the pianist who fails to master the Franck repertory has missed supreme moments.

THE PRÉLUDE, CHORALE, AND FUGUE

This work is in B minor and contains 380 measures. Franck's manner of writing is often difficult for the eye. One measure at the beginning of the prelude contains an E, an E♭, and an E#. His unusual harmonic scheme becomes apparent at once. The piece opens without preliminaries, disclosing the first theme, A, which is not structurally of great importance, but it is interesting because it so closely resembles the celebrated B-A-C-H theme. The accompanying figure is destined to considerable prominence both in the prelude and later in the fugue.

At the short measure, 2/4 time, theme B appears. This is the germ of the fugue theme, but one hears only a phrase, and then the music begins to preludize. Presently, modulating, it begins again from the beginning, but in the dominant. The music is repeated literally in F# minor, whereupon the preludizing starts afresh, is prolonged and merged with the figure in thirty-second notes, and comes to a conclusion after fifty-seven measures, counted from the beginning.

The chorale is introduced by a bold modulation from B minor to E♭ major, the F# of the first chord changes enharmonically to G♭ and becomes a suspension before the third of the E♭ major chord. The chorale has fifty-nine measures, although they occupy only two pages, whereas the prelude with an identical number covers six. The interludes are used later again.

The chorale is followed by a transition which one might designate as a meditation on the fugue theme in the style of the chorale interludes; this contains an inversion of part of the fugue theme. The bass begins to rouse itself, and a little phrase of five notes develops into a running passage which eventually leads the pianist dramatically to another phrase which, after making two statements, finally launches itself into the fugue theme, complete at last.

The fugue consists, broadly speaking, of three sections: the first, of seventy-four measures, has the usual structure; the second begins in the dominant with triplet eighth notes (thus intensifying the development) and has fifty-four measures on a short fermata; the third section begins with a cadenza-like passage based on the running accompaniment figure of the prelude and introduces the theme of the choral. It has ninety-three measures in all and repeats much of the music of the first section of the fugue transposed into other keys. The themes of the chorale and of the fugue are made to march simultaneously, accompanied by the running figure in thirty-second notes of the prelude, reduced here to sixteenths. The piece closes triumphantly with the chorale, which by the way recalls a noted motif from *Parsifal,* in an agitated and brilliant apotheosis.

THE PRÉLUDE, ARIA, AND FINALE

This work is longer, and in one sense more elaborate than the "Prélude, Chorale, and Fugue," but it is not more difficult. It consists of about 550 measures. One may consider it Franck's suggestion of a possible destiny of the sonata form. Students of form should compare it with Liszt's B minor Sonata and with Scriabin's ninth (if with no other) for the ideas of these composers on the broadening of the sonata form. These two sonatas represent genuine additions to the form.

The Prélude.—This section of 190 measures is of far greater importance to this work than the prelude of the preceding work was to its succeeding movements, since nearly all the themes appear in it either in germ or fully developed. The first theme, A, opens the piece in its final form and is not developed further. It is a long, marchlike affair which dominates the entire movement and sometimes interrupts other themes. It is sometimes heard cut down to one-third or two-thirds of its length.

After a strong close in E, the key of the composition, theme B appears. It consists of only four measures, but continues for over a page in various modifications and arrangements. It suggests the organ. After twenty-one measures of B there is a re-entry of A for twelve bars.

C now appears five times. It is a *cantus firmus* that appears now in the soprano and now in the bass and is beautifully surrounded by contrapuntal devices. During its fourth entrance theme D winds chromatically about it and finally stifles it. D develops later into the chief theme of the finale and takes on unexpected importance. Almost immediately E enters. In this theme is seen the germ of one of the subjects of the aria, also destined to considerable importance. B is used in this section as counterpoint and is of assistance in connection with E in leading back to A, which holds the stage for forty-three measures to the end and passes through such remote tonalities as E♭ and F before returning to E major at the close.

The Aria.—This movement opens with what seems to be a free improvisation and reminds one of a phrase from *Tristan*. It is, however, only the first three measures of a long melody not heard in its entirety until the end of the aria. It may be designated F. The germ theme, E, is stated and becomes so long and elaborate that a new letter is necessary, G. The main body of the movement consists of G, a long and developed melody in three sections. G1 and G2 follow without intermission, but a short interlude, H, is inserted between G2 and G3. After its complete presentation it is repeated in its entirety, but with different counterpoint and embellishments. When this repetition is completed theme F occurs in its entirety for the first time.

The Finale.—This movement opens with D developed at length. It works up over two pages to a climax and leads to new material, I. This section appears twice in the finale (the second time curtailed) as contrasting music, never as part of the structure of the work. Thereafter D appears again, but its surging, agitated character suddenly softens and subsides into accompaniment, over which appear G1 and G2 in slow and at the same time quadruple tempo. It is broken off by D in its original character; this modulates from D minor through E♭ to E minor, when it is again presented in its entirety.

After this section I appears again and reaches a brilliant climax which calls for some technical display of octaves and scales—one of the rare occasions when Franck uses these devices. At the peak of this brilliance the very first theme, A, appears suddenly in half time, resounding like a chorale accompanied by counterpoint octaves in the bass. The brilliance subsides little by little, and theme A recurs for the last time, accompanied for its entire length by F. The music becomes plaintive and wistful through the introduction of G3, but loses this character shortly and ends like a sunset. H appears at half speed, and at the very close E returns as in the aria in a series of slowly descending chords.

The work may be summed up as follows: There are eight themes in all. Section I is not counted for the reason that it is not used structurally. Theme E develops into theme G, and therefore it is not strictly correct to note it twice.

A. B. C. D. E...Five themes appear in the prelude.

F. G. H.......Three themes appear in the aria.

I. ....A section of as yet unheard music, but material not used structurally, appears in the finale.

The themes may be presented according to the number of movements in which they appear:

A. D. F. G. H...appear in two movements.

B. C..........appear in one movement.

E. ....appears in three movements.

The prelude thus discloses itself as the real body of the work, for it contains five of the themes. The sonata form in the old sense is rejected in favor of a new plan, which brings about blood relationship, so to speak, as against key relationship. In this new plan the first movement introduces most of the thematic material, the second provides a songlike contrast, and the third gathers up a number of the motifs and closes with a short résumé and a commingling of the subjects. This architectural structure is not set or rigid; on the contrary, the piece has the effect of perfect freedom.

The two compositions just discussed are Franck's finest contributions to the solo literature, but the two works for piano with orchestra are also masterpieces. For those who prefer the symphonic to the virtuoso manner in treating the piano in conjunction with the orchestra, the "Symphonic Variations" are supremely beautiful. They are complicated structurally by the presence of two themes. "Les Djinns" is much less known, but does not deserve its neglect, for it is in the best Franckian style and will well reward the student, although it does not quite reach the altitude of the "Variations." Harold Bauer's transcription of the contemplative, Peruginesque "Prélude, Fugue, and Variation" is highly recommended to the Franck devotee, and Blanche Selva's transcriptions of the three chorales he will find glorious but difficult. The hard digging one has to do with Franck is always richly compensated, and one's pleasure grows with the hard work necessary to master his music.

Much of César Franck's early work has been lost.

MISCELLANEOUS FRENCH, BELGIAN, AND DUTCH COMPOSERS

GEORGES AURIC
(1899—)

Sonatina, 1925.
Adieu à New York.

Three Pastorales.

ÉMILE R. BLANCHET
(1877—)

Le Pont des caravanes.
Suite "Turquie," six pieces.
Op. 31. Two Études, F, and Am.
Three Ballades.
Three Ecossaises.

Fourteen Preludes.
Concertstück, with orchestra.
  (All C.M.C.)
Sixty-four Preludes (Eschig).

CHARLES BORDES
(1863-1909)

Rhapsodie basque, with orchestra.
Caprice à cinq temps.

Danses, marches et cortèges populaires
  du pays basque espagnole.
  (All R. L.)

LOUIS BRASSIN
(1840-1884)

Transcriptions of Wagner's "Magic Fire"
  music (Schott)
Other transcriptions.

PIERRE DE BRÉVILLE
(1861—)

Portraits de maîtres (1892. Eschig).
Album pour enfants.

Stamboul.
Sonate (1923).
  (All R. L.)

ALEXIS E. CHABRIER
(1841-1894)

Pièces pittoresques (Litolff).
Bourrée fantasque (Enoch).

*España, two pianos.

73

CÉCILE CHAMINADE
(1861—)

La Lisonjera ("The Flatterer").
Op. 30. Air de ballet.
Scarf Dance.

Automne.
Op. 35. Concert Études (Schirm.).

ERNEST CHAUSSON
(1855-1899)

Paysage.
Quelques danses, three pieces with a pro-
logue.

*Concerto, for piano, violin, and quartet.
(All R. L.)

LÉON DELAFOSSE
(1874—)

Douze études de concert (Henn,
Geneva).

PAUL DUKAS
(1865-1935)

Sonata, E♭m (1900).
Variations, intermède, et final, on a
theme of Rameau (1907).

Prélude élégiaque, on the name Haydn
(1910).
(All Durand)

GABRIEL DUPONT
(1878-1914)

Les Heures dolents (1905).
La Maison dans les dunes (1910).
(Both Heugel)

MARCEL DUPRÉ
(1886—)

Variations, Ĉ♯m (A. Leduc.).

GABRIEL FAURÉ
(1845-1924)

Thirteen Nocturnes (No. 6 recommend-
ed by Cortot).
Thirteen Barcarolles (*No. 6).
Six Impromptus.
Nine Preludes, in his last manner (*Nos.
3, 6, 9).
*Op. 73. Theme and Variations.

Dolly Suite, in six parts (four hands).
Ballade, with orchestra (1881).
Fantaisie, with orchestra (1919).
Clair de lune, transcriptions by Guy
Maier.
Après une rêve, transcription by Guy
Maier.

74

LOUIS TH. GOUVY
(1819-1898)

*Variations on "Lilliburlero," for two pianos (Senff; Simrock).

Op. 69. Fantaisie (Breit.).

GABRIEL GROVLEZ
(1879—)

Improvisations on London (Aug.).
Fancies, Seven Child's Pieces (Aug.).
A Child's Garden (Chest.).
Études.
   Naiades (double notes).
   Kobolds (octaves).

Trois valses romantiques.
Trois pièces.
   Evocation.
   Barcarolle.
   Scherzo (1914).
(All Durand)

ERNEST GUIRAUD
(1837-1892)

Allegro de concert, C♯m.

ARTHUR HONEGGER
(1892—)

Le Cahier romand (1923).
Concertino, with orchestra (Senart).

Toccata and Variations.
Three Pieces (Mathot).

JACQUES IBERT
(1890—)

Petite suite en forme de ballet.

*Histoires (No. 2 is "Le Petit âne blanc"), ten pieces.
(Both Leduc)

VINCENT D'INDY
(1851-1931)

Op. 9. Petite sonate.
Op. 15. Poèmes des montagnes.
Op. 16. Four Pieces.
   Serenade.
   Choral.
   Scherzetto.
   Agitato.
Op. 17. Helvetia Waltzes.
   Aarau.
   Schinznach.
   Laufenburg.

Op. 24. Sarabande and Menuet.
Op. 26. Nocturne.
Op. 27. Promenade.
Op. 30. Schumanniana, Three Songs Without Words.
   (All Hamelle)
Op. 33. Tableaux de voyage (easy. R. L.).
Op. 63. Sonate, Em.

WITHOUT OPUS NUMBER

Minuet on the Name Haydn.
Two transcriptions from "Le Chant de la cloche."

An elaborate piano part in the *Mountain Symphony*.
(All Hamelle)

JOSEPH JONGEN
(1873—)

Op. 19. Sérénade (R.L.).
Suite en forme de sonate.
Crépuscule au lac Ogwen.
Two Études.

Sarabande triste.
Pages intimes (four hands).
(All Chest.)

LEO KOK
(1893—)

Trois danses exotiques (Chest.).

GUILLAUME LEKEU
(1870-1894)

Sonate (1891).
Tempo di mazurka.

Trois pièces.
   Chansonette sans paroles.
   Valse oubliée.
   Danse joyeuse.

GEORGES MIGOT
(1891—)

Trois épigrammes (1921).
Le Tombeau de Dufault, joueur de luth (1923).

Suite, with orchestra (1926. Senart).

DARIUS MILHAUD
(1892—)

Suite, with orchestra (1913. Durand).
Saudados do Brazil, Suite (2 vols. 1922) (Eschig; Schott).
Sonate (Mathot).

Caramel More.
Printemps, in four parts.
Tano des fratellini.
Three Rag-caprices.

FRANCIS POULENC
(1899—)

Promenades, ten pieces.
Mouvements perpétuels.
Sonate (four hands).
Six impromptus.
Napoli.

Suite, in three parts.
  (All Chest.)
Pastourelle (Heugel).
Concert champètre, for two pianos (R. L.).

76

RHENÉ-BATON
(1879—)

Op. 4. Variations on a Theme in the Aeolian Mode, with orchestra.
Op. 13. En Bretagne, six pieces.

Six Préludes.
Au pardon de Rumengol (Durand).

JEAN J. A. ROGER-DUCASSE
(1873—)

Six Préludes.
Barcarolles (No. 1, 1906; Nos. 2 and 3, 1920).
Étude, C#m (1914).

Variations on a Chorale (1915).
Arabesques (1917).
Rhythms (1917).
Sonorités (1919).
(All Durand)

JOSEPH G. ROPARTZ
(1864-1935)

Musique au jardin (1917. Durand).
Croquis d'été (R.L.).

Dix petites pièces (four hands).

ALBERT ROUSSEL
(1869-1937)

Rustiques, three pieces (1906).
Sonatine (1912).
(Both Durand)

Suite, four pieces (1910).
Résurrection, after Tolstoi.
(Both R. L.)

GUSTAV SAMAZEUILH
(1877—)

*Le Chant de la mer, in three parts (1921).
Prélude.
Clair de lune.
Tempête et lever du jour sur les flots.

Suite, Gm, in six parts (easy).
Chanson à ma poupée.
Naiades au soir (Durand).

ERIK SATIE
(1866-1925)

Trois gymnopédies.
Trois valses du précieux dégouté.
Pièces froides.
Pièces en forme de poire.

Gnossienne.
Véritables préludes flasques d'un chien (R. L.).

77

J. M. DÉODAT DE SÉVÉRAC
(1873-1921)

En vacances, seven pieces for children.
Baigneuses au soleil.
Cerdaña, cinq études pittoresques.
En Languedoc, five pieces.

Sous les lauriers roses.
Le Chant de la terre. Poème géorgique, in four parts.
(All R. L.)

ÉDOUARD SILAS
(1827-1909)

*Gavotte, Em (Schirm.).

GERMAINE TAILLEFERRE
(1892—)

Ballade, with orchestra (Chest.).
Concerto, with orchestra.

Jeux de plein air, two pieces (four hands).

ALEX VOORMOLEN
(1895—)

Le Livre des enfants, twelve pieces.
Scène et danse érotique.
Les Éléphants, étude (1920).
Trois tableaux des Pays-Bas (1921).

Sonnet (1922).
Suite, in four parts (1918).
(All R. L.)

VICTOR VREULS
(1876—)

Prélude élégiaque.
(Both Chest.)

Caprice.

LOUIS VUILLEMIN
(1873-1929)

Op. 21. Soirs armoricains (J. Vuillemin, Nantes).
Au large des clochers.
En rivière.
Carillons dans la baie.
Appareillage.

*Op. 16. Quatre danses, for two pianos (Durand).
Bourrée.
Gigue.
Pavane.
Passepied.

CHARLES M. WIDOR
(1845-1937)

Op 39. Concerto, with orchestra (Hamelle).
Op. 62. Fantasie, with orchestra (Durand).

Op. 77. Concerto, with orchestra.

JEAN WIENER
(1896—)

Sonatine syncopée (*Second movement, "Blues").

Concerto Franco-Americain, with orchestra.
(Both Eschig)

Other writers in France and Holland include Koechlin, Roland-Manuel, Fiévet, Inghelbrecht, and Magnard.

Two albums of compositions by the "Six" are published, one by Schott and one by Eschig. They consist of pieces by Auric, Durey, Honegger, Milhaud, Poulenc, and Tailleferre.

The French school offers less to the taste of the Anglo-Saxon than might be expected. With the exception of Saint-Saëns, Debussy, Ravel, and Franck, all of whom have universal appeal, one is surprised to discover little left. There are so many disciples of Franck and Debussy that one can, to a certain extent, describe any French composition as dependent on one or the other of these influences. Of course there is the sophisticated-naïve style of the "ultras" and the older salon style of which the "Arabesques" of Debussy, the better works of Chaminade, and the compositions of Saint-Saëns are general examples. Like most music of today and the recent yesterdays French music has possibly overstressed "atmosphere" to the detriment of melody, but since one may say that the French "invented" atmosphere they have a better right than most to indulge in it. Unfortunately, atmosphere is more easily manufactured than are ideas.

For one brought up on German and Russian masterpieces French music seems tenuous and a trifle futile. German music was for so long a time the paramount influence in France that its sudden removal by Debussy may have caused a void. It is perhaps too soon to expect a revived French idiom of universal appeal to have been developed, but with the influence of César Franck and with that of Debussy, as well as with the older background of elegance and form provided by Saint-Saëns, probably much of value will eventually result. Exactly how the Franck and Debussy ideals may be harmonized is difficult to see, but many mutually antagonistic influences were at work in Russia, and these finally produced a tremendous nationally homogeneous music.

At present the list of works which one must not miss is small. One should not forget, of course, that the great French composers are dealt with elsewhere.

The two sets of pieces by Dupont are sympathetic works in the older salon style. They are melancholy and somber as a rule, and too many of them must not be played in succession, but they are sincere. Roussel is greatly admired by French critics. His work gives evidence of serious thought and skill, but warmth is absent. Dukas, a Franck disciple, offers one more sustenance. His "Variations on a Theme of Rameau" are not worthy of his master, but at least they show warmth of imagination. The sonata also contains much that is attractive. The "Prélude élégiaque" is valueless.

Lekeu, another Franck disciple, has a sonata which is really a suite in the contrapuntal style, a dream of Bach, though much diluted and not to be recommended. His chamber music is superior to that for piano alone. De Bréville, in his "Portraits de maîtres," has set Fauré, D'Indy, Chausson, and Franck to music. This piece is entertaining but not important. Between the portraits he uses the Tarnhelm motif from Wagner's "Ring" to achieve a transition from one master to another. The motif in this French setting acquires a strange aspect. His sonata, a much more recent work, is in the older harmony and is not exciting, but it contains good individual music. Of Chabrier there is nothing except the fine "España" for two pianos and possibly the "Bourrée fantasque," though the French admire greatly his "Pièces pittoresques."

Samazeuilh, critic and writer on musical subjects, has composed a long ballade-like piece in three parts, "The Song of the Sea." It is an interesting work which leans partly on Debussy and, as it covers twenty-seven full pages, would make an excellent substitute for a sonata on a concert program.

Grovlez, a not too inspired writer, has some good keyboard music in his short, though not easy suite "Trois pièces." Spanish influence is in evidence in the "Évocation," which is good in its way. Another ingenious keyboard writer is Roger-Ducasse, whose pieces are rather difficult. Students would perhaps best begin with the "Six Préludes."

Milhaud has in his "Saudodos do Brazil" a number of very entertaining rhythmical studies in more or less dissonant and sometimes bitonal harmonies. They show excellent musicianship and cleverness, and with a well-modulated touch pleasing effects may be secured.

Vuillemin has done admirable and original work in his "Quatre danses" for two pianos. They should not be missed; with careful study they are very rewarding. In his "Soirs armoricains" he presents interesting studies of his own locality.

It is a pity that Chausson did not write more for the piano. In his "Quelque danses," "Paysage," and the gorgeous Concerto for piano, violin, and quartet he made real contributions, especially in the last named. This is really an expanded trio, for the quartet is treated as a unit throughout; but it is listed here because it is entitled a "Concerto," and also because of its little-known beauties. It is a sonorous and thrilling composition, rather difficult, but good from beginning to end. Chausson was a pupil of Franck and possessed a most fervid imagination.

Poulenc offers some amusing pieces in the sophisticated style of the day. The "Mouvements perpétuels" form, paradoxically, a short piece, in which the "perpetual" idea is created by means of repeats, so that one can make the piece as long as is desired. In the "Promenades" there is more difficult music, and perhaps more interesting. The "Promenade en chemin de fer" is a simple diatonic piece in which the bass approaches the Alberti style of accompanying, probably introduced to suggest the deliciously antiquated idea of traveling on the railway. The "Promenade en autobus" roars along with the cutout open—an ingenious musical commentary on transportation.

Ibert has sent his name around the world on a little white donkey, for "Le Petit âne blanc" is a universal favorite, but there are many others among the "Histoires" which are rewarding and quite as good as the donkey.

It is a pity that Gouvy's striking variations on "Lilliburlero" are out of print, for they are rich and effective. They are naturally in the old romantic style. Perhaps some day they will be republished. It is also a pity to forget the vigorous and satisfying Gavotte of Silas, an excellent nineteenth-century imitation. Guiraud's "Allegro de concert" is an excellent study in Wagner and makes a strange impression, for it comes from Debussy's teacher. It is not original, but nevertheless it is melodically interesting and has a certain swing.

Migot is said to have struck a note new in French music. The writer is unfamiliar with his work. Rhené-Baton has little inspiration and much program. Ropartz is mechanical and cold. Widor is old-fashioned. Wiener, a jazz devotee, writes a syncopated sonatina dedicated to the Negro jazz bands with thanks for their salubrious influence on the music of the day.

De Sévérac, a man from the Midi, celebrates his country in his music as all southerners do. His best work is possibly "Baigneuses au soleil" and "Sous les lauriers roses," but some of the études from "Cerdaña" offer interesting material. "Sous les lauriers roses" is a long ballade, a tribute to his friends Bordes, Albéniz, and Chabrier, in which a scene on the Catalonian coast passes before one.

Satie, whose chief charm consists in his knack of finding entrancing titles for dull pieces, should be mentioned. His emotional specialty is supposed to be irony, but closer inspection discloses it as less that than insipidity. One must, however, concede the humor of the titles. What could be more arresting than to play "pieces in the form of a pear?" Saint-Saëns depicted satisfactorily a number of the more prominent animals, but the musical representation of their psychology he left to Satie, who endeavored to portray the feelings of a dog left alone in a house. If the names are amusing and the pieces insufferable, why not put the names on a program and add a note to the effect that these pieces will not be played? Schumann thought of that trick in the "Carneval," where the "Sphinxes" are marked "not to be played." If one asks "what's in a name?" the answer in Satie's case is "everything."

Fauré is an enigmatical figure. He is adored in France, but elsewhere he fails to win an audience. In this respect he resembles Bruckner whom, if one does not visit Vienna, one can easily avoid hearing. Fauré's titles—Nocturne, Impromptu, Barcarolle—recall Chopin, but in his "Theme and Variations," perhaps his greatest work for piano solo, he approaches Schumann in style, and he does show a certain *Innigkeit*. Though approach to him is a bit difficult, it will probably repay one if one is persistent. What the French consider his best work is marked with an asterisk to enable the enquiring student to choose more easily from the list.

MISCELLANEOUS GERMAN AND HUNGARIAN COMPOSERS

Older Writers

EUGÈNE D'ALBERT
(1864-1932)

Op. 1. Suite: *Allemande, Courante, Sarabande, *Gavotte, *Gigue (Schirm.).

Op. 2. Concerto, Bm, in one movement.

Op. 5. Waltzes (four hands).

Op. 12. Concerto No. 2.
(All B. and B.)

Cadenzas for Beethoven's concerto in G.

Op. 16. Four pieces (Peters).
Waltz.
*Scherzo.
Intermezzo.
Ballade.

*Transcription of Prelude and Fugue, D (organ), Bach.

*Transcription of Passacaglia, Cm (organ), Bach (B. and B.).

FRANZ BENDEL
(1833-1874)

Op. 27. Étude in Sixths (U.E.).

*Op. 135. German Fairy Tales, six numbers.

"Wie berührt mich wundersam," a transcription of one of his songs.

*Transcriptions from *Die Meistersinger* and the "Ring." (All Schirm.)

Numerous salon pieces.

FERDINAND HILLER
(1811-1885)

*Concerto, F♯m (Schirm.).

IGNAZ MOSCHELES
(1794-1870)

Op. 45. Gesellschaftsconcert, with small orchestra (Schott).

Op. 47. Sonata, E♭ (four hands).

Op. 49. Sonata mélancholique (Schott).

*Op. 70, *95, 111. Études (Steingr.).

La Tenerezza.

*Cadenzas to Beethoven's concertos.

Op. 73. Fifty Preludes.

Concertos.
*Op. 58, Gm; Op. 87, C; Op. 90, Bm; Op. 93, Cm are considered his best (Haslinger).

*Op. 92. Hommage à Handel, for two pianos.

Schirmer publishes two volumes.
Vol. I contains Op. 3, 18, 29A, 52, 53, 54, 62, 66, 71, 74, 82.
Vol. II contains Op. 51, 77, 101, 103, 120, 127, and the "Oberon" Fantasia.

JEAN L. NICODÉ
(1853-1919)

*Op. 12. Two Études.

Op. 13. Italian Dances and Songs (*"Tarentella").

Op. 22. Ein Liebesleben. (All Breit.)

The Concert Allegro, Op. 48, of Chopin, rewritten, extended, and arranged for piano and orchestra (Aug.).

JOSEPH RAFF
(1822-1882)

Op. 55. Spring Messengers.

Op. 72. Suite, Em.

Op. 91. Suite (containing the Gigue and Variations).

Op. 108. Saltarello.

*Op. 157. No. 2. La Fileuse.

Op. 163. Suite.

Op. 204. Suite (containing the well-known Rigaudon).

Much salon music of little merit.

KARL H. C. REINECKE
(1824-1909)

Op. 13. Scherzo, Waltz, Fughetta, Tale.

*Op. 20. Ballade, A♭ (Schirm.).

Op. 52. Variations on a Theme of Bach (Siegel).

*Op. 61. Impromptu on a Theme from Schumann's *Manfred,* for two pianos.

*Op. 72. Concerto No. 1, F♯m (Breit.).

Op. 84. Variations on a Theme of Handel (Senff).

Op. 86. Bilder aus dem Süden (four hands).

*Op. 87. Forty-two cadenzas for classical concertos (Breit.).

*Op. 120. Concerto No. 2, Em (Kistner).

*Op. 127a. Six very easy sonatinas.

EMIL SAUER
(1862—)

Concertos in Em (No. 1) and Cm (No. 2).

Sonatas No. 1, D, and No. 2, E♭.

Music Box (also in a simplified edition).

Twenty-nine Concert Studies (Schott).

RICHARD STRAUSS
(1864—)

Op. 3. Five Pieces.

Op. 5. Sonata, Bm.

Op. 9. Stimmungsbilder, containing the "Träumerei."
(All U. E.)

*Op. 38. Music to Tennyson's "Enoch Arden" (recitation with piano accompaniment. Forberg).

*Burlesque, with orchestra (Steingr.).

Newer Writers

JOSEPH ACHRON
(1886—)

Symphonic Variations on a Folk Tune "El Jiwne Hagolil."
(Juwal, publisher of Jewish music)

Children's Suite, twenty pieces (U.E.).

KONRAD BECK
(1901—)

Concertino.

Sonatina (Schott).

WILHELM GROSZ
(1894—)

Op. 20. Dance Sonata.

Op. 21. Sonata (U.E.).

PAUL HINDEMITH
(1895—)

Op. 26. Suite "1922."

Op. 36. No. 1. Concerto, with small orchestra.

Op. 37. Two books of small pieces.

Dance of the Wooden Dolls.

Op. 49. Concert music for piano, brass, and harp (Piano Concerto No. 2) (Schott).

PHILIP JARNACH
(1892—)

Op. 17. Ballabile, Sarabande, and Burlesque.

Op. 18. Sonatina.

Ten Piano Pieces (Schott).

ALEXANDER JEMNITZ
(1890—)

Op. 23. Dance Sonata.

Op. 26. Sonata No. 3 (U.E.).

PAUL KADOSA
(1903—)

Op. 9. Sonata.

Op. 11. Al Fresco, three pieces.

Op. 13. Sonata (Schott).

Konzertmusik für Klavier und Orchester.

SIEGFRIED KARG-ELERT
(1877-1933)

Partita (Schirm.).

ZOLTÁN KODÁLY
(1882—)

Op. 3. Nine Pieces.

Op. 11. Seven Pieces.

Op. 11. Eclogues, four pieces (both sets figure as Op. 11).

Valsette.

Dances of Marroszek (U.E.).

ERICH KORNGOLD
(1897—)

Op. 1. Sonata, Dm (U.E.).

Op. 2. Sonata, E (Schott).

Op. 3. Fairy Pictures (Schirm.).
The Enchanted Princess.

The Real Princess, Rübezahl, The Brownies, The Fairy King's Ball, The Brave Little Tailor.

The Fairy Tale Recites an Epilogue.

Op. 25. Sonata No. 3 (Schott).

FRITZ KREISLER
(1875—)

Caprice viennois.

Rondino on a Theme of Beethoven.

The Old Refrain.

Tambourin chinois.

Chanson Louis XIII, and Pavane (L. Couperin).

Indian Lament of Dvořák, transcribed by Chaloff.

Paradise (Viennese Folk Song).

Andantino Padre Martini.
(All C. Fischer)

Kreisler transcribed the above violin pieces for the piano.

Most of the above are also published by Schott, as are also Liebesfreud, Liebesleid, and Schön Rosmarin.

LADISLAS LAJTHA
(1891—)

Aufzeichnungen eines Musikers, nine fantasias, Märchen (atonal).

A small group of pieces.
(Both Roszavölgyi)

ALEXANDER LASZLO
(1895—)

Op. 9. Traüme, five pieces.

Op. 11. Sonatina with Colored Light (Breit.).

WALTER NIEMANN
(1876—)

Three Sonatas.
Romantic.
Northern.
Elegiac.

Op. 21. Schwarzwald Idyllen, ten pieces.

Op. 26. Deutsche Ländler und Reigen, ten pieces.

Op. 55. Twenty-four Preludes.

Op. 51. Old Greek Temple Dances.
(All Kahnt)

Op. 62. Old China, five pieces (Peters).

Op. 76. The Garden of Orchids (Simrock).

Op. 87. Suite (Simrock).

PAUL A. PISK
(1893—)

Op. 3. Four piano pieces.

Op. 7. Six concert pieces (U.E.).

KAROL RATHAUS
(1895—)

Op. 2. Sonata.

Op. 9. Five piano pieces.

Op. 11. Six Little Pieces.

Op. 20. Sonata, No. 3.

Op. 24. Three Mazurkas (U.E.).

ARNOLD SCHÖNBERG
(1874—)

Op. 11. Three pieces.
Op. 19. Six small pieces.
Op. 23. Five pieces.

Op. 25.   Suite.
Op. 33a. Piano piece (U.E.).

HEINZ TIESSEN
(1887—)

Op. 37. Six pieces (U.E.).

ERNST TOCH
(1887—)

Op. 31. Dance Suite.
Op. 31. Three Burlesques (No. 3, "The Juggler").
Op. 32. Three piano pieces.
Op. 36. Five Capriccietti.
Op. 38. Concerto.

Op. 40. Dances and Plays.
Op. 47. Sonata.
Op. 48. Small-town Pictures.
Op. 55, 56, 57, 58, 59. Studies both for beginners and for concert use, in the modern idiom (Schott).

EGON WELLESZ
(1885—)

Der Abend. Cycle of four pieces (Roszavölgyi).
Pastorale.
Angelus.
Twilight.
Wind on the Moors.

Op. 9. Three pieces.
Op. 11. Eclogues.
Op. 17. Epigrams.
Op. 21. Idylls (U.E.).

GÉZA V. ZÁGON
(1889-1918)

Op. 1. Three Poems.

Op. 2. Sonata. (Roszavölgyi).

The Gavotte of D'Albert was once universally popular and still deserves to be remembered. There are a few other pieces worthy of rescue to which asterisks have been attached; among these one should note especially the magnificent transcription of Bach's Passacaglia.

Bendel, whose salon compositions need not be recalled, discloses himself in the "German Fairy Tales"—a classic—in a really delightful light, that will please all lovers of the naïve. The first of the six tales, "Frau Holle," admits of virtuoso treatment and would be a good concert number. The humor of "Red Ridinghood and the Wolf" and of the "Bremen Town Musicians" is exhilarating. Bendel's transcriptions of Wagner are also good and playable.

A rather patronizing attitude toward Moscheles has been fashionable for fifty years. He seemed to be a pretentious sentimentalist, baroque and sweetish; but he is really not so bad as that, and anyone interested in concertos can enjoy his, especially the G minor Concerto. His études are characteristic short pieces and are not very difficult. An open mind will find plenty to admire in him, and one historically minded will welcome him because he bridged between clavichord and piano literature, a period much neglected in these days. The "Gesellschaftsconcert" (with small orchestra) is a welcome addition to a class of pieces which is neither exactly chamber music nor music for a concert hall. Many concertos can be thus arranged. For example, the two concertos of Chopin are far better with the orchestral accompaniment arranged for a string quartet than they are with full orchestra.

The "Two Études" and the "Tarentella" of Nicodé are worth looking into, but his efforts with Chopin's "Concert Allegro" were wasted because the original piece is weak. Nicodé derives from Schumann.

The F♯ minor Concerto of Hiller, now republished by Schirmer, is a very useful and entertaining work, effective and melodious. The middle movement is less interesting than are the other two movements, but the first is vigorous and the finale quite dashing with its well-contrasted themes. The accompaniment of this concerto also might very well be arranged for string quartet.

There is not much that is worth saving from the wreck of Raff except the Rigaudon from Op. 204 and "La Fileuse." What a pity that this abundant musical spring was set the task of turning the mill of cheap potboilers!

Reinecke is noted for his cadenzas for classical concertos and for his charming easy pieces for children, one of which is noted here. As father of a large flock he had their needs constantly before him. His Concerto in F♯ minor is melodious and fluent, though somewhat pattern-made; the E minor Concerto is also good though less noted than the one in F♯ minor. His A♭ Ballade could be taken from its retirement now and then to good advantage, and his Impromptu on a Schumann theme is a great favorite with two-piano players. One finds in him nothing in poor taste, though many pieces are antiquated and dull. His music is to be preferred to that of Raff.

88

Richard Strauss was never much attracted to writing for the piano, and his early works, 3, 5, and 9, do not count for much. The music for "Enoch Arden," however, is beautiful and excellently made on the leitmotif plan. Recitations with piano are now démodé, and this bastard art is to be indulged in only in the strictest privacy, like four-hand playing; but if one conceals oneself with an accomplice in a remote place and performs "Enoch Arden," wallowing in its sentimentality, what a gorgeous time one can have! The "Burlesque," however, is an excellent "solid" composition and might be offered by pianists more frequently. Its name is at fault, "Scherzo serioso" would better express its emotional content.

All of Korngold's pieces date from his child-wonderment except the third sonata, which appeared comparatively recently. The second sonata is surprisingly mature, though it shows the influence of Strauss. The finale, joyous and exuberant, is the freshest part of the work, and the scherzo is good; the slow movement is cold and artificial. Korngold's "Fairy Pictures" are charming little tone poems—Strauss in miniature—and deserve more frequent performance.

Of the other writers no opinion is offered. Kodály and Wellesz are disciples of Schönberg, Hindemith's music is beginning to be very well known, Niemann is one who successfully puts new wine into old bottles (Brahms also did this), and thus keeps the cult of the older style alive among all the welter of the new. Achron endeavors to develop the Jewish note, Toch scampers merrily over the keyboard, Kreisler arranges his violin successes for piano, and the others follow their own bent.

ALEKSANDR GLAZUNOV

(1865-1936)

Op. 2. Suite on a Russian Theme, S-a-c-h-a, five pieces.

Op. 22. Barcarolle and Novelette.

Op. 23. Valse on S-a-b-la (Sabela).

Op. 25. Prelude, and Two Mazurkas.

Op. 31. Three Études: C, *E, *E ("La Nuit").

*Op. 36. Petite valse.

Op. 37. Nocturne.

Op. 41. Grande valse de concert.

Op. 42. Three Miniatures.
  Pastorale.
  *Polka.
  Valse.

Op. 43. Valse de salon (two editions).

Op. 49. Prelude, Caprice-Impromptu, *Gavotte.

Op. 54. Two Impromptus: D♭, A♭.

Op. 62. Prelude and Fugue.

*Op. 72. Theme and Variations (14), in various styles.

Op. 74. Sonata No. 1, Bbm.

Op. 75. Sonata No. 2, Em (both sonatas have been arranged for two pianos by Felix Blumenfeld).

Op. 92. Concerto No. 1, Fm, with orchestra.

Op. 100. Concerto No. 2, Bm, with orchestra.

Publisher: Belaiev.

The work of this writer exhibits a rather hard surface and lacks somewhat in sympathetic imagination. It is academic music with its faults as well as its virtues. The first sonata was long a favorite in Russia and was frequently used for piano-playing contests. The second is warmer in feeling and preferable in many ways. It presents musical ideas well developed and has attractive passage work in the second movement, but the finale is weak.

Concerto No. 1 is in two movements of which the last is a theme with variations (à la Trio, Op. 50, of Tchaikovsky). Concerto No. 2, a more melodious work, is in one movement.

Op. 41 is a good valse, but undistinguished. The Gavotte from Op. 49 is recommended. Prosniz thinks highly of Op. 31, of which No. 3 was formerly much played, and also of Op. 72, written in imitation of the styles of various composers as a sort of musical joke that cannot be taken seriously.

BENJAMIN GODARD

(1849-1895)

Op. 14. Les Hirondelles.

*Op. 16. First Gavotte.

Op. 25. First Mazurka.

Op. 26. First Valse, Ab.

Op. 31. Concerto, Am.

Op. 34. Duo symphonique, two pianos.

Op. 35. Canzonetta.

Op. 40. Bohèmienne.

Op. 41. Légende.

Op. 42. Études artistiques (*Le Cavalier fantastique).

Op. 43. Rêverie pastorale.

Op. 46. Scènes poétiques (also for four hands. Breit.).

Op. 47. Novellozza.

Op. 49. Introduction and Allegro, with orchestra.

Op. 50. Magic Lantern, first part.

Op. 51. Three pieces.

Op. 53. Chemin faisant.
  *En courant.
  En pleurant.
  En chantant.
  En causant.
  En riant.
  En valsant.

*Op. 54. Second Mazurka, Bb.

Op. 55. Magic Lantern, second part.

Op. 56. Second Valse.

Op. 58. Twenty Pieces (also four hands).

Op. 63. Sonata phantastique (Hamelle).

Op. 66. Magic Lantern, third part.

Op. 69. Premier mai—caprice.

Op. 71. Third Valse-sérénade, E♭.

Op. 74. Third Mazurka.

Op. 75. Fourth Valse.

Op. 80. Second Barcarolle.

Op. 81. Second Gavotte.

*Op. 82. Renouveau—étude.

*Op. 83. Au matin.

Op. 85. Au rouet.

*Op. 88. Valse chromatique.

Op. 91. Conte de fée.

Op. 93. Sixth Valse.

Op. 103. Suite de danses anciennes et modernes.

Op. 105. Third Barcarolle.

Op. 107. Twelve Nouvelles études.
Sous la feuillée.
Par monte et vaux.
*Jonglerie.
Avant le départ.
Tournoiment.
Attente.
En songe.
Conte joyeux.
Divertissement.
*Des ailes.
*Guirlandes.
*En route.

Op. 109. Third Gavotte.

Op. 110. Magic Lantern, fourth part.

Op. 111. Magic Lantern, fifth part.

Op. 119. Minuet pompadour.

Op. 120. Romance sans paroles.

Op. 124. Valse à danser.

Op. 126. Scènes italiennes.

Op. 127. Fifth Mazurka, Am.

Op. 130. Fileuse.

Op. 134. Tziganka.

Op. 143. Fantaisie, in three parts.

Op. 145. Second Concerto.

*Op. 149. Études.
Vol. I. Beginners.
Vol. II. Advanced.
Vol. III. Amateurs.
Vol. IV. Artists.

Op. 150. Fourth Nocturne.

Op. 151. Valse de concert.

Op. 153. Fifteenth Valse.

There are also eighteen posthumous pieces.

Publishers: Hamelle, Joubert, Grus, Schirm.

The works of Godard maintain themselves to a certain extent in the lighter literature in spite of their being a trifle old-fashioned. Their form is always good, their harmonic scheme sufficient, and their melodic line attractive enough to enable them to hold their own in an age which produces no similar pieces. The études ("En route," "En courant," "Le Cavalier fantastique," for example) are good for technical development and are entertaining music; they fill a real want. Schirmer publishes a library volume containing eighteen pieces, and forty other compositions.

LEOPOLD GODOWSKY
(1870—)

Sonata, Em.

Walzermasken, twenty-four pieces in ¾ time.

Triakontameron, thirty pieces in ¾ time (Schirm.).

Cadenzas to Beethoven's Concerto in G.

Studies Based on the Études of Chopin, for the left hand (Schlesinger).

Miniatures (four hands), several books (U.E.).

Concert Paraphrases of the Works of Weber.
    Momento capriccioso.
    Perpetuum mobile.
    Invitation to the Dance.

Symphonic Metamorphoses of Themes of Johann Strauss.
    Künstlerleben.
    Fledermaus.
    Wein, Weib, und Gesang.

Phonoramas—Tonal Journeys for the Pianoforte.
    No. 1. Java Suite, in four parts of three pieces each.

Suite, in eight parts, for the left hand alone.

Prelude and Fugue, for the left hand alone.

Étude macabre, Impromptu, Meditation, for the left hand alone (Schirm.).

*Renaissance, sixteen transcriptions of old music (Schlesinger).

OTHER TRANSCRIPTIONS

*Bach . . . . . Solo Sonatas and Suites, for violin and for cello. (C. Fischer).
    Sonata No. 1, Gm (violin).
    Sonata No. 2, Bm (violin).
    Sonata No. 3, Am (violin).
    Suite No. 2, Dm (cello).
    Suite No. 3, C (cello).
    Suite No. 5, Cm (cello).

Schubert . . Moment musicale, Op. 94, No. 3.

Schubert . . Twelve Songs.

Schubert . . Ballet Music from "Rosamunde."

Strauss, R. . Serenade.

Bohm . . . . . . "Calm as the Night."

Schumann . "Du bist wie eine Blume."

Chopin . . . Posthumous Waltz.

Albéniz . . . Tango.

Weber . . . . Invitation to the Dance, for two pianos and an optional third.
    (all C. Fischer)

Publishers: U.E., Schirm., C. Fischer, Schlesinger.

This specialist in $\frac{3}{4}$ time is also a remarkable master of counterpoint, a combination which produces recondite dances and erudite salon music—Johann Strauss waltzing with Johann Bach. This rather anomalous combination of styles is brought to its logical conclusion with the "Symphonic Metamorphoses" of tunes by Johann Strauss. These are probably the last word in terpsichorean counterpoint.

It is a question whether these pieces, remarkable though they are, do not defeat their purpose, for their essential complication demands a performance which shall be interpretive, and to "interpret" a virtuoso piece is pedantic. Their heavy freight of counterpoint would seem to demand a place on the "prelude and fugue" part of the program, but their slender ideation on the other hand would relegate them to the latter end of the evening's entertainment. The question, however, remains purely academic, for they are so difficult that very few virtuosi attempt them.

Godowsky has amused himself with the études of Chopin. These transcriptions are remarkable for being technically transcendent but musically topsy-turvy.

It is to the "Renaissance" and to the transcriptions of the Bach sonatas and suites that one must turn to taste the unique value of Godowsky. Such rebirths of the old music have been compassed by few and surpassed by none. No pianist can afford to miss the delights of these pieces. The "Renaissance" gives one a modernization of Rameau, Couperin, and many others of the pre-Bach era, and the sonatas and suites celebrate the full glory of the high priest himself.

EUGÈNE GOOSSENS

(1893—)

Op. 10. Concert Étude.
*Op. 18. Kaleidoscope, album of twelve
  pieces.
  Good Morning.
  Promenade.
  The Hurdy-Gurdy Man.
  March of the Wooden Soldiers.
  The Rocking-horse.
  Punch and Judy Show.
  A Ghost Story.
  The Old Musical Box.
  The Clockwork Dancer.
  Lament to a Departed Doll.
  A Merry Party.
  Good Night.

Op. 20. Four Conceits.
  The Gargoyle.
  Dance Memories.
  A Walking Tune.
  The Marionette Show.
Op. 25. Nature Poems.
Op. 28. Hommage à Debussy (composed for a collection of pieces by various writers and called "Le Tombeau de Claude Debussy").
Op. 38. Two Studies, No. 1, Folktune, No. 2, Scherzo.
Publisher: Chest.

Goossens is one of the younger members of the British renaissance who has contributed some valuable pieces to the literature. The "Kaleidoscope" and the "Four Conceits" appear successfully on concert programs, but one waits in vain for the brilliant pages of the "Nature Poems." Nature is caught in strange moods which one would enjoy sharing. The "Concert Étude" is a shimmering butterfly piece. The "Two Studies," Op. 38, are short and epigrammatic.

ENRIQUE GRANADOS

(1867-1916)

*Goyescas: Los Majos enamorados (U.M.E.)
    Vol. I. No. 1. Los Requiebros.
             2. Coloquios en la reja.
             3. El Fandango de candil.
             4. Quejas o la maja y el ru-
                señor.
    Vol. II. No. 1. El Amor y la muerte.
              2. Epilogo (Serenata del es-
                pectro.)
Capricho español.
Seis escenas románticas, two series.
Siete valsas poéticas.
Cinco bocetos (easy pieces).
El Pelele.
Allegro de concert.
Dos improvisados.

A la Cubana.
Marche militaire.
Valse de concert.
Celebre danzas españolas, four books containing three each.
Moresca y canción arabe.
Jota aragonesa.
Rapsodia aragonesa.
Album of seven pieces on Spanish Paisaje (popular airs).
Twenty-six sonatas of Scarlatti freely transcribed. These are the sonatas Scarlatti wrote in Spain (Orfeo Tracio).

Publishers: U. M. E., Orfeo Tracio S. A. Madrid, Schirm.

The pieces listed above are all salon music with the exception of the *Goyescas,* which holds out the promise, unfortunately unfulfilled, of what Granados might have been had he lived. This suite is entitled to a high place among the treasures in the piano literature. It is music by a Spanish Wagner. Although one is never allowed to forget the nationality of the composer, yet the music has a sufficiently elemental breadth and sweep to raise it above the merely picturesque and the exotic. It is the unique instance up to the time of its publication of Spanish themes being used symphonically.* It is not only remarkable music but remarkable writing for the piano. It is symphonic, yet it never transcends the bounds of the piano. The suite has a program, but one of so broad an appeal—love and death—that the composer is never tempted into trivialities; and only in "El Amor y la muerte" does the music become descriptive in the narrower sense. This member of the suite sums up all the preceding and cannot be fully understood without a knowledge of the previous pieces. The first volume is the better by far. It is recommended only to advanced players, for it is exceedingly difficult.

---

*De Falla, in his *Nights in the Gardens of Spain,* has produced another, but this is really a composition for orchestra with obbligato piano; it was probably published after *Goyescas.*

EDVARD GRIEG

(1843-1907)

Op. 1. Four Pieces.
Op. 3. Poetic Tone Pictures.
Op. 6. Humoresques.
Op. 7. Sonata, Em.
Op. 14. Symphonic Pieces (four hands).
Op. 15. Lyric Pieces, Vol. I.
*Op. 16. Concerto, Am, with orchestra.
Op. 17. Twenty-five Northern Dances and Folk Songs.
Op. 19. Bilder aus dem Volksleben.
Auf den Bergen.
Norwegian Bridal Procession.
Carneval.
*Op. 24. Ballade in the Form of Variations on a Norwegian Melody.
Op. 28. Albumblätter.
Op. 29. Improvisata on Two Norwegian Melodies.
Op. 35. Norwegian Dances (four hands; also for two).
Op. 37. Valses caprices (four hands).
Op. 38. Lyric Pieces, Vol. II.

*Op. 40. Holberg Suite, in the old style (arranged by Grieg).
Op. 41. Transcriptions of his own songs.
*Op. 45. Lyric Pieces, Vol. III ("To Spring," etc.).
Op. 47. Lyric Pieces, Vol. IV.
*Op. 51. Romance and Variations, for two pianos.
Op. 52. Transcriptions of his own songs.
Op. 54. Lyric Pieces, Vol. V (No. 4, "Nocturne").
Op. 57. Lyric Pieces, Vol. VI.
Op. 62. Lyric Pieces, Vol. VII.
Op. 65. Lyric Pieces, Vol. VIII.
Op. 68. Lyric Pieces, Vol. IX.
Op. 71. Lyric Pieces, Vol. X.
Op. 72. Norwegian Peasant Dances.
Op. 73. Stimmungen ("Moods"), seven pieces.
*A second piano part for four sonatas of Mozart, in F, Cm, C, G.
Publisher: Peters.

Grieg's pictures are chiefly miniatures. The only larger canvases he displays are the Ballade and the Concerto. Sonata Op. 7, the only sonata for piano solo, should be included among pieces in a larger form; though pleasant enough to play, its inconsiderable content and its immaturity make it necessary to dismiss it from this group. The piece of pieces, after the Concerto, is the glorious though melancholy Ballade, in which Grieg strikes a deeper note than is found in most of his work. An emphasis on nationalism weakens a work, but in this piece the composer achieves an elemental and therefore international grandeur in spite of the obviously Norwegian style. This music needs care in presentation, and on the part of the auditor a certain responsiveness and imagination. It is symphonic in structure and slightly monotonous in mood. Structurally, it has the fault of coming to a stop between variations. It is, like the Polonaise-Phantasie of Chopin, primarily a piece to play for oneself or for one or two congenial spirits. But who shall say that this is not the highest compliment one can pay a piece? The climax at the end of the Ballade might very well be arranged to produce a better effect.

The Concerto is so well known that it is not necessary to dwell in this place on its beloved harmonies. Its first critics were horribly shocked by its "informalities," and it may be interesting to quote from the first edition of Weitzmann:

> The concerto in A minor is written in a cheerful vein and with brilliant passages; but harmonic harshnesses and sharp cross-relations are sometimes disturbing. The first movement closes in A minor and the following short Adagio begins quite without connection with the D flat major chord. Even if the hearer conceive this as the C sharp major chord, the affinity between the two harmonies must be constructed very sophisticatedly through A minor-A major, and C sharp minor-C sharp major.

Weitzmann evidently forgot that Beethoven, whose word was law, committed this identical crime in the C minor Concerto, in which the second movement begins in E, and that he allowed almost as great an irregularity in the Eb Concerto. It is hard to realize that audiences ever were wrought up over such innocent liberties. Weitzmann disapproved also of parallel fifths in the Ballade and of the major sixth rather than the minor sixth in an A-minor waltz. Those were the good old days when one *knew* what was right.

Op. 40 and 51 and the "Lyric Pieces" are undoubtedly the best of the smaller works. The second piano parts to the Mozart sonatas are also excellent.

GEORG FRIEDRICH HANDEL

(1685-1759)

First Suite de pièces, eight pieces (1720).

Second Suite de pièces, eight pieces (1733).

Third Suite de pièces, eleven pieces (written over a very long period).

Fourth Collection, Six Fugues (1753).

Universal has the pieces arranged in three volumes with the third and fourth sets in the third volume.

Augener has an "Album" of favorite pieces; 2 vols. of "easy pieces"; sixteen suites; three lessons; six fugues.

Breitkopf publishes the complete works (Handel Society) and also an edition based on the work of the Handel Society for practical use. Also many volumes of collections.

Steingräber publishes two concertos in Gm and F.

Peters also publishes the works complete.

Schirmer publishes an excellent transcription of a suite in Gm done by Whiting.

There are innumerable reprints of the various pieces, notably of the "Harmonious Blacksmith."

96

Handel, in his piano works, is one of the least attractive of the great composers. He is brief, however, and, unlike Bach, does not require profound study. His manner is broad, placid, and somewhat portly like a florid country gentleman of the old school. The "Harmonious Blacksmith," his most noted piece, and in fact one of the most celebrated pieces in existence, is very wholesome music; but like many of the older sets of variations it gives one the feeling of being shut up in an E major cage from which there is no escape. It is thought that the melody was not original with Handel but was a popular tune of the day. The melody and variations are from the Fifth Suite.

The complete editions by Breitkopf and by Universal give the pieces in chronological order, with the exception that the third volume contains leftovers from a period of nearly fifty years. The fugues are the last works written for the piano. The suites are the best for investigation, and, generally speaking, those pieces in variation form, including passacaglias and chaconnes, are the best. Many of these are impressive in their calm stateliness. Some of the gigues and courantes will also be found attractive. Arthur Whiting has pointed the way with an excellent transcription of a suite in G minor (Schirm.) toward the reclamation of Handel.

There is no reason why one should not play the organ concertos on the piano. In Handel's day the line between the instruments was not very finely drawn, and much of the music written for one was played on the other. The music of the organ concertos is of far greater power and beauty than that written specifically for the piano, and some of the organ concertos are even published for piano. It is interesting to note that the first book of suites was published at approximately the same time as the first volume of Bach's *Welltempered Clavichord*.

JOSEPH HAYDN

(1732-1809)

Sonatas, numbered according to Breitkopf.
(In the complete edition there are fifty-two in all, but usually only thirty-four are printed.)

No. 1. E♭.
No. 2. Em.
No. 3. E♭.
No. 4. Gm.
No. 5. C.
No. 6. C♯m.
No. 7. D.
No. 8. E♭.

No. 9. Eb.

No. 10. Ab.

No. 11. D.

No. 12. B.

No. 13. G.

No. 14. B.

No. 15. D.

No. 16. C.

No. 17. F.

No. 18. G.

No. 19. Cm.

No. 20. D.

No. 21. G.

No. 22. D.

No. 23. G.

No. 24. Eb.

No. 25. F.

No. 26. A.

No. 27. E.

No. 28. Bm.

No. 29. C.

No. 30. E.

No. 31. E.

No. 32. D.

No. 33. A.

No. 34. E.

Concertos in F, G, D (Schott; Peters).

Kindersymphonie, for piano and toy instruments.

Il Maestro e lo scolare, Andante and Variations (four hands).

*Andante varié, Fm.

Arietta con variazioni.

Tema con variazioni.

Air varié, Cm.

Adagio, F.

Fantasia, C (after the variations in Fm the most important piece).

Capriccio, G.

Rondo, A.

(Mostly Peters or Breit.)

Breitkopf publishes the complete edition and has in addition a volume of sonatas as noted above, and a volume of "Twelve Little Pieces."

Universal has the above sonatas (in a different order) and a volume of other compositions, including variations and short pieces.

Steingräber also publishes the Concerto in D.

Augener has the sonatas in two books, variations and pieces, minuets, German Dances, and two volumes of "Easy Pieces."

Saint-Saëns has made a fine *transcription of the Andante from the *Surprise Symphony* (Presser).

The only work of Haydn the pianist need study is the Variations in F minor, which is certainly his most important work; it is effective in recitals. The sonatas have charm in spots, but only a specialist would care to play many of them. Haydn expressed himself best through the medium of the string quartet and the symphony, where his humor seemed to find full play. The colder harpsichord did not inspire him to such an extent. The Concerto in D is a good piece and may be performed in a room with a string quartet, oboes, and horns, or may be adapted for other instruments.

ADOLF HENSELT

(1814-1889)

Op. 1. Variations on a Theme of Donizetti from "Der Liebestrank" (also with orchestra).

Op. 2. Twelve Characteristic Études (Hofmeister).
Orage, tu ne saurais pas m'abattre.
Pensez à moi qui pense toujours à vous.
Exauce mes voeux.
Duo.
Vie orageuse.
Si oiseau j'étais à vous je volerais.
C'est la jeunesse qui a des ailes dorées.
Tu m'attires, m'entraines, m'englouties.
Jeunesse d'amour, plaisir celeste, et tu m'enfuis.
Comme le ruisseau dans la mer se répand.
Dors-tu ma vie?
Plein de soupirs, inquiet, le coeur me bat.

*Op. 3. Poème d'amour.

Op. 4. Rhapsody.

Op. 5. Twelve Études de salon (Breit.).
Eroica.
G.
Witches Dance.
Ave Maria.
Lost Home.
Hymn of Thanks after the Storm.
Dance of the Elves.
A.
Romance with Choral Refrain.
Lost Happiness.
*Love Song.
Ghostly Nocturnal Procession.

Op. 6. Two Nocturnes.

Op. 7. Impromptu in Cm.

Op. 8. Pensée fugitive.

Op. 9. Scherzo.

Op. 10. Romance.

Op. 11. Variations on a Theme from "Robert le Diable," also with orchestra (Breit.).

Op. 12. Two Études written for the "Méthode des méthodes" (*No. 2, "La Gondola." Schlesinger).

Op. 13. Six Pieces, transcriptions (Schlesinger).

*Op. 15. Spring Song (Cranz; Schott).

*Op. 16. Concerto, Fm, with orchestra (Breit.).

Op. 16b. Pastorale, Scène champêtre.

Op. 17. Impromptu.

Op. 18. Songs Without Words (Schott).

Op. 20. Pressentiment, Romance.

Op. 23. Marche funèbre.

*Op. 25. Toccatina.

*Op. 28. Deux petites valses (Breit.).

Op. 29. Cadenza for Beethoven's Concerto in Cm (Schlesinger).

Op. 30. Valse.

Op. 31. Ballade.

Op. 32. Nocturne.

Op. 33. Songs Without Words.

*Op. 34. Illusions perdus (Schlesinger).

Op. 35. Coronation March for Alexander II.

Op. 36. Valse romantique.

Op. 37. Impromptu (Schott).

Op. 39. Morgenständchen (Schott).

Op. 40a. Deux romances russes, transcriptions (Siegel).

Op. 40b. No. 1, Duo, No. 2, Evening Star, transcriptions (Siegel).

WITHOUT OPUS NUMBER

Rondo from E major Concerto of Hummel, transcribed for piano solo.

Romance de Thal.

Mon chant de cygne.

Canon (four hands).

Abschiedsklänge.
(Last three Rahter.)

A second piano part for the fifty études of Cramer.

Cradle Song, Gb (Schlesinger).

Rondoletto.

Six celebrated overtures for concert use.

Two romances of Comte de Wielhorsky (Schuberth).

Das ferne Land.

Preludes, in all keys.

Breitkopf publishes a good "Album."

Publishers: Schlesinger, Breit., Hofmeister, Schirm., Siegel.

Henselt was the minister of salon ecstasy and passion. His titles recall the effulgent romanticism of the Victorian era. His Études, Op. 2, are full of sighs, tears, vows, storm, youth, love, beating hearts, celestial happiness, flying birds, and sentimental delights. In his second group there are witches (refined ones), elves, ghostly nocturnal processions, lost happiness, Ave Marias, hymns of thanks after storms, all rather less ecstatic than the first group. In this group one also comes across further melancholy—presentiment, a funeral march, lost illusions, sad waltzes—which was fashionable in the days of the old soul-sicknesses, about which no one was quite clear.

This sort of thing has outlived its day and the perfumed elegance and polished style are a trifle overpowering to present taste. One does not care to live in this sultry atmosphere for long, but there is, all the same, in this perfection of form and finish something not to be despised. Its superficialities are at least sincere and make no pretensions, like certain superficialities of some composers, to profundity. Henselt understood his gifts and wisely refrained from pulling a long face musically. He wrote no sonatas or fugues—only love songs.

The Concerto, his large work, is indebted to Chopin, but deserves to be rescued from oblivion. The chorale which replaces the development section in the first movement should be reorchestrated to include brass (on its appearance with the piano figuration), then it becomes stirring. The larghetto and the finale are more characteristically Henseltian than the opening allegro. The larghetto contains a middle section which appears suspiciously like the ancestor of the C♯ minor Prelude of Rachmaninoff. The charming waltz in 6/8 time of the finale and the massive yet melodious close of the whole work, as well as the graceful figuration entrusted to the piano, are extremely effective.

Henselt's influence on the Russian renaissance was far-reaching. He lived long in St. Petersburg, and his style is easily traced in such composers as Balakirev ("Au Jardin"), Liadov, and others. This influence was not only in matters of style, polish, and elegance, but was technical, for instance in the spidery arpeggios and passages in the left hand in which Henselt delighted. He appears thus in a new light.

"If I Were a Bird" has become an established classic, and the "Love Song" from Op. 5 is almost equally a favorite. The charming little "Spring Song," Op. 16, will be a treat to those who still care for a melody, and the "Toccatina," a piece of the more vigorous type, shows another aspect of his style.

JOHANN NEPOMUK HUMMEL
(1778-1837)

*Op. 11. Rondo favori, Bb.
*Op. 13. Sonata, Eb.
*Op. 18. Fantasia, Eb.
*Op. 55. La Bella capricciosa.
*Op. 56. Rondo brillant, with orchestra.
 Op. 73. Concertino, G.
*Op. 81. Sonata, F♯.
*Op. 85. Concerto, Am.
*Op. 89. Concerto, Bm.
*Op. 92. Sonata, Ab, for two pianos.
 Op. 106. Sonata, D (Finale has been ed. by Henselt).

*Op. 107. Bagatelles.
*Op. 109. Rondo, Bm.
 Op. 110. Concerto, E, with orchestra.
*Op. 113. Concerto, Ab, with orchestra.
*Op. 116. Grand Fantasia, "Oberon's Magic Horn," with orchestra.
 Op. 120. Rondo "La Galante," Eb.

The profusion of asterisks means merely that the pieces so marked were immensely popular in their day.

Many publishers have volumes dealing with Hummel (Aug., "Sixteen Characteristic Pieces").

This great rival of Beethoven is now practically forgotten as anything more than a name, but it is interesting to turn his musty pages once in a while. They show an inventive, fluent, sophisticated, attitudinizing, and somewhat shallow mind which planned compositions on a pretentious scale, and one can easily understand how in his day many people preferred his music to that of Beethoven. It is usually brilliant, well written, and easy of comprehension. As art it is a trifle baroque, but the old concertos can still teach much about technique; and one should remember that they were (as was Hummel in general) an inspiration to Chopin. It is unlikely that they will ever return to concert programs except as curiosities or for special occasions and special audiences, but pianists should know Op. 85 or Op. 89, preferably the latter. Hummel's technique is much more varied than is Beethoven's, and his concertos are much more difficult, so that he is very far from being what he was so long considered as being—a poor Beethoven. The concertos are the direct precursors of Op. 11 and Op. 21 of Chopin, who used Hummel's compositions constantly in teaching. Some of Hummel's frankly frivolous music should be sampled by the enterprising connoisseur. Op. 11, 18, 55, and 120 are in this category.

JOHN IRELAND

(1879—)

Amberly Wild Brooks.
*Decorations (1913).
  The Island Spell.
  Moon-Glade.
  The Scarlet Ceremonies.
Equinox.
For Remembrance.
*London Pieces (1920).
  Chelsea Reach.
  Ragamuffins.
  Soho Forenoons.
On a Birthday Morning.
Soliloquy.
Sonata (1918-20).
The Darkened Valley (1921).
The Towing Path (1918).
Prelude, E♭.
  (All Aug.)

Preludes.
  The Undertone.
  Obsession.
  *The Holy Boy.
  Fire of Spring.
Leaves from a Child's Sketch, three pieces.
Rhapsody (1915).
  (All W. Rogers.)
Merry Andrew (Ascherberg).
Sonatina.
Spring Will Not Wait (O.U.P.).
Ballade.
Aubade.
February's Child (Schott).
Concerto, E♭, with orchestra (Chest.).

Publishers: Aug., Winthrop Rogers, Schott, Chest., O.U.P.

John Ireland is one of the most significant and fundamentally English of the British school. He is a thoughtful artist who with painstaking slowness composes in an ecstasy chastened by a stern critical mentality. Ruggedness and mysticism give his work its essential character, and the effect of austerity and sincerity which emanates from his pieces makes a pleasant impression.

It is noteworthy that Ireland attained his present eminence with comparatively few works; the compositions published before 1920 accomplished this. The sonata, a solid and thoughtful work thirty-one pages long, represents his greatest attainment up to that time; it is colored by his personal harmonic scheme and is not for the casual player.

Previous to it the "Rhapsody" was considered his best composition. It covers only fourteen pages, but is fairly difficult. Technically, this work leans on Brahms rather than on Liszt. With Ireland the technique is the outcome of the musical material and is not decoration.

For those who find the above mentioned works difficult there are a number of shorter pieces which will be greatly enjoyed. "Decorations," "London Pieces," "The Holy Boy," and others have attained great celebrity.

MISCELLANEOUS ITALIAN COMPOSERS
Older Writers
MARCO E. BOSSI
(1861-1925)

Children's Pieces.
  Iridescenza (Ric.).
  Juvenilia (Ric.).
  Album pour la jeunesse (Carisch).
  Miniatures (Carisch).

Cinque pezzi (Pizzi, Bologna).
  Pagliacetto.
  Capitan Fracassa.
  Pierrot in ambascia.
  Libellule.
  La Danzatrice.

ALLESANDRO LONGO
(1864—)

Fifth Suite romantica.
Op. 26. No. 6. Piccola suite.
  (Both of the above for children.)
Op. 32. Scherzo (Rahter).

Op. 40. Ventiquattro pezzi caratteristi-chi.
Op. 61. Tre intermezzi.
  (Ric., except where noted.)

GIUSEPPE MARTUCCI
(1856-1909)

Op. 53. No. 2. Scherzo.
Op. 82. Tre pezzi.
Concerto, B♭.

Improvviso.
Ric. publishes all his pieces in several volumes of which the first, "Twenty Studies and Concert Pieces," is perhaps the best.

EUGENIO PIRANI
(1852—)

Op. 27. Chansons populaires italiens (four hands. Rahter.)

Op. 44. Scene veneziane, with orchestra, in three movements (Schlesinger).
Twelve Études (Schirm.).

EDUARD POLDINI
(1869—)

Op. 15. No. 2. Marche mignonne (Dieck-mann).
Op. 27. No. 2. Japanese Étude (Rosza-völgyi).

Poupée valsante.
Op. 28. Lin-da-po. Five Japanese Pieces (Roszavölgyi).
Folies d'autrefois suite (Chest.).
Schirm. publishes a number of his pieces.

GIOVANNI SGAMBATI
(1841-1914)

Étude triomphale.
Sérénade valsée.
Prelude and Fugue, Ebm.
Fogli volanti.
Op. 10. Études
   (All Ric.)

Concerto, Gm.
Op. 18. Four Pieces (*No. 2, Vecchio
   menueto, and *No. 4).
Suite, Bm.
   (All Schott.)

MARIO TARENGHI
(1870—)

See under Children's Pieces.

EDGARDO DEL VALLE DE PAZ
(1861-1920)

Preludi.
Menuets drolatiques.
Sonata (a prize composition).
Suite in the Old Style.

Canzonette amorose (Aug.).
Schirm. and Aug. publish many opus numbers
of this composer.

Recent Writers

DOMENICO ALALEONA
(1881-1928)

La Città fiorita (Ric.).

ALFREDO BERISSO
(1876-1931)

Eidyllia, five pieces.
   Psiche femminile.
   Invocazione.
   Notte stellata.
   Serenatina.
   Il Pescatore solitario.
Impressioni (first series).
   Solitudine nel crepuscolo.
   Stalatitti.
   Riflessi nel acqua.
   Pioggia.

Impressioni (second series).
   Pirotecnica sul mare.
   Iberica.
   Libellule.
   Il Gatto e il topo.
   Il Tombolo.
Suite de danses, five pieces.
Danza sacra e danza profana.
   (All Ric.)

ALFREDO CASELLA
(1883—)

A la maniere de . . . (a collection of pieces
in the styles of various composers done
in conjunction with Ravel. Mathot).
Eleven Children's Pieces (U.E.).
Variations on a Chaconne (Mathot).
Deux contrastes (Chest.).
Sonatina (atonal).
A Notte alta, also with orchestra
(atonal).
Cocktail Dance.
Pupazetti, five pieces (four hands;
atonal).

Nove pezzi in modo di . . .
Toccata (older harmonies).
Barcarola (older harmonies).
(All Ric., except where otherwise
stated.)
Two cadenzas for Mozart's Dm Concerto
(K466. Chest.).
Inezie (Chest.).
Partita, with small orchestra (U.E.).

MARIO CASTELNUOVO-TEDESCO
(1895—)

Cantico, a prize composition (Ric.).
*"Alt-Wien," Rhapsodie viennoise, in
three parts (Forlivesi).
Alt-Wien (Waltz).
Nachtmusik ("Notturno").
Memento mori ("Fox-trot tragico").
Tre corali su melodie ebraiche.
Concerto (U.E.).
Tre poemi campestre.
Le Danze del re David.

Questo fù il carro della morte.
"Il Raggio verde."
Alghe.
I Naviganti.
Cipressi.
Vitalba e biancospina.
La Sirenetta e il pesce turchino.
Epigrafe.
(Forlivesi, Florence)

VINCENZO DAVICO
(1889—)

Six Nocturnes (E. Demets).

Impressions crepusculaires (Joseph
Williams).

VICTOR DE SABATA
(1892—)

Tre pezzi (Ric.).
Caline.
Habanera.
Quasi Cake-Walk.

La Morte dell'usignuolo.

ADOLFO GANDINO
(1878—)

Nel Bosco.

ALBERTO GASCO
(1879—)

La Danzatrice di Jodhpur (Ric.).

G. FRANCESCO MALIPIERO
(1882—)

A Claudio Debussy (Chest.).
Armenia (Senart).
Bizzarrie luminose dell'alba, del meriggio,
    della notte (Schmidl, Trieste).
    Giuochi.
    Il Sole.
    Fantasmi.
Barlumi (Chest.).
Cavalcate (Senart).
Maschere che passano (Chest.).

Omaggi (Chest.).
    To a Parrot.
    To an Elephant.
    To an Idiot.
Pasqua di resurrezione (Rouart; Lerolle).
Poemetti lumari (Senart).
Poemi asolani (Chest.).
Preludi autunnale (R.L.).
Risonanze (Pizzi).
Six Pieces (Carisch).
Variazioni senza tema, with orchestra
    (Ric.).

RENZO MASSARANI
(1898—)

Del Lago di Mantova (Ric.).

RICCARDO PICK-MANGIAGALLI
(1882—)

Deux lunaires (Ric.).
    Colloque au clair de la lune.
    La Danse d'Olaf.
Cortèges (Ric.).
    Les Gnomes.
    Les Petits soldats.
    Les Masques.
Prelude and Toccata.

Trois valses caprices (U.E.).
Ombri di sogni, five impressions (A. and
    G. Carisch).
Sortilegi, with orchestra (Ric.).
Silhouettes de carnaval, four pieces.
Burlesca.

ILDEBRANDO PIZZETTI
(1880—)

Three Pieces (Joseph Williams).

Transcriptions of "La Pisanella" by
    Castelnuovo-Tedesco (Forlivesi).

OTTORINO RESPIGHI
(1879-1936)

Tre preludi sopra melodie gregoriane
    (U.E.).
Concerto, with orchestra, in the mixo-
    lydian mode (B. and B.).

Transcriptions of Frescobaldi, etc. (See
    under Clavicinists).

VITTORIO RIETI
(1898—)

Poema fiesolana (U.E.).
Tre marcie per le bestie.
    Funeral March for a Bird.
    Wedding March for a Crocodile.
    Military March for Ants.

Preludio notturno (Pizzi).
Due studi.
Concerto (U.E.).

FRANCESCO SANTOLIQUIDO
(1883—)

Due acquaforte tunisini (Forlivesi).

FRANCO DA VENEZIA
(1876—)

Danse burlesque (Ric.).

AMILCARE ZANELLA
(1873—)

Il Passero solitario (Schmidl, Leipzig).
Canto d'anima (Schmidl).
Due poemetti.
Due valzer melodici.
Introduzione e fuga a due soggetti.
Scherzo—Studio.

"Lachrymae rerum."
Umoresca.
Tempo di menuetto.
Fantasia e fuga sinfonica, with orchestra.
Concerto, with orchestra (Carisch).
Two Studies (Schmidl).
    (Mostly Ric.)

Although they invented the instrument, Italians have never felt so much at home in writing for the piano as they have in writing for the voice. In the days of the clavichord there were a number of excellent composers, headed by Scarlatti, whose works are now being republished and transcribed (see under Clavecinists). Since the arrival of the modern pianoforte, however, only Clementi can be cited as being worthy of remembrance among the writers of his day (see p. 56). The work of the writers of the more recent past will likewise not long detain the seeker after new thrills. Bossi, Martucci, Longo, and Sgambati are respectable routine writers and nothing more. Of the older salon writers, Pirani and Poldini offer better entertainment. The "Poupée valsante" is everybody's friend, and the "Japanese Étude" and "Marche mignonne" have had many appearances on concert programs. Pirani's "Scene veneziane" is worth bringing out now and then. It needs a full orchestra, for it has a good many effects not attainable with its orchestral parts reduced to a string quartet. Tarenghi writes extremely well for young people. His pieces are harmonically interesting and melodically good, and there is considerable variety among them. Although not deeply original they are not commonplace.

Lovers of atonality will find among Italian writers of today many who produce the most exquisite dissonances. Malipiero seems the most distinguished musician among them, and he has given the piano much of his thought. The "Preludi autunnali" have been extravagantly praised by some critics. Casella, another atonalist, wrote a few pieces in the older manner before he saw the new light. He is an important musician and critic, but his forte is not composition.

Pick-Mangiagalli and Castelnuovo-Tedesco supply a large number of pieces not quite so "advanced" harmonically as those of the atonalists. "Deux lunaires" of the former and "Alt-Wien" of the latter are recommended. Their affectations suggest the influence of Debussy. Berisso, probably a would-be Italian Debussy, is an impressionist, and many of his titles are copied word for word from Debussy. He delights in keyboard pyrotechnics, and his pages are covered with notes. He has discovered a recipe, but, as has been said, one soon discovers that one is dining off the recipe instead of the dish. Respighi has done little for the piano, but he reveals in his "Three Preludes on Gregorian Melodies" a much firmer background than do the other Italians. His transcriptions of Frescobaldi and other clavecin composers are highly recommended. His interest in Gregorian music is also disclosed in a concerto for piano in the mixolydian mode. Zanella is a conservative.

ADOLF JENSEN

(1837-1879)

Op. 2. Innere Stimmen, five pieces.
Op. 7. Fantasiestücke, two books (Schuberth).
Op. 8. Romantische Studien, seventeen pieces.
Op. 12. Berceuse.
Op. 15. Hunting Scenes.

Op. 17. Wanderbilder. (*No. 3, The Mill.)
Op. 18. Three Pieces (four hands. Schuberth).
Op. 19. Prelude and Romance.
Op. 20. Four Impromptus.
*Op. 25. Sonata, F♯m (Senff).

Op. 31. Three Valses Caprices.

*Op. 32. Twenty-five Études (Peters).

Op. 33. Lieder und Tänze.

Op. 36. Suite, Bm (Bahn).

Op. 38. Two Nocturnes.

Op. 42. Two Nocturnes. (*No. 2, "Canzonetta").

Op. 43. Idyllen (Hainauer).

*Op. 44. Erotikon, seven pieces with mythological titles (Ries und Erler).

*Op. 45. Wedding Music (four hands. Hainauer).

*Op. 46. Ländler aus Berchtesgaden (also four hands. Hainauer).

Op. 48. Erinnerungen, five pieces (Peters).

*Op. 59. Abendmusik (four hands. Hainauer).

Op. 60. Lebensbilder (four hands. Hainauer).

Op. 62. Silhouettes (four hands. Hainauer).

Op. 65. Rosenlaube (four hands. Hainauer).

Augener has a Jensen album.

Publishers: Peters, Ries und Erler, Schuberth, Senff, Hainauer, Schirm., complete by U.E.

Jensen was a very gifted composer. Unfortunately for him he was overshadowed by Schumann and Mendelssohn. His music is a distillation of early German romanticism, and as such it is valuable. It shows genuine feeling and bears the unfriendly light of today rather better than most of the minor writers of that period. The sonata, although very long, holds the attention and displays an unexpected gift for sustained flight. The first and last movements are the best. Transcribed and cut, it might still have success. Who does not recall and love that childhood piece, "The Mill"? If for nothing else Jensen should be kept in grateful remembrance. Many others of this set are worth reviving, as are also the pieces of the "Erotikon," inspired by Greek subjects. Lovers of four-hand playing will enjoy Op. 45 and 59. If Mendelssohn and Schumann had not lived, Jensen would have been cherished more, but it is quite possible that without these two he could not have written his pieces. His early death was a loss.

ANATOL LIADOV

(1855-1914)

*Op. 2. Birioulki (Bagatelles), fourteen short pieces.

Op. 3. Six Pieces.
Prelude.
Gigue.
Fugue.
The other three are mazurkas.

Op. 4. Arabesque.

*Op. 5. Étude, A♭ (Schirm.).

*Op. 6. Impromptu.

Op. 7. Two Intermezzi.

Op. 8. Two Intermezzi.

Op. 9. Valse.

Op. 10. Prelude, and two Mazurkas.

Op. 11. Mazurkas, and Prelude (*No. 2, "In the Dorian Mode").

Op. 12. Étude.

*Op. 13. Four Preludes.

Op. 15. Mazurka, *Mazurka rustique.

Op. 16. Scherzo (four hands).

Op. 17. La Douleur, and Pastorale.

Op. 20. Novelette.

Op. 21. Ballade.

Op. 23. Sur la prairie.

*Op. 24. Prelude, and Berceuse (Schirm.).

Op. 25. Idylle.

*Op. 26. Petite valse (Schirm.).

Op. 27. Three Preludes.

Op. 29. Marionettes.

Op. 30. Bagatelle.

*Op. 31. Mazurka rustique, and Prelude.

*Op. 32. Tabatière à musique (Schirm.).

Op. 34. Three Canons.

*Op. 35. Variations on a Theme of Glinka.

Op. 36. Three Preludes.

Op. 37. Étude.

Op. 38. Mazurka.

*Op. 39. Four Preludes, A♭, C, B, F♯.

*Op. 40. Étude, and Four Preludes.

Op. 41. Two Fugues.

*Op. 42. Two Preludes, and a Mazurka on a Polish Theme.

*Op. 44. Barcarolle (Schirm.).

*Op. 46. Four Preludes.

*Op. 48. Étude, and Canzonetta.

*Op. 51. Variations on a Polish Theme.

Op. 52. Three Ballet Scenes.

Op. 53. Three Bagatelles.

*Op. 57. Three Pieces.
  Prelude.
  Valse.
  Mazurka.

Op. 64. Four Pieces.
  Grimace.
  Shadows.
  Temptation.
  Reminiscences.

Bessel (Breit.) has a collection in one volume of twenty-seven pieces; also in three volumes.

Transcriptions by Siloti of four songs (C. Fischer).

Publishers: Bessel up to and including Op. 17, after that Belaiev. The Bessel publications have been taken over by Breitkopf.

The compositions listed above do not make an imposing array as far as numbers go, but the immaculate taste, the refined workmanship, and the restraint and economy of means exhibited in them deserve wider recognition than heretofore has been accorded them. Liadov is known to pianists chiefly as the writer of the "Tabatière à musique," which, amusing though it is, does not represent him. A great many of his pieces are simple technically and may be played by those of only moderate pianistic attainments. Their Chopinesque perfection of form combines with a desirable ease of execution to make them a welcome addition to the literature. For this reason asterisks have been placed more freely than usual. The "Variations on a Theme of Glinka," Op. 35, one of Liadov's more pretentious and difficult works, is modeled closely on Chopin. One can almost give the chapter and verse of the sources. By copying perfection he is foredoomed to failure, although the work is charming aside from this one fault. The "Birioulki," once famous in Russia, are recommended; the little Prelude "In the Dorian Mode" is simple and charming; the Barcarolle fine, but technically difficult. Liadov's pieces appear in many of the Russian albums put out by various publishers, but frequently, as with so many albums, the poorer ones are chosen. Novello has three Liadov albums, and Augener has a volume of twenty pieces. Some of his pieces appear in the Russian collections of Schirmer.

SERGIUS LIAPOUNOV

(1859-1924)

Op. 1. Étude, Intermezzo, Valse.
Op. 4. Concerto, E♭m (B. and B.).
Op. 5. Rêverie du soir.
*Op. 5. Impromptu (B. and B.).
Op. 6. Seven Preludes.
Op. 8. Nocturne (B. and B.).
*Op. 11. Études d'exécution transcend-
    ante (Zimmermann).

    Berceuse, F♯.
    *Carillon, B.
    Rondo of the Phantoms, D♯m.
    *Terek, G♯m.
    Summer Night, C♯m.
    *Tempest, C♯m.
    Idyll, A.
    Epic Song, F♯m.
    Aeolian Harps.
    *Lesghinka, Bm.
    Rondo of the Sylphs, G.
    Élégie in Memory of Franz Liszt.

Op. 16. Polonaise.
Op. 17. Mazurka.
Op. 18. Novelette.
Op. 19. Mazurka.
Op. 20. Valse pensive.
Op. 21. Mazurka.
Op. 22. Chant du crépuscule.

Op. 23. Valse impromptu.
Op. 24. Mazurka.
Op. 25. Tarentella.
Op. 26. Chant d'automne.
Op. 27. Sonata.
*Op. 28. Ukrainian Rhapsody, with or-
    chestra.
Op. 29. Valse impromptu.
Op. 31. Mazurka.
Op. 33. Two pieces from *Russlan and
    Ludmilla.*
*Op. 34. Humoresque.
Op. 35. Six Divertissements.
Op. 36. Mazurka.
Op. 38. Second Concerto.
Op. 40. Prelude, Elegy, Humoresque.
*Op. 41. Fêtes de Noël, four pieces.
Op. 45. Scherzo.
Op. 46. Barcarolle.
Op. 49. Variations on a Russian Theme.
Op. 55. Grand polonaise de concert.
Op. 57. Fugue, Spring Song, At the
    Fountain.
Op. 58. Prelude and Fugue.
Publishers: Zimmermann, B. and B.

Liapounov's chief title to consideration is his Op. 11. The études marked with an asterisk offer problems of charm and variety. The "Carillon" is best known, but the "Terek" and the "Tempest" should be played for their Russian savor, especially "Terek" with its charming shepherd's pipe melody. "Idyll" is an elaborate nocturne, and "Lesghinka" is flattery paid to Balakirev's "Islamey." These pieces are all difficult, but the music is so rewarding and the passage work so interesting that the hard work is worth while. The Concerto falls short of what one has a right to expect, although it does contain passages of interest. The "Ukrainian Rhapsody" and the "Fêtes de Noël" are recommended by Josef Lhevinne.

FRANZ LISZT
(1811-1886)

Works for Piano and Orchestra
ORIGINAL COMPOSITIONS

Concerto pathétique (1850), in three versions.
  For piano solo (see under "Grosses Concert Solo).
  For two pianos.
  For one piano and orchestra (Burmeister).

Concerto, E♭ (1857).
Concerto, A (1863).
Malédiction, with strings (posthumous. Breit.).

PARAPHRASES

Fantasia on Themes from Beethoven's *The Ruins of Athens* (1853).
Totentanz* ("Dance of Death") Variations on the "Dies irae" (1850-55).

Fantasia on Hungarian Themes, arranged from the fourteenth Hungarian Rhapsody (1847).

TRANSCRIPTIONS

Wanderer Fantasia, Schubert, Op. 15 (1858. New edition, 1874).

Polacca brillant, Weber (1852).

Works for Piano Alone
ORIGINAL COMPOSITIONS

I. Pieces Published in Volumes or Groups

Harmonies poétiques et religieuses (1835).
  Invocation.
  Ave Maria.
  Bénédiction de Dieu.
  Pensées des morts.
  Pater noster.
  Hymne de l'enfant à son réveil.
  Funérailles (1849).
  Miserere d'àpres Palestrina.
  Andante lagrimoso.
  Cantique d'amour.

Années de Pèlerinage.
  Vol. I, Switzerland (1842-55).
    1. Chapelle de Guillaume Tell.
    2. Au Lac de Wallenstadt.
    3. Pastorale.
    4. Au Bords d'une source.
    5. Orage.
    6. Vallée d'Obermann.
    7. Eclogue.
    8. Le Mal du pays.
    9. Les Cloches de Genève.

*The original edition of the Totentanz (1849), edited by Busoni, is published by Breit.

Vol. II, Italy (1856).
1. Sposalizio.
2. Il Penseroso.
3. Canzonetta del Salvator Rosa.
4. Sonetto del Petrarca, No. 47.
5. Sonetto del Petrarca, No. 104.
6. Sonetto del Petrarca, No. 123.
7. Fantasia quasi sonata après une lecture du Dante.

Supplement to Vol. II (1861).
1. Gondoliera (transcription of an Italian song).
2. Canzone (transcription of a song by Rossini).
3. Tarentella (paraphrase of Italian melodies).

Vol. III, Italy (1883).
1. Angelus.

2. Aux Cyprès de la Villa d'Este (Threnody).
3. Aux Cyprès de la Villa d'Este (Threnody).
4. Les Jeux d'eaux de la Villa d'Este.
5. Sunt lachrimae rerum.
6. Marche funèbre, for Emperor Maximilian.
7. Sursum corda.

Three Apparitions (1835). The third is a fantasia on a waltz of Schubert (1839).

Consolations, six pieces (1850).

Liebesträume, three nocturnes after his own songs (1850). A new edition of No. 3 appeared in 1886.

II. Études

Twelve Études (published as Op. 1, later revised and published under the title Études d'exécution transcendante 1839; 1879).
Preludio.
Étude, Am.
Paysage.
Mazeppa.
Feux follets.
Vision.
Eroica.
Wilde Jagd.
Ricordanza.
Étude, Fm.
Harmonies du soir.
Chasse-neige.

Three Concert Études (1849).
Db (sometimes called "Un Sospiro").
Ab.
Fm.

Six Études after Paganini (1841). Several versions (Breit. See also under Busoni).
Gm.
Eb.
La Campanella.
E.
La Chasse.
Variations, Am.

Two Concert Études (1872, written in 1849).
Waldesrauschen.
Gnomenreigen.

Ab-Irato, Étude de perfectionnement (1852), two versions.

Technical Studies, exercises in twelve books (1870-80).

III. Larger Compositions

Sonata, Bm (1854).

Scherzo and March (1854).

Grosses Concert Solo (1850. See also Concerto pathétique).

Fantasia and Fugue on B-A-C-H (1871).

Grand Variations on a basso continuo from the "Crucifixus" of the Mass in Bm and from the cantata "Weinen, Klagen, Sorgen, Zagen" (1875).

IV. Smaller Compositions

Ballade, Db (1854).

Ballade, Bm (1854).

Berceuse (1854), also transcribed by Busoni (Peters).

Allegro di bravura (1838).

Polonaise, E (1852).

Polonaise, Cm (1852).

Prélude on a basso continuo from the Mass in Bm and the cantata "Weinen, Klagen, Sorgen, Zagen."

Mazurka brillant in A (1851).

Trois caprices valses (1840-52).
Valse de bravoure.
Valse mélancholique.
Valse de concert.

Feuilles d'album (Schott).

Deux feuilles d'album (Schuberth).

Grand galop chromatique (1838).

Valse impromptu (1843).

Two Legends of St. Francis.
St. Francis of Assisi Preaching to the Birds.
St. Francis of Paul Walking on the Waves.

Impromptu, F♯ (1877).

Three Elegies (to Marie Moukhanoff, Marie Lipsius, the last-named also called the "Funeral Gondola").

Bilder aus Ungarn, five Hungarian Folk Songs. Mosonji's Grabgeleit, Dem Andenken Petöfi's, Puszta Wehmut, etc., (U.E.).

Romance oubliée.

Valses oubliées.

Hymne du pape (1865).

Via crucis (1865).

Trauervorspiel und Trauermarsch.

Valse impromptu (1843).

Weihnachtsbaum ("The Christmas Tree"), twelve small pieces (1882).

Ave Maria, E (written for the Lebert and Stark piano method).

Heroic March in the Hungarian Style.

Grande valse de bravoure.

V. Recitations with Piano Accompaniment

Lenore .... Bürger.

The Sad Monk....... Lenau.

The Dead Poet's Love.. Jokai.

Helge's Loyalty....... Strachwitz.

The Blind Bard....... Tolstoi.

The Wandering Jew.... Victor Hugo.
(Written between 1860 and 1876.)

VI. Hungarian and Spanish Rhapsodies

Hungarian Rhapsody.

No. 1. C♯.

No. 2. F♯.

No. 3. Bb.

No. 4. Eb.

No. 5. Em, Héroïde élégiaque.

No. 6. Db.

No. 7. Dm.

No. 8. F♯, Capriccio.

No. 9. Eb, The Carneval of Pesth.

No. 10. E, Preludio.

No. 11. Am.

No. 12. C♯.

No. 13. Am.

No. 14. Fm (the original of the Hungarian Fantasia, with orchestra).

No. 15. Am, the Rakoczy March, transcribed literally.

No. 16. Szozat and Hymnus.

No. 17. From the Figaro Album.

No. 18. For the Buda-Pesth Exposition Album (1886).

No. 19. After Abranyi's Czardas Nobles (1886).
Nos. 16, 17, and 18 are rather short and comparatively simple; No. 19 is long and elaborate.

Spanish Rhapsody (based on "The Follies of Spain," an old tune, the "Jota aragonesa," and a third unnamed theme).

Fantasia on Spanish Themes (a virtuoso piece of little musical value).

TRANSCRIPTIONS

I. Organ, Piano, and Violin Works

Bach . . . . . . Six organ Preludes and Fugues (1869). Am, C, Cm, C, Em, Bm.

Fantasia and Fugue, Gm (1872), organ.

Schubert . . Divertissements à l'hongroise, three books, piano.

Four Marches (1838-46), piano.

Soirées de Vienne, nine parts (there are two versions of the most famous one, No. 6), piano.

David . . . . . Bunte Reihe, twenty-four pieces, violin.

1. Scherzo.
2. Erinnerung.
3. Mazurka.
4. Tanz.
5. Kinderlied.
6. Capriccio.
7. Bolero.
8. Élégie.
9. March.
10. Toccata.
11. Gondellied.
12. Im Sturme.
13. Romance.
14. Allegro.
15. Menuet.
16. Étude.
17. Intermezzo.
18. Sérénade.
19. Ungarisch.
20. Tarentella.
21. Impromptu.
22. In russischer Weise.
23. Lied.
24. Capriccio.

Paganini . . . . . Fantasie sur la clochette, violin.

Dargomyzhsky Tarentella (an arrangement of the four-hand piece. The bass is an organ point).

Bulhakov . . . . Russian Galop (1846).

Conradi . . . . . Gypsy Polka (1849).

Vegh . . . . Valse de concert.

Zichy . . . . . . Valse d'Adèle (1877).

———— . . . . . Mazurka by an Amateur (1883).

Herbeck . . . . . Tanzmomente (1881).

Louis, Prince
of Prussia . . Elegy on Themes by . . . .

Cui . . . . Tarentella.

II. Smaller Song Forms

Alabiev . . . . . . The Nightingale.

Beethoven . . . An die ferne Geliebte.

Auf dem Hügel sitz ich spähend.
Wo die Berge so blau.
Leichte Segler in den Lüften.
Diese Wolken in den Höhen.
Es kehret der Maien.
Nimm sie denn, diese Lieder.

Geistliche Lieder, six songs (*No. 3 "Penitential Song." Schirm.; Schuberth).

Adelaïde.

Mignon's Song.

Mit einem gemalten Band.

Es war einmal ein König.

Freudvoll und leidvoll.

Wonne der Wehmut.

Die Trommel gerühret.

Bülow . . . . . . Tanto gentile (sonnet of Dante).

Chopin . . . . . Six Polish Songs.
Maiden's Wish.
Spring.

The Ring.
Bacchanale.
My Joys.
The Return.

Dessauer .... Three Songs.
Lockung.
Zwei Wege.
Spanisches Lied.

Franz .... Thirteen Songs.
Auf geheimem Waldes-
pfade.
Drüben wird die Sonne
scheinen.
Trübe wird's, die Wol-
ken jagen.
Sonnenuntergang.
Auf dem Teich, dem
regungslosen.
Er ist gekommen.
Der Schalk.
Der Bote.
Meeresstille.
Treibt der Sommer seine
Rosen.
Gewitternacht.
Das ist ein Brausen und
Heulen.
Frühling und Liebe.

Goldschmidt .Two Songs.
Lassen ...... Two Songs.
Lessmann .... Three Tannhäuser Songs.
Liszt .... Die Zelle in Nonnen-
wörth.
Es muss ein Wunderbares
sein.
Six Songs.
Lorelei.
Am Rhein.
Mignon's Lied.
Es war einmal ein Kö-
nig.
Der du vom Himmel
bist.
Angiolin dal biondo
crin.

Kahnt publishes twelve songs, "Lieder
und Gesänge," by Liszt, transcribed
by August Stradal. Since Stradal has
no list of compositions, this collection
is noted here.

Mercadante ..Les Soirées italiennes.
La Primavera.
Il Galop.
Il Pastore avizzero.
La Serenata del mari-
naro.

Il Brindisi.
La Zingarella.

Mendelssohn .Nine Songs.
Auf Flügeln des
Gesanges.
Sonntagslied.
Reiselied.
Neue Liebe.
Frühlingslied.
Winterlied.
Suleika.
Der Jäger Abschied.
Wasserfahrt.

Meyerbeer ...The Monk.
Rossini ...... Les Soirées musicales.
La Promessa.
La Regata veneziana.
L'Invito.
La Gita in gondola.
Il Rimprovero.
La Pastorella.
La Partenza.
La Pesca.
La Danza (Tarentella).
La Serenata.
L'Orgia.
I Marinari.
Two fantasias on the
"Soirées Musicales."
La Serenata, and
L'Orgia.
La Pastorella, and
I Marinari.

Rubinstein ..."O, wenn es doch immer
so bliebe."
Der Asra.

Schubert ..... About fifty songs in all,
variously grouped by
publishing houses.
For detailed infor-
mation in regard to
these transcriptions
see Corder's *Liszt*.

Winterreise, twelve songs.
Gute Nacht.
Die Nebensonne.
Muth.
Die Post.
Erstarrung.
Wasserfluth.
Der Lindenbaum.
Der Leiermann.
Täuschung.
Das Wirthshaus.
Der stürmische Morgen.
Im Dorfe.

116

Schwanengesang.
   Die Stadt.
   Das Fischermädchen.
   Am Meer.
   Abschied.
   In der Ferne.
   Ständchen.
   Ihr Bild.
   Frühlings-Sehnsucht.
   Liebesbotschaft.
   Der Atlas.
   Der Doppelgänger.
   Die Taubenpost.
   Kriegers Ahnung.

Sei mir gegrüsst.
Auf dem Wasser zu singen.
Meeresstille.
Frühlingsglaube.
Hark, Hark, the Lark.
Der Wanderer.
Lebewohl.
Das Sterbeglöcklein.
Ungeduld.
Lob der Thränen.
Geistliche Lieder, four songs.
Müllerleider, six songs.
Du bist die Ruh'.
Erlkönig.
Die junge Nonne.
Gretchen am Spinnrade.
Rastlose Liebe.

Ave Maria.
Mädchens Klage.
Trockne Blumen.
Die Forelle (two transcriptions).

Schumann, R. An den Sonnenschein.
Widmung.
Provenzalisches Minnelied.
Frühlingsnacht.
Weihnachtslied.
Die wandelnde Glocke.
Frühlings Ankunft.
Des Sennen Abschied.
Er ist's.
Nur wer die Sehnsucht kennt.
An die Thüren will ich schleichen.

Schumann, C. Warum willst du and're fragen.
Ich hab' in deinem Auge.
Geheimes Flüstern hier und dort.

Spohr . . . . . . Rose, Softly Blooming.
Weber . . . . . . Einsam bin ich.
Schlummerlied.
Leier und Schwert.
Lützow's wilde Jagd.
Wielhorsky . . . Autrefois.

III. Church Music

Arcadelt . . . . . Allelujah, and Ave Maria.
Mozart . . . . . . Confutatis, and Lagrimoso from the Requiem.
Mozart and Allegri . . . À la chapelle sixtine (Miserere of Allegri, and Ave Maria of Mozart).
Rossini . . . . . . Aria from Stabat Mater, La Charité.
Soriano . . . . . . Élégie.
Verdi . . . . Agnus Dei, from the Requiem.

IV. National Melodies

English ......God Save the Queen, and Rule Britannia.

French ......La Marseillaise.
Chanson du Béarn.
Faribolo pastour.

German .....Paraphrase on "Gaudeamus igitur."

Hungarian ...Hungarian Folk Songs, five numbers.

Italian ......La Romanesca (a melody of the sixteenth century).

(Other transcription from Salvator Rosa, Rossini, etc., in the *Années de pèlerinage,* Vol. II and Supplement.)

Polish ......Glanes de Woronince.
Ballade Ukraine.
Mélodie polonaise.
Complainte—Doumka.

Russian .....Parting; Folk Song.

Spanish ....Il Contrabandista (a rondo on a Spanish theme. See also under rhapsodies).

Swiss ....Three Swiss pieces.
Ranz des vaches.
Un Soir dans la montagne.*
Ranz des chèvres.

Fantaisie romantique sur deux melodies suisses (1836).

V. Paraphrases and Transcriptions of Arias and Scenes from Operas

Auber ......Fantasia on "La Tyrolienne," from *La Fiancée.*

Tarentella, from *Masaniello.*

Berlioz ......Two motifs from *Benvenuto Cellini.*

Bellini ......Reminiscences, from *I Puritani.*

Grande Fantasie sur *La Sonnambula* (two versions).

Grande Fantasie sur *Norma.*

Introduction and Polonaise, from *I Puritani.*

Hexameron. Grand Variations on a theme from *I Puritani.*

(Liszt contributed a variation to this piece. The other composers were Thalberg, Pixis, Herz, Czerny, Chopin.)

Donizetti ....Fantasia, on motifs from *Dom Sébastian.*

Reminiscences of *Lucia di Lammermoor.*

Reminiscences of *Lucrezia Borgia.*

Marche funèbre, from *Dom Sébastian.*

Glinka ......Tscherkess March, from *Russlan e Ludmilla.*

Goldschmidt .Two pieces from *Die sieben Todsünden.*

Gounod .....Berceuse, from *Reine de Saba.*

*This piece later becomes (somewhat changed) the "Mal du pays" of the *Années de pèlerinage.* The air is used by the organist of the church at Lucerne in his celebrated Fantasia, "A Storm in the Alps." There are many more "Swiss" pieces in the complete edition of the early works, but they are not to present-day taste.

Les Adieux, from *Roméo et Juliet*.
Valse, from *Faust*.

Halévy . . . . . Reminiscences, from *La Juive*.

Handel . . . . . Sarabande and Chaconne, from *Almira*.

Lassen . . . . . Hagen und Kriemhilde. Symphonic Intermezzo to a Drama of Calderon.

Liszt . . . . Salve Polonia, from *Stanislaus*.

Meyerbeer . . . Fantasia on *L'Africaine* (two parts).
Reminiscences of *Les Huguenots*.
Fantasia on *Le Prophète* (four parts).
Fantasia on *Robert le Diable*.

Mendelssohn . Wedding March and Elfin Dance, from *Midsummer Night's Dream*.

Mosonyi . . . . Fantasia on *Szep Ilonka*.

Mozart . . . . . Reminiscences of *Don Giovanni* (also a version for two pianos).
Fantasia on *The Marriage of Figaro* (left incomplete; finished by Busoni).

Pacini . . . . . . Grand Fantasia on *Niobe*.

Raff . . . . Fantasia on *König Alfred*.

Ernest, Duke of Saxe-Coburg . . Hunting Chorus and Steyrer, from *Tony*.

Tchaikovsky . Polonaise, from *Eugène Onegin*.

Verdi . . . . Two Illustrations, from *Don Carlos*.
Three Paraphrases on *Il Trovatore*, *Ernani*, and *Rigoletto*.
Fantasia on *Simone Boccanegra*.
Salve Maria, from *I Lombardi*.

Wagner . . . . . Fantasia on *Rienzi*.
Spinning Song, from *Der fliegende Holländer*.
Senta's Ballade, from *Der fliegende Holländer*.
The Overture, from *Tannhäuser*.
The Evening Star, from *Tannhäuser*.
Entry of the Guests, from *Tannhäuser*.
Chorus of Pilgrims, from *Tannhäuser*.
Isolde's Love-Death, from *Tristan und Isolde*.
"Am stillen Herd," from *Die Meistersinger*.
Entry of the Gods in Walhalla, from *Das Rheingold*.
March to the Castle of the Grail, from *Parsifal*.

VI. Orchestral Works

Beethoven ... All nine symphonies.
Septet.

Berlioz ...... L'Idée fixe, Le Bal, and Marche au supplice, from the *Symphonie fantastique*.
March of the Pilgrims, from *Harold in Italy*.
Dance of the Sylphs, from *The Damnation of Faust*.
Overture to *Les Francjuges*.
Overture to *King Lear*.
The symphony, *Harold in Italy*.

Donizetti .... Paraphrase of the March of Sultan Abdul Medjid Khan.

Hummel ..... Septet.

Liszt .... "Gretchen" movement, from the *Faust Symphony*.
Two Episodes, from Lenau's *Faust*.
Mephisto Waltz (he later wrote other "Mephisto" waltzes).
Der nächtliche Zug.
Hungarian Quick March (two versions).
The one published by Schirmer is the better.

Festival March for the Goethe Festival.
Huldigungsmarsch for the Grand Duke of Weimar.
Vom Fels zum Meer (a German victory march).
Parts of the Oratorio St. Elizabeth.
Festzug zur Schillerfeier.
Von der Wiege bis zum Grabe (a symphonic poem).
Excelsior, Prelude to Die Glocken von Strassburg.
Second Mephisto Waltz.
Third Mephisto Waltz.
Mephisto Polka.
All his own symphonic poems and his two symphonies.

Meyerbeer ... March for the Schiller Centenary.
Overture to *William Tell*.
Impromptu on themes of Rossini.

Saint-Saëns .. Danse macabre.

Szechenyi .... Introduction, and Hungarian March.

Weber ...... Overtures to *Der Freischütz, Oberon,* and the *Jubel*.

Liszt Pedagogium. The piano compositions of Liszt, together with hitherto unedited changes, additions, and cadenzas, according to the master's teachings, by Lina Ramann (Breit.).

Vol. I. Pieces of Religious Tendency.
Vol. II. Larger and Smaller Forms.
Vol. III. Hungarian Pieces.
Vol. IV. Larger and Smaller Forms of Various Tendencies.

Although Liszt was born in 1811 and has been dead about fifty years, his music has hardly achieved anything like a settled position. Because of his tremendous fecundity and unbounded virtuosity on the keyboard, he allowed an uncritical attitude to govern his composing, and the music written during the early period when he was seeking an audience grew to be better known than the later, more serious work. His inherent greatness, however, as time went on, corrected this fault, if it was one (for those pieces served a real purpose), and his native sincerity asserted itself with the increasing seriousness which the passing of the years brought to him. In his last years he devoted himself to the cultivation of music free from all taint of virtuosity, and these later works are scarcely recognizable to those familiar with his more frivolous side. Like Dr. Johnson he was greater than his works, and his influence will never be lost even should some of his compositions some day be ignored. Since these have given so far no signs of mortality, aside from some obvious exceptions, it may be presumed that they are here to stay.

It is quite impossible to arrange a list of his works which will be satisfactory in every way. Prosniz groups them under four heads with numerous subdivisions; Corder, in his book, *Liszt,* arranges them under six heads without subdivision. The present arrangement differs from both, but makes no claim to superiority. It should be added that the list of compositions is never alike in all particulars and that no list can be perfect without so many explanations in regard to changes Liszt made, that it would be unnecessarily complicated. Since this book aims to be of practical rather than of encyclopedic use, no apologies are offered for certain inaccuracies. One must not take the dates too literally. Liszt had the habit of withdrawing works from publication, to alter and to republish them. The dates thus indicate merely the approximate period in the composer's life in which the pieces were written.

The student will soon find that it is something of a task to master even the titles of the Liszt repertory. Since Liszt was the inventor of modern technique and indisputably the greatest pianistic personality the world has ever known, it is necessary for the cultured player to make this effort. His works contain practically all the secrets of the keyboard and are a compendium of piano virtuosity. Even in the hopelessly frivolous operatic fantasias the student of the keyboard will always find interest of an inventive mechanical order. The musical content of these pieces, however, is so antiquated and dull that one cannot put up with them any more in spite of their pianistic effectiveness. One cannot think otherwise than that Liszt had his tongue in his cheek when writing them, or that, for his own reasons, he was "giving the public what it wanted." That they represent a new departure in pianism is the only reason they survive at all. An exception should be made in favor of the *Don Giovanni* of Mozart and naturally some of the Wagner transcriptions. Mozart's drama is presented in a truly colossal style; there is little superficial decoration, and for once his music dons a guise of modern virtuosity without losing its original character.

Liszt has been unfortunate in that his worst pieces have always been his best known. Ten thousand know the "Rigoletto" Fantasia to one familiar with the "Grand Variations on 'Weinen, klagen.'" How many to whom the Twelfth Rhapsody is a household word realize that the same man wrote the "Fantasia and Fugue on B-A-C-H"? Some of Liszt's works have been prophetic visions of future developments. For instance the "Sonata quasi fantasia après une lecture du Dante" contains a well-developed treatment of the leit-motif usually attributed to Wagner, and it has passages based on the whole-tone scale as well as some curiously "modern" harmonies. The work dates from 1837. That Liszt possessed a fount of genuine musical inspiration cannot be denied by anyone who knows his songs. Here is simplicity, warmth, unaffectedness, and an entire absence of that pomposity, that grandiosity, which mars so many of his piano pieces.

Since it is the endeavor of this book to rescue pieces worth saving, it seems worth while to proceed on the basis that although Liszt is not one of the greatest composers he was a great writer and pathfinder. There is in him at times the ecstasy of a journalist rather than that of a littérateur, but since a variety of ecstasies have been conceded this kind also might be admitted.

HARMONIES POÉTIQUES ET RELIGIEUSES

The student will find in this collection much genuinely good work that is comparatively unknown. The first and last pieces are weak, the third, "Bénédiction de Dieu dans la solitude," is very long and somewhat theatrical, but the others all bear closer inspection. The "Bénédiction," by the way, if drastically cut, might appear at times on programs.

No. 2, "Ave Maria," is conceived with all the delicacy of the early Renaissance: archaic, yet warm and full of religious feeling. How effective and how simple is the appearance in B minor of the "Nunc et in hora mortis nostrae" out of a general atmosphere of B♭ major. It must be confessed, however, that the piece is more adapted to orchestral treatment.

No. 4, "Pensées des morts," is probably the most original and certainly one of the most beautiful and interesting of the collection. Written in 1834 this "Thoughts of the Dead" has lost nothing of its grandeur, its gloomy rigor, its mystery, and its general fascination. Its rhythms, 5/4, 7/4, 4/4, 3/4, and its augmented chords, unusual at that date, give it distinct coloring. Some of the passages in major thirds and sixths are difficult, but they give it a specifically intended character and are inherent in the general atmosphere of "augmentation." The piece is in two sections; the first is introspective and in the nature of a lamentation; the second is softer in feeling, as if time had mitigated the pain of the grinding irrevocability of death. This part is as lovely as any song of Schubert and lacks entirely the rather insincere and theatrical character of the "Bénédiction." The theme of the first part consists merely of three notes, which slowly descend and then slowly ascend. Nothing could be fundamentally simpler.

No. 5, "Pater noster," is ancient church music without additions. The Latin words are followed literally. The prayer is repeated and very slightly embellished by a wavering tiny arpeggio figure so insignificant that it serves to reinforce rather than to beautify the theme.

No. 6, "Hymne de l'enfant à son réveil," is a charming modification of the solemnity characteristic of this suite in general. Its 6/8 rhythm flows so easily after the uncompromising "Pater noster" that one is relieved and relaxed. The actual hymn is preceded by four very lovely pages probably intended to depict the mood of a child on awakening.

No. 7, "Funérailles," is the only one of the set to have won much renown. Recently it has been forgotten. The clashing dissonances of the introduction are perhaps the most interesting and striking part, although the octaves toward the middle of the piece, in passages which inevitably recall Chopin's Polonaise, Op. 53, are magnificent. It was written at a much later date than any of the other pieces.

No. 8, "Miserere d'après Palestrina," is another piece in the old church style. It consists of twelve measures of the Miserere with two variations, the first with a tremolo accompaniment, the second with arpeggios. It is hardly worth playing except for oneself in certain moods. No. 9, "Andante lagrimoso," is what the name implies, a lament, containing some excellent music. It also will be acceptable or not according to one's mood.

ANNÉES DE PÈLERINAGE

There are twenty-six pieces in this suite, divided into three books with a supplement to the second book. Many pieces in the first volume are on the borderline between good and bad, but in the following volumes there are none which can be said to be really bad or out-of-date. The three pieces forming the supplement are of a rather frivolous nature, but only the "Canzona" is uninteresting; the "Gondoliera" and "Tarentella" both have their individual appeals. To understand the difference in the quality of the music in the three volumes the student must observe the dates of composition.

In the first volume, dedicated to Switzerland, the following are valuable in one way or another: "Au Lac de Wallenstadt," strikes the Swiss note very charmingly; "Au Bords d'une source" is a very noted "water" piece; "Eclogue" has its quietly pastoral effect; "Orage" is slightly theatrical but still a rather good veteran, if one does not mind a musical thunderstorm. To see how much better it is than the old-fashioned descriptive music one might compare it with "The Battle of Prague." The "Mal du pays," achieves a dreariness equal to the subject. The "Cloches de Genève," the "Chapelle de Guillaume Tell," and the "Vallée d'Obermann" are worth no more than a glance; they have more program than inspiration and lapse sometimes into grandiosity.

The second of the "Years of Pilgrimage" is a different matter. Liszt had reached Italy and had found greater and more serious inspiration. He rises to greater inspiration in all the compositions in this volume. The "Sposalizio" is as rich in coloring as one of his own tone poems and suggests orchestral instruments at every step; "Il Penseroso," one of his most perfect inspirations, is without blot of any sort; and who does not love the "Canzonetta del Salvator Rosa," for which Liszt wrote both words and music. He has transcribed it in such a manner that none of its perfection of form, delicate brilliance, or unencumbered naïveté is lost.

The three following pieces appear both as songs and piano pieces in

Liszt's collected works. These three sonnets of Petrarch were favorites of his own. They are eminently Italian in character, expansive, melodious, rhapsodic, but very lovely and well suited to the ecstasy of the lover in contemplation of his lady's eyebrows.

The last piece is the "Fantasia quasi sonata après une lecture du Dante." Much should be said to do justice to this thrilling and epoch-making work. Its 380 measures fall into three main subdivisions of which the second and third are further subdivided. There is no pause in the work. Six themes are used in the leitmotif manner, which I designate as follows: (1) Virgil's call to Dante, (2) Dante's grudging and weary response, (3) the first tentative steps of the journey, (4) the wailings and groanings of the tormented, (5) the promise of release, and (6) the vision of paradise. The first four themes appear at once, but there are several repetitions of the "call" theme before Dante is fully aroused. This section is introductory, the main movement begins with the entrance in full of the theme of the tormented, a chromatic scale harmonized in minors.

The "promise of release" theme appears glowing and brilliant in F♯, as the second theme of the sonata. Interesting developments and transformations of the themes follow, and the wails of the tormented are harmonized with major chords. One of the most striking harmonic ventures of the piece is a chord of C♯, G♯, and D struck repeatedly, over which the "call" theme resounds in B and F. It seems impossible that this passage could date from 1837. Wagner had not yet begun even *Rienzi*. The whole-tone scale is used in two places in the piece. It is not necessary to proceed with the analysis of the work, enough has been said to indicate its importance and interest.

Of the three pieces in the "Supplement" which is here inserted, it must be pointed out that two are transcriptions, and the third is a paraphrase or fantasia. The "Gondoliera" is a transcription of an Italian air, the "Canzona" a worked-over aria of Rossini from *Otello,* and the third, the "Tarentella," rhapsodizes on two Neapolitan tunes. The first and third are well known and popular, the "Canzona" is deservedly unknown.

Many years later an older Liszt made another pilgrimage, seeing things Italian with more weary and disillusioned eyes. He published a third volume in 1883, which differs vastly from the other two; it is little known to this day. It is less gay, and the quality of the music is more introspective and pensive. The most curious part of the matter is that Liszt wrote this music with no thought of the piano qua piano. Its idiom was completely forgotten. The pieces are pure music in the same sense that the music of the clavichord writers was pure music and was to be arranged for any instrument or combination of instruments. It is, of course, possible that he published some of these pieces for orchestra and a version for the piano at the same time, without designating which was the original, and in this sense there was no original. The first number, the "Angelus," is not well adapted to the piano, but when played by a string quartet it is an exquisite piece.

Of the two "Threnodies" inspired by the ancient cypresses of the Villa d'Este the second is arranged better for piano, though both are beautiful and full of tears. No one should miss their sad glory. The third piece inspired by the villa, the "Jeux d'eaux," also retains the atmosphere of sadness which this gorgeous place sends forth like a fragrance in spite of the living waters which everywhere sparkle or roar or whisper or trickle. A quotation from St. John, *"Sed aqua quam ego dabo ei,"* makes it plain, if it had not been obvious before, that Liszt did not intend this as an ordinary "jeu d'eau" piece.

The atmosphere of solemnity is still strong in the following "Sunt lachrymae rerum" in the Hungarian mode, and in the "Marche funèbre" for the Emperor Maximilian; but in the seventh and last piece, "Sursum corda," he lets the sun in on all this ancient sadness in a welcome manner. It is short and based almost entirely on an organ point. Liszt "lifts up his heart," unconquered at the end, in spite of the sadness of memories.

It is obvious that one must be in the right mood to enjoy this music. It is distinctly sad, though rich in beauty. One may regard these three volumes as three phases of his life and genius. The first year, Switzerland, is superficial, brilliant, spectacular, and in places bombastic; the second year is still decorative, picturesque, and descriptive, but it is also mature and more emotional; the third year the piano, the companion of a lifetime, is thrown over as a virtuoso instrument, and the music is abstract, religious in tendency, withdrawn from the earlier brilliance, grave, and solemn.

There is no need to remark on the other pieces published as collections —the "Consolations," the "Apparitions," the "Liebesträume"—for they are well known. These and the études are the only pieces published in sets.

THE ÉTUDES

Among the *Études d'exécution transcendantes* are some which deserve more attention than they are receiving. The best one, musically speaking, is the unnamed Étude in F minor, No. 10, not to be confused with the well-known one in the same key. "Harmonies du soir" is also worth playing. In both of these the difficulties are not "transcendent," and the musical value is greater than in many of the others. "Feux-follets" should also not be overlooked. It is rather difficult, but musically it is attractive even if one must play it in a slower tempo. "Chasse-neige" is beautiful, but the great reaches combined with tremolos and great speed remove it from the sphere of most players. "Mazeppa" is technically interesting but musically arid. "Ricordanza" is a perfect example of the baroque style, florid and meretricious. "Wilde Jagd" is entertaining in the early German romantic manner: a kind of "Freischütz."

ÉTUDES AFTER PAGANINI

It is another matter to turn to the Paganini études, which Liszt formed from that composer's Caprices. Here is the highest art and most excellent taste. Only one of them, "La Campanella," achieved the fame which they all deserve, although No. 5, "La Chasse," is well known. Every one of these études deserves long continued study by the pianist, and even the amateur may obtain genuine pleasure from a careful, slow reading of these masterpieces. No. 6 is the original "Theme and Variations" by Paganini, of which Brahms used only the theme for his two books of variations. To transcribe these transcriptions seems like painting the lily, but Busoni thought he could improve them (see under Busoni).

The complete edition of Liszt's works (Breit.) gives a number of interesting drafts of the études before Liszt decided on their ultimate form. These sketches give an illuminating and intimate glimpse into Liszt's mind. The student should also be familiar with the original version for violin solo. It may be said in passing that Paganini shines rather brightly as a composer in these pieces. He possesses something of the ecstatic brilliance of Scarlatti.

OTHER ÉTUDES

"Ab-Irato," an unduly neglected étude, is a work of great beauty. It is a rugged conception in general, but ends in two pages of softer loveliness.

The Db étude, sometimes called "Un Sospiro," and the lacelike, tenuous Étude in F minor of the same series ("Three Concert Études") require no mention, because they belong to the recognized recital program, and the third one is undeserving of comment. It would be almost impertinent to praise such perfect masterpieces as "Waldesrauschen" and "Gnomenreigen." They are of the highest standard.

SONATA, B MINOR

The suggestions contained in the works of Liszt and César Franck for a further development of the sonata form are among the most important offered by musicians since Beethoven's time. In his B minor Sonata Liszt presents the following plan. The usual beginning of the first movement with two subjects, passage work, etc., is followed, without a pause and in the place of the usual development, by the andante and the scherzo; after this comes the recapitulation of the exposition transposed into the proper sets of keys and, finally, the coda. It will readily be seen how this scheme unifies the four movements: recapitulation serves as finale, and the development of the themes proceeds throughout the entire work.

Of the five themes used, the first three to be sounded are grouped together and form, in a sense, the first subject, although they do not always appear together. The fourth theme is the usual second subject, and the fifth is the subject of the adagio. After the adagio no new thematic material is introduced, and the scherzo-fugue is built up entirely on the first group of themes. There are 760 measures in all, and of these only about one hundred are not made out of or suggested by the five themes.

Liszt was perhaps the first to transmute his thematic material by means of rhythmic and agogic as well as dynamic changes, and in this sonata he succeeded in producing the most startling and sometimes almost unrecognizable variants. The composition unfolds itself in such gorgeous splendor and with such strong internal evidence of masterly scholarship that one hesitates to criticize certain spots which betray a tendency to overripeness and the baroque. The ground plan of this work is unique and is an admirable suggestion for obtaining cohesion of the movements of a sonata. One may regard the work as one of the most striking compositions of the period.

GRAND VARIATIONS ON A BASSO CONTINUO FROM THE
B MINOR MASS AND FROM THE CANTATA
"WEINEN, KLAGEN, SORGEN, ZAGEN" OF BACH

This superb work appears so rarely on concert programs as to be practically a novelty, and yet it is a serious composition of pronounced value and
effectiveness. Those who love the Gothic gloom of the great cathedrals will
find in this composition, translated into music, the shivering elevation of
spirit effected by those incomparable buildings. In the "Harmonies poétiques
et religieuses" Liszt translates the Catholic ritual into piano music. Here he
does the same for the Protestant ritual, and it is breath-taking to observe the
Catholic Liszt in an evangelical mood. He does it impressively, gravely, even
thrillingly. To me, at all events, this work is one of the climaxes of his art and
one might add of all piano music.

The variations are less true variations than is a chaconne or a passacaglia
style of composition, since the basso continuo is very short and little can be
done in a four-measure phrase. If the middle part is found over long, a cut
may easily be made. This section is doubtless rather complaining and whin-
ing, but when the variations begin again the piece draws to a tremendous
close amid music so well written for the instrument that a great climax of
sound is attained with a minimum amount of effort. After this whirlwind
comes a peaceful ending with the chorale "Was Gott thut das ist wohlge-
than." It is a veritable Book of Job, and in it Liszt has apotheosized Protes-
tantism, at least in its gloomier aspects. As it dates from 1875 it represents
Liszt at his maturity. There is no virtuosity for its own sake in the piece.

GRAND CONCERT SOLO (GROSSES CONCERT SOLO)

This piece is better in its form for piano and orchestra ("Concerto pathétique"). It lapses, unfortunately, into the pomposity of the composer's weaker
moments, but it is an effective virtuoso piece.

FANTASIA AND FUGUE ON B-A-C-H

This is another instance, which no one should miss, of Liszt's power of
transmuting his thematic material. A close study of it will reveal this many-
sided man in a new light. It is a suggestion for the fugue of the future. In its

austere grandeur it has affinity with the "Grand Variations on 'Weinen, Klagen'," but it is more cheerful.

WORKS FOR PIANO AND ORCHESTRA

The two concertos in E♭ and A need no mention, for they are only too well known. The first with its pompous theme, forever associated with the words *"Das versteht ihr alle nicht,"* applied jokingly to it, is now understood very well. These threadbare concertos are still used by prima-donna pianists for exhibition purposes just as prima-donna singers use the old trivial Italian arias to show off their voices. The Concerto in A is less hackneyed, but it also has musical drawbacks, for its unfortunate themes are transmuted overvigorously.

The "Totentanz" based on the gloomy old "Dies irae" is infinitely better, for the medieval atmosphere is admirably retained throughout, and the clashing dissonances, excellent use of the glissando, canonical variation, and marvelously appropriate cadenzas (one of them a hunting scene suggested by hornlike passages) give a musical reproduction of that favorite motif of the Middle Ages, the dance of death.

The "Concerto pathétique" has been mentioned under the heading "Grand Concert Solo," of which it is an arrangement. The transcription of Weber's Polacca is an excellent piece of lighter nature, and the Fantasia on themes from Beethoven's *Ruins of Athens* is well worth doing. The latter has been entertainingly transcribed for band instruments and piano and contains two marches and the "Dancing Dervish" music.

The "Wanderer" Fantasia, a transcription from Schubert, is hardly worth reviving, for the original is tedious in parts, especially the finale, which is very bad, though it starts as if it were going to be a grand fugue. The "Hungarian Fantasia" needs no comment.

It is not known what Liszt intended to call that grave piece for piano and strings, "Malediction," for it is a posthumous work. The word "Malediction" was written over the tempo direction, but it is not certain that he intended this for the definitive title. A performance of this piece would be a genuine novelty. It is probably only accessible in the complete edition (Breit.).

SMALLER COMPOSITIONS

Of the two ballades, the second in B minor may be played with some pleasure, but the first one in Db is antiquated. The "Berceuse" is somewhat obviously modeled on Chopin. The E major Polonaise, though rather thread-bare, is still the better of the two, although the other in C minor is more serious and, were it not for a commonplace middle section, might be worth playing. The short Prélude on the same basso continuo as that of the "Grand Varia-tions" is a solemn and beautiful work. The character is identical in both.

St. Francis of Assisi is portrayed in the "Sermon to the Birds," and St. Francis of Paul is represented "Walking on the Waves." The first is charm-ing. The birds twitter during the sermon, which they naturally found pedan-tic. St. Francis seems not to have discovered the fact that one must feed be-fore one converts. I am not sure which of these two saints was the patron of Liszt, and possibly not even Liszt was certain, for, to be on the safe side, he wrote a piece for each. "Paul" (Paolo), of the "St. Francis of Paul," is a little town on the coast of Italy not far from Sicily.

The charming and mature Impromptu in F♯, the "Valse oubliée," and the "Ave Maria" in E (written for the defunct Lebert and Stark piano method) are all worthy of a place in one's heart, especially the "Ave Maria," which must not be confused with the other two, one by Arcadelt (a transcription) and the other in Bb in the "Harmonies poétiques et religieuses."

HUNGARIAN AND SPANISH RHAPSODIES

There are still many admirers of those formless compositions, the "Hun-garian Rhapsodies," and it must be admitted that they have a certain real value. One either admires or dislikes them—there seem to be only two courses. They are undoubtedly better than the operatic fantasias and are very good keyboard music. They were originally written to astound, but since the pub-lic can no longer be astounded, one reason for playing them has been elimi-nated. Formally and musically the second remains the best, on account of its structure as well as its inspiring melodies. The fifteenth, good for the same reasons, is a literal transcription of the "Rákoczy March" (apropos of Hun-garian music, see under Dohnányi and Bartók). Ricordi lists a twentieth rhapsody which I have never seen.

The "Spanish Rhapsody" develops on a more solid musical basis, at least in its first half, than do the Hungarian ones, and is interesting for its contrasting moods. The first part is based on the ancient tune "The Follies of Spain," a grave old melody used as early as Corelli for violin variations. Liszt develops it in the passacaglia manner and achieves an effect of great dignity. The second half is made up of two melodies, the "Jota aragonesa" and an unnamed tune. For a while the music is excellent, but it degenerates and indulges in anticlimaxes, so that the piece is not unalloyed delight; however, cuts may be made. Busoni has arranged it for piano and orchestra. The second venture into Spanish music, made in the "Fantasia on Spanish Airs," has no organic development and is merely technical embroidery of Spanish tunes.

TRANSCRIPTIONS

Among the transcriptions one should know are those of the great G minor "Fantasia and Fugue," and the first A minor of the group of six organ preludes and fugues of Bach. One should delve among the "Soirées de Vienne," for there is much unappreciated beauty hidden there. Only the sixth is generally familiar. Some of the "Bunte Reihe" are most attractive and would be novelties, so entirely are they forgotten. The "Tarentella" of Dargomyzhsky, amusingly written to play with someone who does not play the piano, is good music. In the original the bass player had nothing to do but to play A all through the piece. With the other transcriptions of piano, violin, and organ works the casual student need not concern himself.

The song transcriptions are among Liszt's most inspired and beautiful works. It will be remembered that he invented this style of thing in an endeavor to popularize Schubert's songs. The transcriptions emerge from his hands not merely arranged for the piano, but reconceived, and have in a sense the value of original compositions. One can hardly go amiss on any of them. Fortunately, they are done with entire absence of "technique," although they are hard enough! Only in "Adelaïde" does he allow himself a cadenza, perhaps to stimulate this very long song, which is certainly little adapted to the piano alone.

The Chopin songs display more virtuosity in their reconception for piano and demand considerable smoothness, agility, and finish. Liszt's own song "Die Lorelei" is admirably done, and his other songs show a remarkable gift for lieder writing. The "Penitential Song" of Beethoven should not be forgotten; it is done in the contrapuntal style and comes to a great climax. "On Wings of Song" is exactly as good in his transcription for piano as in the original version. "The Nightingale" by Alabiev is also a standard transcription. Mercadante's "Les Soirées italiennes" and Rossini's "Les Soirées musicales" should be explored, for there is much in them worth playing.

The lover of the mongrel art of recitation with piano will find some good things to pander to this low taste. Transcriptions of church music will not be found very satisfactory except for purposes of playing for oneself, and the transcriptions of national melodies are out-of-date. Over those of the operas it is respectful to Liszt to draw a veil. They were written for a purpose which they served well, but at present they are not needed. Gounod's Valse from *Faust* and Verdi's *Rigoletto* are beloved by some, and I have even heard a noted pianist play the scene in the skating rink from one of Meyerbeer's operas. Of course it was fun to do the glissandi. The title "Two Pieces" from *Die sieben Todesünden* ("The Seven Deadly Sins") is attractive, but one fears that the music by Goldschmidt might not adequately depict them. The Fantasia on *The Marriage of Figaro,* completed by Busoni, is a serious work and may come to the concert stage, though it has not been heard much as yet.

The transcriptions of orchestral works are in the same category as the list just discussed. No one wants to hear a pianist play a symphony of Beethoven, but what fun to bludgeon one's way through, say, the *Tannhäuser* overture! The only two worth noting under this heading are the "Mephisto Waltz," No. 1, and the "Hungarian Quick March" (in two versions, of which Schirmer's is the better).

To know Liszt completely one must have a bowing acquaintance with these pieces and also with the operatic fantasias, if for no other reason than to appreciate his large sympathies. In gratitude to this heroic though very human figure which the gods once sent to earth, one closes an eye to certain failings and forgives freely certain lapses in taste. Liszt made a whole literature for the piano in a manner no one had dreamed of before. What wonder that a few experiments failed!

EDWARD MACDOWELL

(1861-1908)

*Op. 10. First Modern Suite (Breit.).
  Preludium.
  Presto.
  Andantino, Allegretto.
  Intermezzo.
  Rhapsody.
  Fugue.

Op. 13. Prelude and Fugue.

Op. 14. Second Modern Suite (Breit.).
  Preludium.
  Fugato.
  Rhapsody.
  Scherzino.
  March.
  Fantasy-Dance.

*Op. 15. Concerto No. 1, Dm, with orchestra (Breit.).

Op. 16. Serenata.

Op. 17. Two Pieces.
  A Legend.
  *Witches Dance.

Op. 18. Two Pieces.
  Barcarolle.
  Humoresque.

Op. 19. Forest Idylls, four pieces.

Op. 21. Six Poems.

Op. 23. Concerto No. 2, Am, with orchestra.

Op. 24. Humoresque, March, Cradle Song, Czardas (Friska).

Op. 28. Six Idylls after Goethe.
  In the Woods.
  Siesta.
  To the Moonlight.
  Silver Clouds.
  Flute Idyll.
  The Bluebell.

Op. 31. Six Poems after Heine.
  From a Fisherman's Hut.
  *Scotch Poem.
  From Long Ago.
  The Post Wagon.
  The Shepherd Boy.
  Monologue.

Op. 32. Four Little Poems.
  *The Eagle.
  The Brook.
  Moonlight.
  Winter.

*Op. 36. Étude, F♯.

Op. 37. Les Orientales.
  Clair de lune.
  Dans le hamac.
  Danse andalouse.

Op. 38. Marionettes, in eight parts.

Op. 39. Études for Technic and Style.
  Hunting Song.
  Alla Tarentella.
  Romance.
  Arabesque.
  In the Forest.
  Dance of the Gnomes.
  Idyll.
  *Shadow Dance.
  Intermezzo.
  Melody.
  Scherzino.
  Hungarian.

*Op. 44. Sonata tragica, Gm.

Op. 46. Twelve Virtuoso Études.
  Novelette.
  Moto perpetuo.
  Wilde Jagd.
  Improvisation.
  Elfentanz.
  Valse triste.
  Burlesque.
  Bluette.
  Träumerei.
  *March Wind.
  Impromptu.
  Polonaise.

Op. 49. Air and Rigaudon.

*Op. 50. Sonata Eroica, "Flos regum Arthurus."

*Op. 51. Woodland Sketches.
  *To a Wild Rose.
  Will o' the Wisp.
  At an Old Trysting Place.
  In Autumn.
  From an Indian Lodge.
  *To a Waterlily.
  From Uncle Remus.

A Deserted Farm.
By a Meadow Brook.
Told at Sunset.

Op. 55. Sea Pieces.
To the Sea.
From a Wandering Iceberg.
A.D. 1621.
Starlight.
Nautilus.
In Mid-ocean.

Op. 57. Sonata No. 3, Norse.
Op. 59. Sonata No. 4, Celtic.
Op. 61. Fireside Tales.
An Old Garden.
Midsummer.
Midwinter.
With Sweet Lavender.
In Deep Woods.

Indian Idyll.
To an Old White Pine.
From Puritan Days.
From a Log Cabin.
The Joys of Autumn.

Op. 62. New England Idylls.

PIECES PUBLISHED UNDER THE
PSEUDONYM OF EDGAR THORN

Amourette.
Forgotten Fairy Tales, four pieces.
Six Fancies.
In Lilting Rhythm, two pieces.

MacDowell also edited about fifty compositions for teaching purposes and published
valuable technical exercises.

Publishers: Schmidt, Breit., Schirm.

It is unnecessary to enter here into an extended review of MacDowell's works, since they have always enjoyed immense popularity and celebrity. Attention might, however, be called to the four sonatas, which are infrequently played. Their difficulties are not as serious as are those of many works in this form, and they offer excellent opportunities for sonata playing to the student who wishes to get away from Beethoven. Op. 44 and 50 are especially recommended. Concerto No. 1, in D minor, is also a useful and effective work. It presents an interesting use of the "cyclical" idea—use of identical themes in all movements. The Concerto in A minor is less known and has a more subtle charm than the one in D minor, for that reason it is, perhaps, less immediately effective.

The pieces in the smaller forms have, as a rule, little variety of mood, and if many are played in succession monotony easily supervenes. Isolated, they appear to better advantage. Asterisks mark the pieces which have attained the greatest popularity, although there are many more just as good.

NIKOLAI MEDTNER

(1879—)

Op. 1. Eight Musical Pictures.
Op. 2. Three Improvisations.
Undine.
Reminiscences of the Dance.
Scherzo.

Op. 4. Four Pieces.
Étude.
Caprice.
Moment Musicale.
Prélude.

Op. 5. Sonata (*Largo).
Op. 7. Three Arabesques.
  1. An Idyll.
  2. and 3. Tragedy-Fragments.
Op. 8. Two Fairy Tales.
  Andante.
  Allegrissimo.
Op. 9. Three Fairy Tales, Fm, C, G.
*Op. 10. Three Dithyrambs, D, Eb, E.
Op. 11. A Triad of Sonatas, Ab, Dm, C.
Op. 14. Two Fairy Tales, Fm, Em.
*Op. 17. Three Novelettes, G, Cm, E.
*Op. 20. Two Tales, Bb, Bm.
*Op. 22. Sonata, Gm.
Op. 23. Lyric Fragments, *Cm, Am, Fm, *Cm.
Op. 25. No. 1. Sonata-Tale, Cm.

*No. 2. Sonata, Em.
*Op. 26. Four Fairy Tales, Eb, Eb, Fm, F#m.
*Op. 27. Sonata-Ballade, F#.
*Op. 30. Sonata, Am.
Op. 31. Three Pieces.
  *Improvisation.
  Funeral March.
  Fairy Tale.
Op. 33. Concerto, Cm.
Op. 34. Four Fairy Tales, Bm, Fm, Am, Dm.
Op. 35. Four Fairy Tales, C, G, Am, C#m.
Op. 38. Vergessene Weisen.
Op. 39. Vergessene Weisen.
Op. 40. Vergessene Weisen.
Op. 42. Three Tales.

WITHOUT OPUS NUMBER

Sonata-Vocalise (Zimmermann).
Tale, Dm.
Étude of Medium Difficulty.
Two Cadenzas for Beethoven's Concerto in G (E.M.R.).
Concerto No. 2.

Three Hymns in Praise of Toil (Chest.).
  Before Work.
  At the Anvil.
  After Work.

Publishers: Jurgenson up to Op. 14, after that E.M.R. and U.E.

As Medtner has called about two dozen of his pieces "fairy tales" ("conte" or "skazka"), and of the nine sonatas, two bear additional subtitles which advise the player that he thought of them as tales, he may be regarded as a program writer who withholds the story. His inspiration derives from a love of fantastic literature of which he is said to know everything ever written. But his music is not fanciful in the lighter sense. The tales are told by a Brahms rather than a Bendel, and, as a rule, they are grave and portentous. He is a scholar who loves the grotesque. Conservative and reserved, he does not indulge in cacophony, unless one applies the epithet to the strange harmonic scheme at the climax of Op. 30, the Sonata in A minor. It is hardly that, but it sounds curiously uncontrolled.

Medtner is primarily a man of ideas, and he affords one, when at his best, the unwonted luxury of reveling in an inexhaustible imagination. He is never caught in the impasse of a set rhythm, nor does he ever dwell tediously on a pet phrase. As with Brahms one must first get the feel of his technique before it goes easily. There is an admirable abstention from technique as such, and from all high or facile coloring. He is a direct descendant of the great tree of Bach, Beethoven, and Brahms—Bülow's three B's—and he reminds one somewhat of all of them. Medtner will have none of the wavering line of the impressionists, nor any "atmosphere"; for him only classic firmness will suffice.

The appearance of this reincarnation of the old masters is arresting, and one may well watch his career with interest. He achieves an ecstasy of his own, quite different from that of Scriabin, which branched from the old at Chopin. His is the old familiar German genius buried for a while in Russia, but blossoming afresh and tinged with the Muscovite atmosphere. He suggests the example of Franck, whose German ancestry asserted itself in his Latin surroundings. In Franck the hybridization was successful. It is of great interest to study Medtner from this point of view.

As with Scriabin, rhythm plays a vital part in his music, but the rhythmic life is less nervous, though at times altogether as complicated. In the finale of the G minor Sonata, Op. 22, he even thought it necessary to suggest a manner of study for mastering its intricacies. In his first Concerto Medtner made a valuable technical change in descending chromatic thirds. He devised it to fit the keyboard by writing now major now minor thirds to eliminate awkwardness and promote speed, the fifth finger is not used. Certain notes are entirely omitted without being missed by the ear.

Medtner really offers nothing new either formally or harmonically; but his mastery of counterpoint and of rhythm and his solidity, when it does not degenerate into heaviness, present an adherence to the past which is a good balance wheel to the new music. Some critics damn Medtner because he brings nothing new; but one should look on him as one who cultivates an ancient historic garden and raises there old familiar plants which he has crossed in a novel way with plants of a new country. His accomplishments in the sonatas are little short of imposing. No other modern writer except Scriabin has written nine sonatas. It must remain for time to decide whether his thought, couched as it is in the idiom of the past, is sufficiently weighty to carve a place for itself among the lasting things. Meanwhile he has enlarged the literature considerably.

Aside from an excellent largo in the first sonata, and the group of Op. 10, there is little to detain one in the early works. Op. 20 forms a good introduction to Medtner, especially the second piece which gives admittance to his fairyland. It is probably permissible under the circumstances to hear a frightful giant taking clumsy steps in the bass toward a captive blond princess, who twitters away in the treble, nervously awaiting the alarmingly delayed arrival of the hero.

Sonata Op. 22, in G minor, is written in what may be described as the bravura-contrapuntal style. It is a good recital sonata, though difficult, and it in his first sonata and also in the Concerto. It is what one may call his Bach bitious work; it is a powerful piece and full of beauty. It has fine themes, unusual harmonies, clever passage work, and remarkable rhythms. Most of the sonata is in the rare time of 15/8, but the impression is somehow conveyed that he did this not merely to be odd, but in an endeavor to escape the tyranny of the bar lines without degenerating into license, for the music flows along springily enough. The sonata is in two movements, although there is no pause between them. The first is in free sonata form, whereas the second develops along original and personal lines. The first movement finishes at the foot of page 24, and the second begins at once with a passage which is theme A slightly altered and played *allegro sfrenatamente,* accompanied by an alteration of theme E. Presently a short fugato enters, based on what is practically an inversion of theme E. This rhythm seems to haunt Medtner, for it is found in his first sonata, and also in the Concerto. It is what one may call his Bach mood. It is the exact rhythm of the second subject of the C♯ minor fugue of the *Well-tempered Clavichord.* This sonata is somber without being dull, intellectual without being cold, and contrapuntal and architectural without being muddy or sluggish.

Op. 27, the "Sonata-Ballade," is in a softer though no less scholarly vein. It is narrative and lyric, feminine in contrast to the very masculine Op. 22, but equally, if not even more, difficult. It is in two movements, though the introduction to the last movement seems like a separate section. A humorous attempt to start a fugue three times before the inspiration comes is an amusing feature of the finale. It is cyclical in form, and the opening theme is used for the brilliant and triumphant ending. The work shows the most careful and imaginative scholarship and affords the serious and advanced student much real delight—as well as much hard work.

Sonata Op. 30, mentioned above as containing the only approach to cacophony in his compositions, is well made, but the thematic material is less interesting. Concerto Op. 33 was introduced by Medtner himself in this country. A certain feeling of disappointment in regard to it is inescapable, though it has strong points. The "Vergessene Weisen" are of small value and may possibly be from early compositions.

FELIX MENDELSSOHN-BARTHOLDI

(1809-1847)

*Op. 5. Capriccio, F♯m.
Op. 6. Sonata, E.
*Op. 7b. Seven Characteristic Pieces.
*Op. 14. Rondo capriccioso.
Op. 15. Fantasia on "The Last Rose of Summer."
*Op. 16. Three Fantasias or Caprices.
Op. 19. Songs without Words.
*Op. 22. Capriccio brillant, with orchestra.
*Op. 25. Concerto, Gm, with orchestra.
Op. 28. Fantasia, F♯m.
Op. 29. Rondo brillant, E♭.
Op. 30. Songs without Words.
*Op. 33. Three Caprices.
Op. 35. Six Preludes and Fugues (*No. 1).
Op. 38. Songs without Words.

*Op. 40. Concerto, Dm, with orchestra.
Op. 43. Serenade and Allegro giojoso, with orchestra.
Op. 53. Songs without Words.
*Op. 54. Variations sérieuses.
Op. 62. Songs without Words.
Op. 67. Songs without Words.
Op. 72. Children's Pieces.
*Op. 82. Variations, E♭.
Op. 83. Variations, B♭.
Op. 85. Songs without Words.
Op. 92. Allegro brillant (four hands).
Op. 102. Songs without Words.
Op. 104. Three Preludes, and Three Studies.
Op. 105. Sonata, Gm.
Op. 106. Sonata, B♭m.
Op. 117. Albumblatt, Song Without Words, Em.

WITHOUT OPUS NUMBER

Étude, Fm.
Scherzo, Bm.
Andante cantabile, and Presto agitato.

Prelude and Fugue, Em.
Clavierstücke, two pieces, B♭ and Gm.
*Scherzo a capriccio, F♯m.

Time is bringing Mendelssohn again into favor. After his enormous success during his life a reaction was to be expected, for his triumphs seemed very easy, his works sweet, simple, and superficial. But one comes to realize that, after all, sweetness, simplicity, and even superficiality have a place. Surface beauty again has an appeal after the recent cult of ugliness. The mountain of atonality has in its portentous travail produced as yet only a rather small mouse, and one turns to Mendelssohn with a feeling that he was not very bad.

One domain is peculiarly Mendelssohn's own—the scherzo. His scherzi are true fairy music, and anyone who believes in fairies must believe in Mendelssohn. Conversely, anyone who believes in Mendelssohn must believe in fairies. No one who had not held converse with them could adequately portray the delectable little creatures. Is there any music more exquisitely gay and eternally fresh than that which he wrote for *Midsummer Night's Dream* or for the finale of the violin Concerto? To the piano he did not give such ecstatic pieces, but there are several for which one must be profoundly grateful. Op. 16, No. 2, hackneyed though it is, never loses its charm. It opens with Oberon's fairy horns, which dominate the whole elfin dance. The "Scherzo a capriccio" (without opus number) is also genuine fairy music, though a trifle heavier — perhaps for fatter fairies. It has exciting rhythms and excellent tunes. There is another tiny two-page scherzo listed under pieces without opus number as "Scherzo, B minor." The "Rondo capriccioso," although it does not appear very capricious to our ears, is also for fairies. If the introduction is played without enervating sentimentality, one can win through to the scherzo part without damage, and then what delicious rhythms! There is still another fairy piece, Op. 7, No. 7. Many numbers of this opus are pleasant to play. In the fairy-scherzo style appears the finale of the G minor Concerto, which should ripple along light as air and bubbling with vivacity. Finally, one has Op. 5, Capriccio, F♯ minor, of which Rossini is said to have observed on first hearing it, *"Ça sent de Scarlatti."* Does this penetrating remark not give the key to Mendelssohn's style, or at least one side of him? Scarlatti, of course, never wrote anything remotely resembling the "Songs without Words." Mendelssohn's best and most characteristic work for the piano at least has the freshness, the gaiety, the classic abandon which one associates with Scarlatti.

The G minor Concerto is better than the one in D minor, and might with reason be brought forward by artists now and then. The "Capriccio brillant" also has attractions. It pays Weber's "Concertstück" the compliment of imitation. Of the three variation sets Op. 54, "Variations sérieuses," should be known and played by every pianist. It is Mendelssohn's longest and possibly greatest work for piano. In it he shows all his technical tricks and gives an excellent repertory piece at the same time. It is difficult to tell why the other sets, Op. 82 and 83, have been neglected, for they are attractive and not as difficult as is Op. 54. The "Prelude and Fugue," Op. 35, No. 1, in E minor, is strongly recommended. It is one of the permanent things in the piano literature.

Op. 72, the "Children's Pieces," is charming; Op. 33, No. 3, has a lovely melody, the andante cantabile and allegro agitato are worth playing, and the less familiar "Songs without Words" will be rewarding.

MORITZ MOSZKOWSKI
(1854-1925)

Op. 1. Scherzo.

Op. 2. Albumblatt.

Op. 4. Caprice.

Op. 5. Fantasia, Hommage à Schumann.

Op. 6. Fantaisie-Impromptu.

Op. 7. Three Moments musicaux, B, *C♯m, F♯.

Op. 8. Five Waltzes (four hands).

Op. 10. Sketches.
  *1. Melody.
  2. and 3. Theme and Mazurka.
  4. Impromptu.

Op. 11. Polonaise, Waltz, Hungarian Dance (four hands).

*Op. 12. Spanish Dances (four hands).

Op. 14. Humoresque.

Op. 15. Six Pieces.
  *Serenata.
  Arabesque.
  Mazurka.
  Canon.
  Waltz.
  Barcarolle.

Op. 16. Ballade, and Bolero.

Op. 17. *Polonaise, Minuet, Waltz.

Op. 18. Melody, Scherzino, Étude, Marcia, Polonaise.

Op. 20. Allegro scherzando.

Op. 21. Album espagnole.

Op. 23. From Foreign Parts.
  Russia.
  Germany.
  Spain.
  Poland.
  Italy.
  Hungary.

*Op. 24. Three Concert Études, *G♭, C♯m, C.

*Op. 25. Reigen, five pieces (four hands).

*Op. 27. Barcarolle, and Tarentella.

Op. 28. Miniatures. *No. 3.

Op. 31. Six Pieces (Ries and Erler).
  *Monologue.
  Melody.
  Valse.
  Scherzetto.
  Impromptu.
  Caprice.

Op. 33. Four Pieces (four hands).

*Op. 34. Three Pieces.
  *Valse, E.
  Étude.
  Mazurka.

Op. 35. Four Pieces.

*Op. 36. Huit morceaux caractéristiques (Hainauer).
  Pièce rococo.
  Rêverie.
  Expansion.
  *En automne.
  *Air de ballet.
  *Étincelles.
  Valse sentimentale.
  Pièce rustique.

*Op. 37. Caprice espagnole.

Op. 38. Four Pieces.
  Bourrée.
  Berceuse.
  Mazurka.
  Mélodie, italienne.

Op. 40. Scherzo Waltz.

Op. 41. Gondoliera.

*Op. 42. Romance, Siciliano, Momento giojoso (Peters).

Op. 43. Two Pieces (four hands).

Op. 44. "Der Schäfer putzte sich zum Tanz," Scene from *Faust*.

Op. 45. Polonaise and *Guitarre.

Op. 46. Valse Mazurka.

Op. 47. Preludio, Intermezzo.

Op. 48. Two Études de concert, D, C.

Op. 50. Suite in G—Allegro, Air, Capriccio, Presto.

Op. 51. Fackelzug ("Torchlight Procession").

Op. 52. Six Fantasy Pieces (Peters).
  Landscape.
  Night Piece.
  Duo.
  *Juggleress.
  *Masks and Unmasking.
  At the Feast.

Op. 53. Danse fantastique.

*Op. 54. Polish Dance (four hands. Peters).

Op. 56. Six Pieces to Grabbe's "Don Juan and Faust."
  Entr'acte.
  Sarabande.
  Passepied.
  Intermezzo.
  Phantasmagoria.
  Menuet.

Op. 57. Spring, five pieces.
  *Impatience.
  Spring Sounds.
  Flower Pictures.
  *Zephyr.
  Love Waltz.

Op. 58. Tristesses et sourires.
  *Effusions.
  Consolation.
  Près du berceau.
  Vieux souvenir.
  Historiette.
  Mélancolie.
  Rêve étrange.
  Resignation.

*Op. 59. Concerto, E (Peters).

Op. 60. Three Mazurkas.

Op. 61. Romance in A, Scherzo in Gm.

Op. 63. Three Bagatelles.

*Op. 64. School of Double Notes (Enoch).

Op. 65. New Spanish Dances (four hands).

Op. 66. Pensées fugitives.

Op. 67. Deux morceaux.

Op. 69. Valse de concert, F.

Op. 77. Ten Pieces (Schott).

Op. 81. Six Pieces (Schott).
  Canon.
  Allegro agitato.
  Étude de legato.
  Humoresque.
  Romance.
  Mélodie appassionata.

Op. 83. Six Pieces (Aug.).

Op. 84. Four Moments musicales (Aug.).

Op. 86. Three Pieces.
  Album Leaf.
  Gavotte.
  Scherzo Étude (Schott).

Op. 89. Tanzmomente (Aug.).

Op. 91. Dexterity and Style, études (Aug.).

Op. 97. Esquisses techniques ("advanced studies." Aug.).

Hainauer publishes most of the pieces up to Op. 28.

WITHOUT OPUS NUMBER

*Scherzo-Valse from *Boabdil*.

*Valse brillante, A♭ (Peters).

Valse mignonne (Hainauer).

A Parody, "Anton Notenquetscher am Klavier," with text. (Steinitz).

Mazurka, from *The Bazar*.

Two Concert Paraphrases (Peters).
  Isolde's Love Death.
  Venusberg Bacchanale.

Publishers: Simon, Schirm., Ries and Erler, B. and B., Steinitz, Peters, Hainauer, Aug., Enoch, Schott.

Moszkowski is truly the model salon music writer. He is is brilliant, melodious, polished, light without being trivial, formal, and elegant. To appreciate his achievement one should compare him with the writers who purveyed music to the people of the first half of the last century. What an improvement on the "Home, Sweet Home and Variations" type of entertainment! Who shall say that the public taste has not improved when he looks at Moszkowski's success? In the sense that he wrote only to amuse, he is akin to Scarlatti. He did not take himself seriously, and only on one occasion did he compose a work in a large form, the Concerto, which might be performed oftener were it less difficult and somewhat shorter. It contains some most beautiful music.

The player of Moszkowski's music needs well-developed fingers capable of executing spidery passage work and wide skips with delicacy and accuracy, without both of which qualities the pieces make little appeal. His "Caprice espagnole" belongs to the rather restricted class of long-short compositions. It is neither in the sonata nor the short-piece class. In a sense it is a dance piece, but its scope is broader. Its length being considerable it is able to create the effect of a longer scene and is comparable to Tchaikovsky's "Doumka," Balakirev's "Islamey," or, in a modest way, to Chopin's ballades, though, of course, it lacks their genius. It is thus useful in a certain part of the program. Asterisks in the list denote the famous pieces, but it is not to be understood that many others just as good cannot be found. Attention is called to the "School of Double Notes" and to the wealth of four-hand music.

MODESTE MOUSSORGSKY
(1835-1881)

Night on the Bare Mountain (first published as a piano piece).

Eight Pieces.
Intermezzo.
Une Plaisanterie.
Au Village.
Une Larme.
*La Couturière.
Près de la côte d'Azur en Crimée.
Sur la côte d'Azur.
Méditation.

Ein Kinderscherz, Intermezzo (Peters. The pieces published under these titles are the first two of the above "Eight Pieces").

*Pictures at an Exhibition (Peters).
Promenade.
Gnomus.
A Medieval Castle.
Tuileries.
Bydlo.
Ballet of the Chickens in the Eggs.
Samuel Goldenberg and Schmuyle.
The Market-place at Limoges.
Catacombae.
Baba-Yaga's Hut.
The Great Gate at Kieff.

Six Pieces (Aug.; Breit.).
Scherzo.
Niania et moi.
Première punirion.
Impromptu passione.
Souvenir d'enfance.
Rêverie (Duma).

A Collection was published by Bessel (now Breit.) of fourteen pieces.

Publishers: Jurgenson, Bessel, Hamelle, Peters, Schirm.

143

Moussorgsky, as a writer for piano, is almost negligible, but his renaissance as a musician makes the inclusion of these few pieces desirable. The explorer will find "Pictures at an Exhibition" the best. The "pictures" are connected by a section representing, it may be supposed, a person viewing them. This section becomes a trifle tiresome and may be omitted. Aside from this collection the best piece is "La Couturière," a most charming thing, and a good exercise for the left hand.

WOLFGANG AMADEUS MOZART

(1756-1791)

THE SONATAS

No.	No.
1. C.	10. B♭.
2. G.	11. C.
3. C.	12. B♭.
4. F.	13. D.
5. C.	14. D.
6. F.	15. D.
*7. F.	*16. A.
8. B♭.	17. F.
*9. A ("Turkish March").	*Fantasia and Sonata, Cm.

CHIEF WORKS IN SMALLER FORMS

*Fantasia, Dm.
Fantasia, Cm.
Fantasia and Fugue, C.
Rondo in D, 4/4.
Rondo in F, 2/4.
*Rondo in Am, 6/8.
Overture, Andante, and Allegretto in the Style of Handel.

Adagio, Bm, 4/4.
Menuetto in D.
Gigue, G.
Romanza, A♭, 6/8.
Allegro, G.
*Pastorale variée, B♭ ("work of doubtful authenticity"—Köchel).
Thirty-six cadenzas for the concertos.

WORKS FOR FOUR HANDS

Four Sonatas in D, B♭, C, F.
Unfinished Sonata, G.

Two Fantasias in Fm, Adagio and Allegro.
Andante and Variations, G.

WORKS FOR TWO PIANOS

Fugue
*Sonata, D.

*Concerto, E♭ (see below).

THE CONCERTOS

Nos. 1-28 are from the Breitkopf catalogue; the numbers in parentheses are from Köchel's catalogue.

No.
1. (37) F.
2. (39) Bb.
3. (40) D.
4. (41) G.
5. (175) D.
6. (238) Bb.
7. (242) F, for three pianos; arranged for two pianos (Steingr.).
8. (246) C.
9. (271) Eb.
*10. (365) Eb, for two pianos.
11. (413) F.
12. (414) A.

No.
13. (415) C.
14. (449) Eb.
15. (450) Bb.
16. (451) D.
*17. (453) G.
18. (456) Bb.
19. (459) F.
*20. (466) Dm.
*21. (467) C.
22. (482) Eb.
23. (488) A.
*24. (491) Cm.
25. (503) C.
*26. (537) D (*Coronation*).
27. (595) Bb.
28. (382) Concerto-Rondo, D.

CADENZAS FOR THE CONCERTOS

Beethoven ...... for 466.
Brahms .... for 446, 453, 491.
Busoni .... for 271, 466, 491, 503.
Casella .... for 466.
Hummel, Op. 4 .. for seven.
Moscheles ...... for 363.

Mozart .... thirty-six, as above.
Rubinstein ..... for 466.
Saint-Saëns ..... for 482, 491.
Schumann, C. ... for 466 (Riet. Biedermann).

The publishers of these cadenzas are given in the lists of their composers' works.

VARIATIONS

No.
1. (24) Eight Variations on an Allegretto in G.
2. (25) Seven Variations on "William of Nassau," in D.
3. (179) Twelve Variations on a Minuet of Fischer in C.
4. (180) Six Variations on "Mio caro Adone" of Salieri in G.
5. (269) Nine Variations on "Lison dormait" in C.
6. (265) Twelve Variations on "Ah vous dirai-je maman" in C.
7. (352) Eight Variations on a March from "Mariages samnites" in F.
8. (353) Twelve Variations on "La belle Françoise" in Eb.

No.
9. (354) Twelve Variations on "Je suis Landor" in Eb.
10. (398) Five Variations on "Salve tu domine," Paisiello, in G.
11. (455) Ten Variations on "Unser dummer Pöbel meint."
12. (460) Eight Variations on "Come un agnello," Sarti, in A.
13. (500) Twelve Variations on an Allegretto in Bb.
14. (573) Nine Variations on a Minuet of Duport in D.
15. (613) Eight Variations on "Ein Weib ist das herrlichste Ding."
(54) Six Variations on an Allegretto in F.

Nos. 1-15 are published by Breit., the other set is published by Köchel.

Mozart's music shines nowadays with increasing brilliance. The passing years, far from dimming it, only add luster, for the people of the twentieth century are returning to this joyous carefree fount to refresh themselves after the turgid thunderings and harmonic extravagances of recent times, with a feeling of genuine thankfulness to the astounding genius who could write immortal music which was neither "deep," nor "epoch-making," nor "pregnant," nor even "thoughtful"—but merely refreshing and gay. There is room for every kind of great art, but there is especial need for a genius who writes neither to elevate, nor to tear the soul, nor to build musical architecture, but only to entertain. What a difficult task, and how very few have accomplished it!

Pianists regret that the Mozart literature is not the equal of his writing in other fields. There is a dearth of smaller pieces and a plethora of sonatas, some of the latter having been written almost before he could talk. There are plenty of concertos, but these are less usable than are solo pieces. The best of the shorter pieces have been collected by Schirmer in a volume which will be found most attractive. With a few sonatas and concertos it will probably constitute one's Mozart library, though everyone will want to add that delightful though possibly illegitimate piece "Pastorale variée." One can hardly believe that the theme was not written by Mozart, yet the variations are undoubtedly by someone else. They preserve the Mozartian quality in an admirable manner.

The enthusiast will enjoy browsing among the concertos, for there are many which are to all intents and purposes quite unknown, and just as good as the familiar ones, though the one in D minor is probably the most dramatic and advanced, in the same way that the Fantasia and Sonata in C minor is the most advanced among the sonatas. Gieseking introduced No. 21 (467) with great success. No one knew it. The four-hand and the two-piano literature should also be looked into, for the two-piano Sonata in D and the four-hand fantasias, as well as the two-piano Concerto, are first class.

How lovely are the Fantasia in D minor, the great Rondo in A minor, and the quaint little Rondo in D! They must be played from the knuckles down, with forgetfulness of the arm. The music must become softer and softer until one can scarcely hear it, and then what fairy music it is! It is health-giving and childlike after the dramatic composers. Periodic study of Mozart restores one's ear to a normal condition and one's technique to sensitiveness.

The best way to enjoy the sonatas is through performances of single movements, since the harmonic scheme is limited, and they easily become monotonous. The last one in C minor with the Fantasia is different and is grander in conception. Here the singing tone, the serious air, and the grand manner are more in keeping with the music.

SELIM PALMGREN
(1878—)

Aria (Breit.).
Barcarolle (Chest.).
Berceuse (Breit.).
Bird Song (Chest.).
Concerto No. 2 ("The River").
Dance on a Place of Execution (Chest.).
Deux contrastes (Breit.).
Deux impromptus.
Dragonfly.
Dream Melody.
En Route (Chest.).
Evening Whispers (Chest.).
Entr'acte valsante.
*Finnish Lullaby (Chest.).
Finnish Lyric Pieces (2 vols. Chest.).
Finnish Rhythms (Chest.).
Folk Song Intermezzo (Chest.).
Gavotte and Musette (Breit.).
Gnistor étude (Breit.).
Graceful Rhythms, two pieces.
Harlequinade (Chest.).
Humoresque, Db (Breit.).
Humoresque (Chest.).
Light and Shade (Chest.).
Lyric Intermezzo (Chest.).
Minuet célèbre de Mozart.
Minuet.
Mephisto Waltz.

*Night in May.
Northern Summer, five pieces.
Preludes.
*Preludium (Chest.).
Piano Sketches.
Pastorale in Three Scenes.
Presto-prélude (Chest.).
Piano Pieces.
Postludium.
Prélude funèbre.
*Refrain du berceau (Chest.).
Rococo (Chest.).
Round Dance (Chest.).
Scherzo (Breit.).
Spinning Wheel.
Spring Sounds.
Snowflakes (Chest.).
Stimmungsbilder (Breit.).
Tempo di valse (Chest.).
*The Sea (Chest.).
Valse Vivo Tuhkimo (Chest.).
War, Allegro marziale (Chest.).
Youth, six lyric pieces.
　　Prelude.
　　Isle of Shadows.
　　Saga.
　　The Mother Sings.
　　*The Swan.
　　Round Dance.
Publishers: Breit., Chest., Schirm.

Palmgren is a very unequal writer. Among commonplace things one runs across sincerely felt and delicately executed little gems like the "May Night." He is a typical *Vielschreiber* who unwearyingly provides material for the maw of the publisher. The "Swan" and "The Sea" are worthy of Grieg and appeal to musician and layman alike. This seems to denote that there is something above the ordinary in them. The rather ambitious title "The Finnish Chopin," bestowed on him by the publishers, is not deserved, for he lacks the superb intellectuality of Chopin; at times, however, he is undeniably poetic. The above list of his works is far from complete.

SERGEI PROKOFIEV
(1891—)

Op. 1. Sonata (recomposed, 1909).

*Op. 2. Four Études.

Op. 3. Conte, Badinage, Marche fantôme.

Op. 4. Élan, Désespoir (ostinato effect), *Suggestion diabolique.

Op. 10. Concerto No. 1.

*Op. 11. Toccata.

Op. 12. March, Gavotte, *Mazurka (in fourths), Caprice, *Prelude in C, Allemande, *Scherzo humoristique (in the manner of four bassoons), *Scherzo (_ppp_ throughout).

*Op. 14. Sonata No. 2, Dm.

Op. 16. Concerto No. 2.

*Op. 17. Sarcasms, five pieces.

*Op. 22. Visions fugitives, nineteen pieces.

Op. 25. Gavotte from Symphonie classique, arranged by the composer.

Op. 26. Concerto No. 3 (Breit.).

Op. 28. Sonata No. 3 (after old sketches. 1917).

Op. 29. Sonata No. 4.

*Op. 31. Contes de la vieille grand'mère, four pieces.

Op. 32. Danza, Menuet, Gavotte, Waltz.

Op. 33. March and Scherzo, from _The Loves of the Three Oranges._

Op. 38. Sonata No. 5.

Op. 55. Concerto No. 5.

WITHOUT OPUS NUMBER

Prelude and Fugue for Organ, Buxtehude (transcribed).

Waltzes of Schubert Arranged in the Form of a Suite.
(Both Gutheil).

Publishers: Jurgenson up to and including Op. 14. After that, Gutheil. U.E. also publishes nearly everything.

Schirmer publishes six pieces from Op. 2, 12, 17, 22.

The fantastic imagination of Prokofiev expresses itself in pieces pervaded by an atmosphere of fairy tale and legend. He takes one into strange places and shows one strange sights. Without sentiment, the music is frequently humorous and ironic; it holds one through its diabolic cleverness and freedom. For those who want something a little more old-fashioned by a composer of today, there is always the excellent first sonata, the Étude in C minor, the ethereal Prelude in C, and others in the same opus, some of the "Visions fugitives," and the "Contes de la vieille grand'mère." The latter are singularly quaint.

The "Suggestion diabolique" has of late years become a standard piece with virtuosi and bids fair to take a place among the lasting works of the literature. It represents Prokofiev's most individual manner. Among the concertos, perhaps the third represents him at his best. It is difficult, but rewarding.

In this caveman music there is much that is vigorous and primitive, much that is biting and acid, but there occur also ethereal and humorous moments. There is no doubt that Prokofiev has struck some new emotional notes and that he should be included among the most interesting and worth while Russian composers.

SERGEI RACHMANINOFF
(1873—)

Op. 1. Concerto, F♯m, with orchestra.

Op. 3. Five Pieces.
  Elegy.
  *Prelude, C♯m (the famous one).
  Mélodie.
  Polichinelle.
  Serenade.

Op. 5. Six Pieces, for two pianos.

Op. 7. Suite, for two pianos.

Op. 10. Seven Pieces.
  Nocturne.
  Valse.
  Barcarolle.
  Mélodie.
  Humoresque.
  Romance.
  Mazurka.

Op. 11. Six Pieces (four hands).

Op. 16. Six moments musicaux.

*Op. 17. Second Suite, for two pianos, four pieces.

*Op. 18. Second Concerto, Cm, with orchestra.

Op. 22. Variations on a Theme of Chopin (the Cm Prelude).

Op. 23. Ten Preludes.
  F♯m.
  B♭.
  *Dm.
  D.
  *Gm.
  *E♭.
  Cm.
  A♭.
  *E♭m (double notes).
  G♭.

Op. 28. Sonata No. 2 ("Faust" sonata).

Op. 30. Third Concerto, Dm.

Op. 32. Thirteen Preludes.

Op. 35. Nine Études—Tableaux.

Fm.	*E♭m.
C.	E♭.
Cm.	Gm.
Am.	C♯m.
Dm.	

Op. 36. Sonata, No. 2, B♭m.

Op. 39. Nine Études Tableaux.

Cm.	Am.
Am.	Cm.
F♯m.	Dm.
*Bm.	D.
E♭m.	

Op. 40. Concerto No. 4.

WITHOUT OPUS NUMBER

Polka of W. R. (E.M.R.).

TRANSCRIPTIONS

Kreisler ....Liebeslied.
Moussorgsky ....Hopak (C. Fischer).
Rachmaninoff .. Les Lilas (Gutheil).

Publishers: Gutheil (except where stated), Jurgenson, E.M.R., U.E.

A volume of preludes from Op. 3, 23, and 32 is published by Gutheil.

Rachmaninoff is an inventive and intellectual, rather than a fervid and imaginative writer. Since he lacks mood variety, his shorter pieces are his best. It has been said of his celebrated Prelude in C♯ minor that it tells everything he has to say. This is, in a sense, true, for his two favorite moods in it are rather exhaustingly repeated in the subsequent pieces. The Concerto in C minor is the best; it attains a thrilling climax at the close. The third rambles on, and Rachmaninoff cuts it himself in public playing. The suites for two pianos are good, some of the "Études-Tableaux" interesting, and a few of the preludes extraordinary, especially the frightfully difficult one in double notes. The "Polka of W.R." is a marvelous tour de force.

MAURICE RAVEL

(1875-1937)

*Jeux d'eaux (Demets).
Gaspard de la nuit, Three poems for piano (Durand).
  *Ondine.
  Le Gibet.
  *Scarbo.
*Sonatine (Durand).
Pavane pour une infante défunte (Demets).
*Miroirs (Demets).
  Noctuelles.
  Oiseaux tristes.
  Une Barque sur l'océan.
  Alborado gracioso.
  La Vallée des cloches.
*Le Tombeau de Couperin.
  Prélude.
  Fugue.

  Forlane.
  Rigaudon.
  Menuet.
  Toccata.
*Ma Mère l'oie ("Mother Goose," five pieces, four hands. Demets).
Valses nobles et sentimentales.
A la manière de . . . . (A collection of short pieces written in the styles of various composers in collaboration with Casella. Mathot).
Concerto for the left hand alone (unpublished, but performed in 1933).

Publishers: Durand, E. Demets.
An album has been published by Durand.
The "Miroirs" may be had for four hands (Schott).

Although Debussy was the most important composer to write in his particular manner and was an inescapable influence on all French and many other composers, yet Ravel, who is by no means to be considered merely another Debussy, has an unusual number of excellent pieces which give a glimpse of a new personality. Most noted of them is the shimmering and dazzling "Jeux d'eaux," which since its conception has not ceased its triumphant round of appearances. Somewhat neglected are "Ondine" and "Scarbo," the latter a true virtuoso piece and for virtuosi only. "Ondine," though difficult, may be played by lesser folk. It is a charming piece. "Scarbo" is a little sprite who scratches on the bed curtains and pinches one, and one gets up to see what the matter is, only to catch a glimpse of him disappearing down the stairs or far off in the garden. This airy scherzo contains novel technical effects. The Sonatine is charming and improves on acquaintance. The "Mother Goose" and the "Valses sentimentales" have achieved more success in adaptations for the orchestra. The "Miroirs" are larger canvases, excellent and effective. They are not only good music, but they offer the advanced student valuable studies in contrasting sonorities.

MAX REGER
(1873-1916)

Op. 11. Waltzes (2 vols.).

Op. 13. Lose Blätter.

Op. 14. Lose Blätter.

Op. 17. Aus der Jugendzeit.

Op. 18. Improvisations (2 vols.). (All Schott)

Op. 20. Five Humoresques (U.E.).

Op. 22. Six Waltzes (four hands, also arranged for two. U. E.).

Op. 23. Sonatinas.

Op. 25. Aquarelles (Schott).

Op. 32. Seven Characteristic Pieces (U.E.).

Op. 36. Bunte Blätter, nine little pieces (U.E.).

Op. 44. Ten Little Pieces (U.E.; Breit.).

Op. 45. Six Intermezzi.

Op. 53. Silhouettes, seven pieces (Breit.).

Op. 58. Sechs Burlesken (Senff).

*Op. 81. Variations and Fugue on a Theme of Bach (arranged for piano and orchestra by Pillney).

Op. 82. Aus Meinem Tagebuch ("Leaves from My Diary." 2 vols. of twelve pieces each. U.E.).

*Op. 86. Variations and Fugue on a Theme of Beethoven, for two pianos (U.E.).

Op. 89. Sonatinas (U.E.).

Op. 96. Passacaglia and Fugue, for two pianos.

Op. 99. Six Preludes and Fugues (U. E.).

Op. 114. Concerto, Fm (B. and B.).

Op. 115. Episodes.

Op. 132. Variations and Fugue on a Mozart Theme (Peters).

Op. 134. Variations and Fugue on a Theme of Telemann.

Op. 135a. Thirty Short Chorale-Preludes (Peters).

*Op. 143. Träume am Kamin, twelve little pieces.

WITHOUT OPUS NUMBER

Arrangements and Studies Based on Bach's Choralvorspiele (Aibl; U.E.; Breit.).

Arrangements of Chopin's Works and Studies for the Left Hand Alone (Aibl; U.E.).

Scherzo.

Perpetuum mobile.

Sonatas in Am and F.

Canons (Aug.; Schott).

TRANSCRIPTIONS

Wagner . . . . .
    Walküre, for two pianos (Peters).
Wagner . . . . . .
    Tristan, for two pianos (Peters).
Strauss . . . .
    "Blue Danube."

Wolf, H. . . . . .
    Songs.

Publishers: B. and B., Breit., Lauterbach and Kuhn, Forberg, U.E., Kahnt, Schott, Peters, Senff.

Most of Reger's music is what the Germans call *Kapellmeistermusik* and lacks lightness of touch. Reger called himself "Bach the second," and it must be admitted that as regards contrapuntal facility he had a certain claim to the title; but he seems to have forgotten that Bach had other qualities which he lacks. To see him at his best the student should scan Op. 81 and should not be discouraged by the complicated look of the pages. It is a remarkable composition. There is also good music in the Concerto, and the two-piano pieces might be tried.

JULIUS RÖNTGEN

(1855-1934)

Op. 2. Sonata, A.
Op. 4. Aus der Jugendzeit, three books of small pieces (four hands).
Op. 5. A Cycle of Fantasy Pieces.
Op. 6. Ballade, Dm.
Op. 7. Suite, in four parts.
Op. 8. Fantasie, C.
Op. 10. Sonata No. 2, Db.
Op. 11. Neckens Polska, Variations on a Swedish Folk Song.
Op. 12. Julklapp, nine little pieces.
Op. 16. Introduction, Scherzo, Intermezzo, Finale (four hands).
Op. 17. Theme and Variations (four hands).
Op. 18. Concerto, D, with orchestra.

Op. 19. Improvisata on a Norwegian Folk Song.
Op. 22. Ballade No. 2, Gm.
Op. 25. Variations and Finale on a Hungarian Czardas.
Op. 28. Fugues.
Op. 36b. Ballade on a Norwegian Melody, two pianos (Simrock).
Op. 38. Variations and Finale (Rieter-Biedermann).
Op. 51. Old Dutch Songs Transcribed (2 vols. Aug.).
Op. 59. Azzopardi Studies: Preludes in All Keys, Fugue and Waltz. On a Cantus Firmus of Azzopardi.

WITHOUT OPUS NUMBER

Cadenzas for Beethoven's Concerto in G (Alsbach).
    (All Breit. except where noted.)

Publishers: Breit., Rieter-Biedermann, Alsbach, Simrock, Aug.

Julius Röntgen is a Dutch composer who escaped being a notable writer by a narrow margin. He remains more or less unknown. His work displays good taste and invention, and much pleasure may be derived from its perusal. In style he leans a little too heavily on Schumann and Brahms—but what excellent crutches! He does not always succeed in avoiding respectable dullness, and his ecstasy is sometimes a trifle traditional.

The "Old Dutch Songs" are excellent and very easy. "Neckens Polska" slightly cut would make a fine piece. The theme is beautiful (Ophelia sings it in Thomas' "Hamlet"), and the variations are Brahmsian. For lovers of four-hand and two-piano playing there is a wealth of material.

ANTON RUBINSTEIN
(1830-1894)

Op. 1. Undine.

Op. 2. Russian Fantasia.

Op. 3. Two Melodies, F and B.

Op. 4. Mazurka-Fantasie.

Op. 5. Polish Dances.
Polonaise.
Cracovienne.
Mazurka.

Op. 6. Tarentella.

Op. 7. Impromptu.

Op. 8. Voix intérieures.

Op. 10. Album of Portraits, twenty-four pieces, among which is "Kammenoi Ostrow."

*Op. 12. Sonata, Em (Peters).

Op. 14. Le Bal, ten pieces (B. and B.).
1. Impatience.
2. Polonaise.
*3. Contradanse, six pieces.
4. Valse.
5. Intermezzo.
6. Polka.
7. Polka-Mazurka.
8. Mazurka.
*9. Galop.
10. Le Rêve.

Op. 16. Three Pieces.
Impromptu.
Berceuse.
Sérénade.

Op. 20. Sonata No. 2 (*Theme and Variations).

Op. 21. Three Caprices.

Op. 22. Three Serenades.
(Last three Breit.)

*Op. 23. Six Études (No. 1 is the celebrated "Staccato Étude." Peters).

*Op. 24. Six Preludes (*Fm. Peters).

Op. 25. Concerto No. 1, Em, with orchestra (*First Movement).

*Op. 26. Romance and Impromptu.

Op. 28. Nocturne and Caprice.

Op. 29. Two Funeral Marches.
For an Artist.
For a Hero.

*Op. 30. Barcarolle, Fm, and Appassionata.

Op. 35. Concerto No. 2, Fm, with orchestra.

Op. 37. Acrostic (L) F, (A) Gm, (U) B, (R) Dm, (A) F.

Op. 38. Suite (Schott).
Prélude.   Passacaille.
*Menuet.   Allemande.
Gigue.   Courante.
Sarabande.   Passepied.
*Gavotte.   Bourrée.

*Op. 41. Sonata No. 3, F (Breit).

Op. 44. Soirées de St. Pétersbourg.

*Romance, E♭.   Impromptu.
*Scherzo.   Nocturne.
Preghiera.   Appassionata.

Op. 45. Concerto No. 3, G, with orchestra.

*Op. 45a. Barcarolle.

Op. 50. Characterbilder (four hands).

Nocturne.   Capriccio.
Scherzo.   March.
*Barcarolle.

Op. 51. Six Pieces.

Melancholy.   Caprice.
Enjoyment.   Passion.
Revery.   Coquetry.

*Op. 53. Preludes and Fugues in Free Style (Peters).

(The preludes are those of Op. 24.)

Op. 69. Five Pieces (Siegel).

*Caprice, A♭.   Romance, Bm.
Nocturne.   *Toccata, Dm.
Scherzo, Am.

*Op. 70. Concerto No. 4, Dm, with orchestra (Senff).

Op. 71. Three Pieces.

Nocturne, A♭.
Mazurka, Fm.
Scherzo, Am.

*Op. 73. Fantasia, Fm, two pianos (Senff).

Op. 75. Album de Peterhof (Senff).

Souvenir.   Pensées.
*Aubade.   *Nocturne.
Funeral March. Prélude.
*Impromptu.   Mazurka.
Revery.   *Romance.
Caprice.   Scherzo.

Op. 77. Fantasia, Em (Senff).

*Op. 81. Six Études.

Op. 82. Album of Popular Dances.

Lesghinka.   Valse.
Czardas.   Trepak.
Tarentella.   Polka.
Mazurka.

Op. 84. Fantasia, with orchestra.

*Op. 88. Theme and Variations, G (Senff).

Op. 93. Miscellaneous Pieces.

Ballade after Bürger's "Lenore."
Two Grand Études.
Doumka and Polonaise.
*Fifth Barcarolle, Am.
*Scherzo.
Two Russian Serenades.
Nouvelle mélodie and Impromptu.
Variations on "Yankee Doodle."
Miniatures.
  1. Près du ruisseau.
*2. Menuet.
  3. Berceuse.
  4. Hallali.
*5. Sérénade.
*6. L'érmite.
  7. El Dachterawan.
  8. Valse.
  9. Chevalier et paysanne.
10. À la fenêtre.
11. Revoir.
12. Le Cortège.

Op. 94. Concerto No. 5, E♭, with orchestra (Senff).

Op. 100. Sonata No. 4, Am (*Scherzo. Senff).

Op. 102. Caprice russe, with orchestra (Senff).

Op. 103. Ball costumé, twenty pieces (four hands. B. and B.).

Op. 104. Six Pieces.

Elegy.   *Sixth Barcarolle.
Variations.   Impromptu.
Étude.   Ballade.

Op. 109. Soirées musicales.

Prélude.   Rêverie.
Valse.   Caprice.
Nocturne.   Badinage.
Scherzo.   Thème varié.
Impromptu.   Étude, E♭.

Op. 113. Concertstück, E♭.

Op. 114. Second Acrostic.

Op. 118. Souvenir de Dresde.

Simplicitas.   Caprice.
Appassionata. Nocturne.
Novelette.   Polonaise.

WITHOUT OPUS NUMBER

*Barcarolle No. 4, G (B. and B.).
Chanson à boire.
Étude, E♭.

*Étude on "Wrong Notes."
Sérénade russe (for Album Bellini).
*Valse caprice, E♭ (Senff).

Bluette.

Cadenzas for Beethoven's first four concertos (Schott).

Fantasia on Hungarian Melodies (Roszavölgyi).

Euphemia Polka.

Four Polkas.

Polish Dances.

Finger Exercises (ed. by Villoing. Simrock).

Cadenzas for Mozart's concerto, Dm (K466. Schott).

Lesghinka, from *The Demon,* transcribed by Pabst (Simrock).

The *Barcarolles have been collected in one volume and published by Schirmer.

Publishers: Senff (the chief one), B. and B., Peters, Schirm., Kahnt, Spina, Roszavölgyi, Hamelle, Schott, Breit.

The music of Rubinstein is almost completely in eclipse. Aside from the D minor Concerto, the "Melody in F," the "Valse Caprice," "Kammenoi Ostrow," the "Romance in Eb," and the "Staccato Étude," most people would find it difficult to name another piece. The other compositions fell like the stick of a rocket after their vivid but short life under his fingers. The critical estimate of his work during his lifetime was blinded by the dazzling manner in which he presented many works intrinsically of little value, and it was only the morning after, so to speak, that the world awoke to the fact that in his death it had not lost a Beethoven. Rubinstein, however, considered himself the last composer, and honestly thought that composition ended with him. The situation recalls the bon mot regarding the relative merits of Brahms and Liszt, to the effect that Liszt's music sounds better than it is, and Brahms's music is better than it sounds. Rubinstein's music under his fingers certainly sounded better than it was, and now under the less sympathetic fingers of later pianists it does not have the same effect.

His chief value at present seems to lie in the wonderful melodies he was able to spin. The magnificent tunes of the D minor Concerto, the E minor Sonata, the finale of the Cello Sonata, even the hackneyed "Kammenoi Ostrow" and the "Romance in Eb" soar. What expansiveness do they not radiate! Such pieces as Rubinstein wrote could never please a taste confined to the recent vogue of terseness, irony, atonality, bitonality, and the abhorrence of sentiment; but should one tire of these newer joys and feel a longing for a good tune again, one can turn to some of the compositions by Rubinstein. Unfortunately, he has to be classed as a *Vielschreiber,* and one has to exercise judgment and knowledge of the repertory to pick the worth while pieces. Like many fecund composers he offers two kinds of failures. First, the pieces which are essentially tedious because of aridity of thought, and second, those which are ineffective through careless writing, though they contain good ideas. Many an unfortunate work of the second class could be reclaimed through transcription, and probably—or should one only say perhaps—some day excursions into this music will be made. The asterisks attached to his compositions are in general the taste of Josef Lhevinne, to whom I am indebted for a sympathetic appreciation of many of Rubinstein's forgotten works and for advice concerning them. The reader is also referred to pages 215-217 for the programs Rubinstein gave in his great historical recital series, which will give the works he himself chose as most worthily representing him. From these two points of view the student can get opinions worth having.

Rubinstein's genius manifests itself best in the great Variations, Op. 88, an enormous work that requires forty minutes to play and deserves to rank with the great sets of Bach, Beethoven, Mendelssohn, and Brahms. He had a special sympathy with the barcarolle mood—all his pieces called "barcarolle" are good (see the collection by Schirmer)—and among the études of Op. 23 will be found other good ones besides the "Staccato Étude." The Prelude in F minor is fine, and the Gavotte from Op. 38 is fresh and gay. It contains an inspiring melody. Its form, A-B-A-B, instead of the usual A-B-A, is original. The "Étude on Wrong Notes" has vigorous dash and a fine middle section in double notes that will commend it to players of a large grasp. Sonata Op. 12 contains most excellent ideas, intrinsically good, except that the first theme of the slow movement might be considered a trifle "angel-serenady." Transscribed for two pianos it gives a fine effect. The finale is a whirlwind impossible on one piano. Those who like descriptive music will enjoy Op. 93, No. 1, the Ballade after Bürger's "Lenore," with its galloping horse and rattling bones. The variations on "Yankee Doodle" are entertaining to an American for the theme, but are mediocre as music.

MISCELLANEOUS RUSSIAN AND POLISH COMPOSERS

FELIX BLUMENFELD
(1863-1931)

Op. 3. Études.

Op. 4. Sonata.

Op. 14. Sur mer, étude.

*Op. 17. Twenty-four Preludes.

Op. 24. Étude de concert.

*Op. 25. Two Études-fantaisies, G, Eb.

Op. 23. Polish Suite.

Op. 31. Polish Suite.

*Op. 34. Ballade in Form of Variations.

Op. 40. Cloches.

Op. 44. Four Études.

Op. 46. Sonata-Fantasie.

Allegro de concert, with orchestra.
  (All Belaiev)

ALEXANDER BORODIN
(1833-1887)

*Au couvent (Schirm.).

SERGEI BORTKIEWICZ
(1877—)

*Concerto Op. 16, Bb, with orchestra
  (Kistner, 1913).

A second concerto and a number of pieces in the smaller forms.

ALEXANDER DARGOMYZHSKY
(1813-1869)

Tarentella slave (four hands, to play with someone who does not play the piano).

ISSAYE DOBROVEN
(1893—)

Op. 1. Eight Preludes.

Op. 2. Ballade.
  (Both E.M.R.)

Op. 4. Four Mazurkas.

Op. 6. Two Valses.

Op. 9. Second Ballade.

Op. 10. Second Sonata.

Op. 13. Seven Pieces.

Op. 14. Impromptu.
  (All U.E.)

SAMUEL FEINBERG
(1890—)

Op. 13. Sonata.

Op. 15. Three Preludes.

Transcriptions of four Bach Choralvorspiele.
  (All U.E.)

IGNAZ FRIEDMANN
(1882—)

Transcriptions for concert use of compositions by the following writers: Dandrieu, Rameau, Grazioli, Gluck, Beethoven, Scarlatti, Dalayrac, Couperin, Shield, Dornell, Field, and Schubert.

A large number of original compositions in salon style.

REINHOLD GLIÈRE
(1875—)

Op. 15. Scherzo.
Op. 16. Deux Morceaux.
    Prélude.
    Romance.
*Op. 17. Five Sketches.
Op. 19. Three Pieces.
    Mazurka.
    Intermezzo.
    Mazurka.
Op. 21. Three Pieces.
    *Tristesse.
    Joie.
    Chagrin.

*Op. 26. Six Pieces, for two pianos.
Op. 29. Three Mazurkas.
*Op. 30. Twenty-five Preludes in All Keys.
Op. 31. Twelve Pieces for Children.
Op. 34. Twenty-four Characteristic Pieces for Young People.
Op. 40. Esquisses.
Op. 41. Five Pieces.
Op. 43. Eight Easy Pieces.
    (All Jurgenson)
    (An album is published by Chest.)

ALEXANDER GOEDICKE
(1877—)

Op. 18. Sonata.
Op. 19. Two Preludes.

Op. 20. Prelude, "The Blind," of Maeterlinck.
    (All E.M.R.)

ALEXANDER GRETCHANINOV
(1864—)

Op. 3. Pastels, five miniatures (Belaiev).
Op. 37. Two Pieces (E.M.R.).
Op. 53. Four Mazurkas, easy (Zimmermann).
Op. 61. Pastels, eight miniatures (second set).

Op. 92. Das Kinderbuch.
Op. 99. In the Meadows, ten pieces.
Op. 110. Two Sonatinas.
Op. 116. Three Pieces.
    (All Schott)

PAUL JUON
(1872—)

Op. 1. Six Sketches (*No. 6, Petite valse. Easy).
Op. 12. Six Concert Pieces (*No. 3, Humoresk).
Op. 18. Satyrs and Nymphs (*No. 1, Naiads at the Spring).

Op. 20. Child Suite, four pieces.
Op. 14 and Op. 24. Dance Rhythms (Four hands, seven books).
Op. 45. Triple Concerto, for piano, violin, and violin cello, with orchestra.
    (All Schirm.)

LUCIAN KAMIENSKI
(1885—)

Op. 17. Fantaisie sur deux Noëls polonais
(Gebetner und Wolff).

THEODOR LESCHETIZKY
(1830-1915)

*Op. 39. Souvenirs d'Italie (B. and B.).   Danse à la russe.
   *Barcarola.
   Canzonetta toscana.
   Le Lucciole.

STEFAN MALINOWSKI
(1887—)

Op. 12. Tema con variazioni (Gebetner
und Wolff).

IGOR MARKEVITSCH
(1912—)

Concerto, with orchestra.   Partita, with small orchestra (Overture,
                                          Chorale, and Rondo).

NICOLAI MIASKOWSKY
(1881—)

Four Sonatas (*No. 2. No. 3 is atonal).   Op. 25. Bizarreries (U.E.).

IGNACY PADEREWSKI
(1860—)

Op. 17. Concerto, Am, with orchestra.   Variations, A.
Op. 19. Fantasie-Polonaise, with orches-   Variations and Fugue, Am.
   tra.   Caprice in G.
   (Both Schirm.)   Chants du voyageur.

VLADIMIR REBIKOV
(1866-1920)

Op. 2. Six Pieces.
Op. 5. Seven Pieces.
Op. 6. Four Pieces.
Op. 8. Rêveries d'automne (album of
   eighteen pieces).
Op. 9. Autour du monde (album for
   the young).
Op. 11. Mélomimiques.
   Naiade.
   Les Démons s'amusent.
   Le Faune.
   La Néréide.
   Dans la fôret.

Op. 17. Mélomimiques.
   Rêveries.
   Idylle.
Op. 22. Mélomimiques.
   Tableau musical-psychologique.
   Esclavage et liberté.
Op. 25. Tableau musical-psychologique.
   Chanson du coeur.
Op. 25. Tableau musical-psychologique.
   "Aspirer et atteindre."
Op. 26. Tableau musical-psychologique.
   Cauchemar, for two pianos.
Many other small pieces with and with-
   out opus number.
   (All Jurgenson).

NIKOLAI RIMSKI-KORSAKOV
(1844-1908)

Op. 30. Concerto, C♯, with orchestra (Belaiev).

Variations on B-A-C-H (Rahter).

NIKOLAI ROSLAVETZ
(1881—)

Prelude.
Two Compositions.
    Quasi Prelude.
    Quasi Poem.

Three Compositions.
Three Études.
(All U.E.)

LUDOMIR VON RÓZYCKI
(1883—)

Op. 11. Fantaisie (Gebetner und Wolff).
Op. 18. Ballade, with orchestra (Piwarski).
Op. 25. Balladnya Poema (Piwarski).
Op. 26. Contes d'une horloge (Gebetner und Wolff).
Op. 37. Danses polonaises (3 vols. Hansen).

Op. 43. Concerto, with orchestra (Hansen).
Op. 46. Fantasiestücke (Roszavölgyi).
Op. 50. Italie (2 vols. of five simple melodies each. Gebetner und Wolff).
Polish Dances (3 vols. Hansen).
There are many more preludes, nocturnes, and intermezzi.

VASSILY SAPELLNIKOV
(1868—)

*Op. 3. Dance of the Elves (Andre).

EDUARD SCHÜTT
(1856-1933)

*Op. 48. Carnaval mignonne (Simrock).
Paraphrases on "Die Fledermaus" and on many other of the Strauss waltzes (Cranz).

Also innumerable salon pieces of good quality.

ARTUR SCHULZ-EVLER
(1854-1905)

*Arabesques on the "Blue Danube" Waltzes (Schirm.).

IGOR STRAVINSKI
(1882—)

Piano Rag.
Five-finger Exercises.
Three Pieces, with an easy bass part.
Five Pieces, with an easy treble part.
Scherzino.
    (All Chest.)

Caprice, with orchestra (Schott).
Concerto, with orchestra.
Sonata.
*Three Movements from "Petrouchka,"
    transcribed by the composer.
    (Last three, E.M.R.)

ALEXANDER TANSMAN
(1897—)

Twenty Easy Pieces, Modern Studies on
    Polish Folk Songs.
Sonatina.
Three Études transcendantes.
Sonata rustica.
    (All U.E.)
Two Concertos, with orchestra.
Concertino, with orchestra.
Symphonie concertante, for piano, quartet, and orchestra.
Suite, for two pianos and orchestra.

Three Preludes.
Petite suite.
Four Preludes.
Five Impromptus.
Mazurka.
Second Sonata.
Arabesques.
Tempo americano.
Suite in the Old Style.
    (All Eschig)

ALEXANDER TCHEREPNIN
(1899—)

Toccata.
Nocturne and *Dance.
    (Both Belaiev)
Five Arabesques, short pieces in étude
    style, the last one with violin.
Sonata, A.
Deux Novelettes.
Transcriptions slaves.
    *Les Bâteliers du Volga.
    Chanson pour la chérie.
    *Chanson grandrussien.
    Le Long du Volga.
    *Chanson tchèque.
    (All Heugel)
Sonatine romantique.
Petite suite.
    (Both Durand)
Canzone (Simrock).

Bagatelles.
*Concerto in F, with orchestra.
Six Études.
Four Transcriptions.
    Bortniansky .. Chants du cherubim.
    Bortniansky .. Chants du cherubim.
    Digtiarov .... Concerto spirituel
                  pour l'annonciation.
    Beresovsky ... Un Mouvement du
                   concerto spirituel.
    (All Chest.)
Op. 39. Message (U.E.).
*Bagatelles.
Nine Inventions (Eschig).
Op. 31. Four Romances.

Lovers of piano music will find in the modern Russian school by far the largest and most interesting field for research. Since music branched from Bach, Mozart, and Beethoven to a more or less consciously national form, the Russians have made an incomparable record. At first they were divided in two distinct groups: the nationalists and the eclectics. The second group included the two Rubinsteins and Tchaikovsky; in the first were the celebrated "Five" —Rimski-Korsakov, Cui, Balakirev, Borodin, and Moussorgsky. Of the rivalries and the final amalgamation of ideals this is not the place to speak, but it is necessary for the understanding of the true greatness of the Russian contribution to know that these two influences were constantly at work, each rectifying the other, and that this, no doubt, contributed very definitely to the magnificence of the outcome. The contributions of such writers as Scriabin, Liadov, Tchaikovsky, Balakirev, Medtner, Glière, Prokofiev, Tcherepnin, and others, as a group, are unparalleled in the history of the postromantic era. Among the older salon writers not included in this book are Wihtol, Shcherbatschev, Amani, Pachulski, Zolotarev, and Kryjanowsky, some of whom have done good work.

The greatest Russian composers have been given attention outside this section, so that it only remains to consider the lesser lights in this place.

Blumenfeld, a very excellent "journalist," is too good to miss. He is fluent and ripples agreeably. His music is good for immediate effect, and many of the pieces would be excellent on concert programs. Some of the preludes from Op. 17 are acceptable.

Borodin was not primarily a piano composer, but the little piece "Au Couvent" is so distinctive that it should not be forgotten.

Bortkiewicz has written what may be described as a Russian-Wagner-salon concerto. The finale is the Russian section, the first movement the Wagner section, and the slow movement the salon section; the last is the least successful. The Concerto, though obviously indebted to Wagner, is big and effective in style; and since good concertos do not grow on every tree it behooves us to be properly grateful for it. The Russian tunes in the finale are glorious. The second Concerto, though musical, is less striking.

Dobroven attempts high things, but is a trifle turgid and gives the impression of not having altogether found himself. His thought is difficult to disentangle. His list includes a second Sonata but no first—what a good idea!

The entertaining Tarantella of Dargomyzhsky for four hands, to play with a friend who does not play the piano, fills a longfelt want. One of the chief troubles with piano literature is that it requires so much playing. Here is one piece which on the part of the bass player at least needs no previous knowledge of the piano. He sits there fearlessly playing two A's in each measure, while the treble player has all the hard parts. Liszt transcribed this piece for two hands.

Feinberg, Roslavetz, and Evseiev are recent writers who uphold new lines of musical thought.

Glière provides some excellent salon music, possibly a trifle more original than that of Blumenfeld. It is melodious and often individual. Op 17, 26, and 30 are recommended. There are many good pieces for young people. An album is published by Chester. The pathetic little piece "Tristesse," which might have been called "Tristan," so obvious is its inspiration, is a charming bit and worth playing for its own sake. It is only two pages long.

Gretchaninov, writer of much excellent liturgical music, has written a few pieces for piano. For some inexplicable reason they are unsatisfactory and are included merely because Gretchaninov wrote them. They are short but obscure. His thought processes perhaps are unsuited to expression on the keyboard. He has written many pieces for children.

Goedicke has very little to say, and his texture is flimsy, but a keen hunter may fancy reading him through once.

The imposing Paul Juon presents a list of more than three hundred compositions. He has ventured into every field, but seems to have been most successful in that of chamber music. Some of his pieces have attained popularity and appear on programs of virtuosi. The best known are listed. Nearly every opus number contains from six to twelve pieces.

Kamienski, a Polish writer, has written a rather engaging piece transcribing two Polish Noëls, which unfortunately falls short in places; otherwise it would have made an unusual concert piece. Perhaps someone can arrange it. Malinowski is another Polish writer who shows promise. He leans on Schumann.

Leschetizky's "Souvenirs d'Italie" is possibly the only thing of this salon writer worth saving, although the "Two Larks," "La Piccola," and the "Sextet from Lucia" for the left hand alone are still popular in certain quarters.

The "Barcarola," the "Canzonetta toscana," and "Le Lucciole" have enough character and distinction to make them acceptable.

Miaskowsky is interesting chiefly for his orchestral compositions; he has written some symphonies considered valuable, but his piano music remains largely unplayed. The four sonatas constitute his chief work for the instrument. I have heard only the third, which seems very wild in the atonal manner. No. 2 is said to be excellent.

The compositions of Paderewski are well known. They are of the salon type, but some will undoubtedly live on, helped by his enormous fame. The "Variations" in A and one of the "Chants du voyageur" are charming, and personal taste will select many others.

Rebikov's music is difficult to procure and, as far as is known to me, is rather slight in texture. The title "A Nightmare for Two Pianos" piques the curiosity.

Rimski-Korsakov wrote a short and not too interesting, though very cleverly made, Concerto prized for its characteristic brevity. It takes only ten minutes to play it. Aside from this there is a group of very short and conventional pieces, and the "Variations on B-A-C-H."

Rózycki is considered by some to be, after Szymanowski, Poland's most prominent piano composer. But his music lacks originality and, when all is said, is only more good music in the older style, contributing no new quality to the art. He is a very prolific composer.

Sapellnikov's "Danse des elves" deserves to be remembered. It is a difficult bravura piece and has long been popular. It was his sole inspiration.

Eduard Schütt has been a mainstay of the sentimental for years. "À la bien aimée" and its sister pieces have ministered to their easy-going tastes, and, one must hasten to add, ministered in a good style resembling Moszkowski's manner. The transcriptions of the Strauss waltzes might give pleasure, and the "Carnaval mignonne" has excellent material in it.

When Schulz-Evler brought out his "Arabesques on the Blue Danube Waltzes," the "Blue Danube" found, at last, an able and satisfactory transcription. It will be long before anyone does a better one.

Stravinski, another devotee of color, is, like Rimski-Korsakov, not at his best in his piano music. Of his early pieces the Étude in F♯ is about the best thing he did, of his later works the "Petrushka" transcription is by far the best. The sophisticated-naïve return to the classics was not a success in the Sonata. It is amusing to find Stravinski writing five-finger exercises and "easy" pieces.

Alexander Tcherepnin, not to be confused with the elder Tcherepnin, Nicholas, who was a respectable writer of no particular distinction, has an enormous fund of rich vitality. His works are not atonal, and it is pleasant to find originality and freshness still possible without recourse to an arbitrarily arranged harmonic scheme. The one-movement Concerto is rugged, the Sonata is short and good, the Suite is good, and the five transcriptions are interesting; all of these add entertainingly to the useable literature. The "Nine Inventions" are dull.

Tansman is a recent Polish writer of whom great things are expected. After Szymanowski he is said to be the most original and personal composer and therefore more important than is Rózycki. His Concerto won a prize.

CAMILLE SAINT-SAËNS

(1835-1921)

Op. 3. Six Bagatelles.
Op. 17. Concerto No. 1, Dm.
Op. 21. Mazurka, Gm.
*Op. 22. Concerto No. 2, Gm (it has been arranged as a solo by Bizet).
*Op. 23. Gavotte, Cm.
Op. 24. Second Mazurka, Gm.
Op. 29. Concerto No. 3, Ebm.
*Op. 35. Variations on a Theme of Beethoven, for two pianos.
*Op. 44. Concerto No. 4, Cm.
Op. 52. Six Études.
  Prelude.
  Independence of Fingers.
  Prelude and Fugue, Fm.
  Study in Rhythms.
  Prelude and Fugue, F.
  *In Form of a Waltz.
Op. 56. Minuet and Waltz.
Op. 59. Harald Haarfager. Ballade (four hands).
Op. 61. Rêverie du soir.

Op. 63. A Night at Lisbon.
Op. 66. Third Mazurka, Bm.
Op. 70. Allegro appassionata.
Op. 72. Album of Six Pieces.
  Prelude.
  Carillon.
  Toccata.
  Valse.
  Chanson napolitaine.
  Finale.
*Op. 73. Rhapsodie d'Auvergne (two editions, with or without orchestra).
Op. 76. Wedding Cake, Caprice Valse (two editions, with or without orchestra).
Op. 77. Polonaise, for two pianos.
Op. 80. Souvenir d'Italie.
Op. 81. Feuillet d'album (four hands).
Op. 85. Les Cloches du soir.
Op. 86. Pas redouble (four hands).
*Op. 87. Scherzo, for two pianos.
Op. 88. Valse canariote.

*Op. 89. Africa (two editions, with or without orchestra).

Op. 90. Suite in the Old Style (*Nos. 2 and 3).

Op. 93. Sarabande and Rigaudon.

Op. 97. Thème varié.

Op. 99. Prélude No. 2.

Op. 100. Souvenir d'Ismailia.

Op. 103. Concerto No. 5 (*Finale. Arrangement of finale for solo, see below).

Op. 104. Valse mignonne.

Op. 105. Berceuse (four hands).

Op. 110. Valse, nonchalante.

Op. 111. Six Études.
Major and Minor Thirds.
Chromatics.
Prelude and Fugue.
Les Cloches de Las Palmas.
Chromatic Thirds.
*Toccata, after the finale of the fifth concerto.

Op. 120. Valse langoureuse.

*Op. 135. Six Études, for the left hand alone.

Op. 139. Valse gai.

Op. 161. Six Fugues.

Op. 169. Feuillet d'album.

WITHOUT OPUS NUMBER

*Mandolinata of Paladilhe (Schott).

*Dervish Chorus, from Beethoven's *Ruins of Athens*.

Two Fantasias for the Lute (fourteenth century), by Milan de Valence.

*Caprice on Airs de ballet, from Gluck's *Alceste*.

*Andante, from Haydn's *Surprise Symphony* (Presser).

Cadenzas for Beethoven's Concerto in G.

Chanson des Maucroix, by Durand.

Scherzo, from Mendelssohn's *Midsummer Night's Dream*.

TRANSCRIPTIONS

Beethoven . . Adagio, from the sixth quartet.

Beethoven . . Scherzo, from the seventh quartet.

Beethoven . . Finale, from the ninth quartet.

J. S. Bach . . . *Twelve Pieces.

From his own operas—*Henry VIII, Étienne Marcel, Samson et Dalila*.

From the operas of Gounod and Massenet.

Cadenzas for Mozart's concertos in Cm (K491) and Eb (K482).

Minuet, from Gluck's *Orpheus*.

Le Cygne, poem of Sully-Prudhomme (a recitation with piano accompaniment).

POSTHUMOUSLY PUBLISHED

The Carnival of Animals, for two pianos and orchestra. One number only, "The Swan," was published before his death.

Durand publishes an album, "Six Pieces," and another containing all the valses.

Publishers: Durand.

Saint-Saëns' quality may be characterized as that of a mirror rather than that of a prism, and his compositions as reflections rather than as paintings. His art, always elegant and polished, shines unequally, the thought is spun out to inconceivable tenuosity in places. His urbanity and eclecticism preclude pronounced personal convictions, and he gathers atmosphere from Timbuctoo to Teheran. This is spread like jam and is not transmuted into the inevitableness of great art. His Gallicism is indeed evident, but his personality is so covered with conventions that his compositions as a group, unlike the works of the greatest writers, do not display a composite soul. A Saint-Saëns harmonic scheme, to put it differently, does not exist in the larger sense.

Now that the worst is said one must do him justice by seeking out those pieces one cannot do without, and surprisingly enough there are a large number of them. Who does not admire the genius that conceived the Concerto in G minor? It has grandeur and originality of form in its first movement, delicious delicacy and freshness in its second, and riotous abandon in its third. Such an all-around, well-balanced concerto is hard to duplicate and impossible to surpass. The finale of Concerto No. 5 (otherwise a dull work), published as a solo in Op. 111, No. 6, is a fine virtuoso piece and good music. The "Variations on a Theme of Beethoven," Op. 35, have long since passed into a classic. What lovelier piece than the "Caprice on Airs de ballet," from *Alceste,* is to be found in the whole range of the literature? His presentation of the "Dervish Chorus" and the deliciously frivolous "Mandolinata" are also admirable in their exceedingly diverging ways; and they show his broad sympathies. For a short, easy, poetic piece for piano and orchestra the "Rhapsodie d'Auvergne" is useful and hardly known. "Africa," although a bit more difficult, is interesting, and much more brilliant. Op. 52, No. 6, 56, 61, 63, and 70 have many admirers, and the Andante from Haydn's *Surprise Symphony* and the Bach transcriptions will give real pleasure. The "Carnival of Animals" is humorous and vastly entertaining. It is a pity he did not give freer vent in his other compositions to the bubbling humor he exhibits here.

DOMENICO SCARLATTI
(1683-1757)

COLLECTIONS

Twenty-nine Compositions (Aug.).

Fifty Harpsichord Lessons (Aug.).

Sixty Compositions (Breit.).

Twenty Compositions, selected by Clara Schumann (Breit.).

Eighteen Compositions, selected (some of them transposed) and arranged in suites by Hans von Bülow (Peters).

Fifty Compositions (Ricordi). This will eventually become the complete edition.

Twenty-two Compositions, edited by Buonamici (Schirm.).

Seventeen Compositions (published in the *Golden Treasury,* Vol. II. Schirm.).

Seventy Compositions (4 vols. U.E.).

Twenty-one Compositions (each one also published separately. Schott).

TRANSCRIPTIONS

Five Sonatas, transcribed by Tausig (published in many editions).

Twenty - six Sonatas, transcribed by

Granados (Orfeo Tracio, Madrid. These are the sonatas Scarlatti wrote in Spain).

It is a pity that the uniquely pleasant music of Scarlatti is known to very few. It is unique because, aside from J. S. Bach, he was by far the greatest clavecinist. He sensed technique before anyone else, and he sometimes foreshadowed his successors with uncanny precision. Technically, he was the Liszt of his time. With the possible exception of Clementi he is the most important piano composer Italy has contributed, and he is perhaps the only composer to be ranked with Mozart for the sense of pure enduring beauty as divorced from emotion or intellectuality. Like Mozart he practiced the rare art of amusing—rare, that is, on the high, pure plane whereon he moved; and again like Mozart he was able to turn the trick hundreds of times. This immortal child is the Puck of musicians; his music teases, laughs, pretends to weep, all in an ecstasy of pagan freedom. Its humorous unrestraint, nimble vivacity, and animal spirits are Greek, and no music could have been more appropriate for a Bacchic festival. Sentiment is lacking and quite properly so, and all but a very few of the six hundred odd pieces are in a rapid tempo. The form of the pieces is, with rare exceptions, invariably the same. It is early sonata form, but it never irks Scarlatti in his merry scamperings about the keyboard and is merely the set arena in which his high spirits take their exercise.

It remains to discuss briefly the various editions of his works. None of the collections exactly duplicates any other, although many pieces figure in all of them. The Schirmer is probably the best for the student who is content with only one volume. It is closely duplicated by Bülow's edition, but contains more pieces and gives more variety. Lovers of Scarlatti will not be content with either of these volumes only, but will want at least the first two volumes of the Universal Edition which gives them thirty-seven more pieces. The astonishing fact should be noted here that scarcely a piece is stupid or dull. One cannot go far amiss in buying anything of Scarlatti. Many enthusiasts, however, will only be satisfied with the great Ricordi edition, which is publishing many pieces for the first time since his death.

Like most early music, nearly all the pieces would benefit by some transcribing. A few notes added or changed often make a vast tonal difference and do not require much skill nor do they change the spirit of the music. The student who will compare the "Siciliano" in F, which is published in the collections of both Peters and Schirmer, will understand what is meant. Tausig's work on five of the sonatas is first-class transcribing and is highly recommended. These transcriptions, especially the "Pastorale" and "Capriccio," have become classics.

It must be added that in order to get the true impish, elfin character of this music, one's fingers must be nimble, light, and accurate, for most of it is of a delicate bravura type and far from easy. It is richly rewarding and very healthful for hand and mind.

FLORENT SCHMITT
(1870—)

*Les Soirs, ten pieces.
  En rêvant.
  Gaity.
  Spleen.
  Après l'été.
  Parfum exotique.
  Un Soir.
  Tziganiana.
  Eclogue.
  Sur l'onde.
  Dernières pages.
Mirages, Et Pan, etc., written for "Le Tombeau de Debussy."
*Les Ombres.
  J'entends dans le lointain.
  Mauresque.
  Cette ombre mon image.
À la mémoire de Claude Debussy.
Sur le nom de Gabriel Fauré.
Two Pieces, for chromatic harp or piano.
  (All Durand)
*Nuits romaines.
  Chanson de l'Anio.
  Le Lucciole.
Danse orientale.
Chanson mélancholique.
Romance sans paroles.
Gitana.

L'Heure immobile.
Chanson tendre.
Nocturne.
Sérénade antique.
  (All Hamelle)
*Musique intime (2 vols.; the first Heugel, the second Mathot).
Trois valses nocturnes (Mathot).
Seven Pieces (four hands. Leduc).
Feuillets de voyage (2 vols., ten pieces, four hands).
Trois rhapsodies, for two pianos.
  Française.
  Polonaise.
  Viennoise.
Reflets d'Allemagne.
Crépuscule (Aug.).
Trois Préludes (R.L.).
  Prélude triste.
  Obsession.
  Chant des cygnes.
Ballade de la neige (R.L.)
Humoresques, six pieces (four hands).
Petites musiques (La Sirène musicale, easy pieces).
Publishers: Durand, Rouart, Lerolle et Cie., Mathot, Leduc.

169

This voluminous composer of salon music is unnecessary to the happiness of pianists. Should anyone care to venture into this not very rich pasture, the pieces marked with asterisks represent the choice of a connoisseur. The music is pallid and unconvincing. Some of the later works lean on Debussy.

FRANZ SCHUBERT
(1797-1828)

With few exceptions Schubert's compositions are available only in volumes published by the leading publishing houses. The Peters edition given here is as follows: Complete Sonatas, Complete Dances, Compositions (Fantasia Op. 15, Fantasia Op. 78, Impromptus, Moments musicales), and a Supplement.

The four-hand music is arranged also in four volumes: Marches, Polonaises, Dances, and an album.

SONATAS

*Op. 42, Am (*Andante).
Op. 53, D.
*Op. 120, A.
Op. 122, Eb.
*Op. 143, Am.
Op. 147, B.

Op. 164, Am. (The andante has a theme identical with one in the finale of the posthumous Sonata in A.)
Posthumous, Cm.
*Posthumous, A.
Posthumous, Bb (*Andante and Scherzo).

"COMPOSITIONS"

Op. 15. Fantasia, C ("The Wanderer").
*Op. 78. Fantasia, G (contains the well-known Minuet).

*Op. 90. Four Impromptus.
*Op. 94. Moments musicales.
Op. 142. Four Impromptus.

DANCES

*Op. 9a, 9b, 50a, 50b, 77, 127. Waltzes.
Op. 18b. Waltzes and Ecossaises.
Op. 33. Ländler and Ecossaises.
Op. 49. Galop and Ecossaises.
Op. 91a and 91b. Grätzer Waltz and Galop.

Hommage aux belles Viennoises (Wiener-Damen-Ländler).

The originals of Liszt's transcriptions "Soirées de Vienne" are found in Op. 9a and Op. 33.

SUPPLEMENT

Sonata, E.
Unfinished Sonata, C.
Op. 145. Adagio and Rondo, E.
Adagio.
Allegretto, Cm.
Three Pieces, Ebm, Eb, C.
Op. 171. Twelve Ländler.

Twelve German Dances and Five Ecossaises.
Sixteen Ländler.
Marsch sammt Trio.
Two Scherzi.

These are scraps left over and are not very interesting.

COMPOSITIONS FOR FOUR-HAND PERFORMANCE

Three Marches.

Six Marches.

Three Military Marches.

Funeral March.

Heroic March.

Two Characteristic Marches.

Children's March.

Rondo brillant.

Lebensstürme.

Phantasie.

Phantasie (1810).

Phantasie (1811).

Overtures in F, C, D.

Sonatas in B♭, C.

Rondos in A, D.

Variations in E, A♭, C.

Introduction and Variations.

Divertissement, and Divertissement à l'hongroise.

Andantino varié.

Six Polonaises.

Four Polonaises.

Four Ländler.

Allegro moderato and Andante.

Phantasie (1813).

The above list of works is compiled from the complete edition (Breit.). The publisher lists his works in their complete edition in twenty-one series, of which Nos. 4, 7, 12, and 21 are for piano.

TRANSCRIPTIONS
BY BAUER

Op. 84, No. 1. Andantino varié, adapted for two pianos.

No. 2. Rondo brillant, adapted for two pianos.

Op. 103. Fantasia in Fm, adapted for two pianos.

Ländler and other pieces, selected and edited.

(All Schirm.)

For transcriptions of Schubert's works see also under Liszt, Tausig, Křenek, Busoni, Prokofiev, and Brahms.

The quantity of Schubert's piano compositions is so great that it is at once obvious that many of them must have been potboilers. His brain seethed unceasingly with melodies which were left on the town, as it were, without education. Witness the thousands of tunes gaily tripping past on the pages of the various dances and marches. They are left undeveloped. What an orphan asylum! Liszt adopted many, brought them up, and left them beautified and cultivated. A dozen Liszts are needed to adopt them all.

In that ancient "war horse," the "Wanderer" Fantasia, the dull parts so outnumber the attractive ones that the piece, though still played occasionally, is no longer altogether acceptable. The other Fantasia, Op. 78, however, is really charming, not only the beloved Minuet, but all the movements. Lovely themes flit across its pages endlessly.

Weitzmann damns the sonatas with the faint praise "they offer refined entertainment." Many are dull and antiquated, and few are worth playing except on special occasions, but there are many movements which deserve to be rescued from oblivion. These movements are marked with asterisks in the general list. The entire posthumous Sonata in A, in which cuts may be made in the finale, is worth playing. Op. 90, 94, and 142 are too well known to need comment.

Liszt and Tausig have best interpreted Schubert for the piano. Liszt with his marvelous sympathy has translated the songs into veritable little ballades. Tausig left three fine interpretations; the "Military March" is a standard work, but people have never taken up the "Andantino varié," a lovely piece. Bauer has recently made excellent transcriptions not yet played enough. Busoni, Prokofiev, and Křenek have also written transcriptions.

ROBERT SCHUMANN
(1810-1856)

Op. 1. Variations on the Name "Abegg."

Op. 2. Papillons.

Op. 3. Studies after Paganini.

Op. 4. Intermezzi.

Op. 5. Impromptus on a Theme of Clara Wieck (two editions).

Op. 6. Davidsbündlertänze (two editions).

Op. 7. Toccata.

Op. 8. Allegro.

Op. 9. Carnaval, Scènes mignonnes sur quatre notes.

Op. 10. Studies after Paganini.

Op. 11. Sonata, F♯m.

Op. 12. Fantasiestücke ("Fantasy Pieces").
Des Abends.
Aufschwung.
Warum?
Grillen.
In der Nacht.
Fabel.
Traumeswirren.
Ende vom Lied.

Op. 13. Études symphoniques.

Op. 14. Sonata, Fm (Konzert ohne orchester).

Op. 15. Scenes from Childhood.
Von fremden Ländern.
Curiose Geschichte.
Hasche-Mann.
Bittendes Kind.
Glückes genug.
Wichtige Begebenheit.
Traümerei.
Am Camin.
Ritter vom Steckenpferd.
Fast zu ernst.
Fürchtenmachen.
Der Dichter spricht.

Op. 16. Kreisleriana, eight pieces.

Op. 17. Fantasia in C.

Op. 18. Arabesque.

Op. 19. Blumenstück.

Op. 20. Humoresque.

Op. 21. Eight Novelettes.

Op. 22. Sonata, Gm.

Op. 23. Nachtstücke ("Four Nocturnes").

Op. 26. Faschingsschwank aus Wien ("Vienna Carnival Pranks").

Op. 28. Three Romances: B♭m, F♯, B.

Op. 32. Scherzo, Gigue, Romance, Fughetta.

Op. 46. Andante and Variations, for two pianos.

Op. 54. Concerto, Am.

Op. 56. Six Studies, for the pedal piano.

Op. 58. Four Studies, for the pedal piano.

Op. 66. Bilder aus dem Osten (four hands).

Op. 68. Album for the young, forty-three short pieces.

Op. 72. Four Fugues.

Op. 76. Four Marches.

Op. 82. Wood Scenes (No. 7 is "Vogel als Prophet").

Op. 85. Twelve Pieces for Four Hands for Great and Small.

Op. 92. Introduction and Allegro, with orchestra.

Op. 99. Bunte Blätter, fourteen short pieces.

> Three Little Pieces: A, Em, E.
> Albumblätter: F♯, Bm, A♭, E♭.
> Novelette, Bm.
> March, Dm.
> Abendmusik, B♭.
> Scherzo, Gm.
> Geschwindmarsch, Gm.

Op. 109. Nine Characteristic Pieces (four hands).

Op. 111. Three Fantasy Pieces, Cm, A♭, Cm.

Op. 118a. Three Sonatas for the Young.

Op. 122. Recitations with Piano Accompaniment.

> Der Haidenknabe.
> Die Flüchtlinge.

Op. 124. Albumblätter, twenty short pieces.

Op. 126. Seven Pieces, in form of short fugues.

Op. 130. The Children's Ball (four hands).

Op. 134. Introduction and Allegro, Dm, with orchestra.

Schumann left some alternatives and additions to his composition which follow:

Op. 46, Andante and Variations, was first published for two pianos, two violin cellos, and two horns.

Presto, a movement originally intended for the Gm Sonata, Op. 22.

Scherzo, a movement originally intended for the Fm Sonata, Op. 14.

Variations, the nonincorporated variations of the Études symphoniques are now printed in the Schirmer edition.

It is interesting to note that the melody of the Aria from the Sonata Op. 11 was used also for a song called "To Anna." The andante of the G minor Sonata has been similarly used. Breitkopf publishes all these pieces in the complete edition.

More than any other composer, Schumann represents for pianists that movement of romanticism which followed the great German classical period. Youth was busy as usual discovering and reforming the world. Mendelssohn was a belated classicist, Weber was chiefly concerned with the theater, Chopin was a foreigner; and Schumann bore the pianists' banner of the best German lyric feeling. It is in this respect that he should be considered, and only in this light is he fully understood.

In his quest for new things Schumann wrote a number of works which suffer from diffuseness. These pieces one might designate as provincial, because they are really only understood and enjoyed in Germany. They have never carried very far into the outside world, though they richly repay sympathetic study. A notable work of this class is the "Davidsbündlertänze," a mag-

nificent collection of eighteen pieces which is impossible for public performance unless on a special Schumann program. It is not cyclic in form, though a
quotation from No. 2 appears in No. 17, but it hangs together psychologically,
even in its contrasting moods. Nos. 2, 14, 15, and 17 are entrancingly lovely;
Nos. 4, 6, and 19 are stormy in character. Humor, pathos, and simplicity also
find expression in them. Students unfamiliar with the meaning of the title
should look it up, since it has to do with the eternal goals of youth and is
intimately connected with Schumann's life and also with his literary works.

Among the pieces little played for one reason or another is the first movement of Op. 14, which is spiritually related to the "Symphonic Variations,"
but is lesser music. It is the only valuable movement. The second and fifth of
the Intermezzi, Op. 4, are good.

The "Kreisleriana" has unfortunately to be classified in this group for the
reason that its eight component parts form too long a unit for a program.
The key relationship in all eight is not sufficiently diversified, and the work
played in its entirety for a large audience becomes monotonous. As music and
as "Schumann" it is of the best. The pieces may, of course, be played separately and would enter a group very well.

The "Humoresque" is probably hopeless, though it contains passages of
beauty; it is a continuous piece from beginning to end and not a collection.
It resembles a garrulous person flitting from topic to topic, who returns now
and again to his main thesis only to stray off when one hopes the end is near.

Theoretically the "Carnaval" should belong in this class, but, in spite of
its scrappy character, it has some strange vitality which affects the audience.
The literary allusions, the puns, the "four notes," and the whole program are
artistically questionable, but somehow the work survives. One likes the humor
of putting "Chopin" between two robust German ladies with Italian names,
"Chiarina" and "Estrella." It is good fun to explore all the many punning
complexities. One must know the German names for the notes. One of the
best jokes, though possibly it is one Schumann did not intend, involves his
excitement about the young lady in Asch; when all was over and done, he
dedicated the piece to the violinist Lipinsky.

The "Studies after Paganini" are recommended for exploration. They
belong in the less-known regions of Schumann's work and suffer from the fact
that Liszt is much better at this, but one may learn interesting lessons from

them. Some, though not many, are duplicates, and a comparison, for example, of Op. 10, No. 2, with the first étude in the Liszt group is enlightening. "La Chasse" has been transcribed by both Schumann and Liszt.

The "Abegg" variations and the "Papillons" will hardly do for concerts; they are pleasant occasionally for oneself. As Schumann is fond of quoting himself, and his favorite phrases appear first in the "Papillons," every pianist ought to have a bowing acquaintance with this opus in order to be able to recognize its phrases when they occur in another piece. The great work of the very early opus numbers is the Toccata, which occupies a high place among pieces dealing with double notes. One groups it naturally with "Islamey," Chopin's étude in thirds, and the first two of the first book of Brahms's "Paganini Variations." The test of its musical value, and whether speed is a sine qua non of its effect, is to play it slowly to see whether its content has sufficient charm to give pleasure. The result will be surprising, for there are musical effects which pass by unenjoyed when one plays it fast. It is a marvelous piece.

Sonata Op. 11 strikes a very exalted note and has a sustained flow. Schumann departs for the first time from the plan of stringing many short pieces together and finds that he can develop themes at length. It is fresh in inspiration and noteworthy in scholarship. The cyclical idea is most happily applied, for the theme of the aria is delicately foreshadowed in the introduction. The main body of the first movement is cleverly and convincingly constructed of two tersely cogent motifs, and it has the architectural "feel" essential in longer works. The finale is weakly put together and is the least impressive part, but a cut suggested in the Schirmer edition helps to strengthen it.

Of the "Fantasiestücke" it is in general unnecessary to speak, except to ask "why always the first pieces and never 'In der Nacht' or 'Das Ende vom Lied'?" With the "Études symphoniques" Schumann succeeded in creating a world piece; no one needs a special outlook to enjoy this glorious composition. One can, by using the theme, the rejected variations, and the finale, create a new set of "Symphonic Variations" (see list). The "Scenes from Childhood" require no comment.

Another very great work is the Fantasia, Op. 17. It may not come amiss to speak somewhat at length concerning it. It is in three movements, of which the first and third are essentially fantastic, or better, impromptu-style, though formally well articulated. All three are to all intents and purposes in sonata form, except that in each the development is replaced by new material. The origin of the work and the original titles of the movements (it was a sort of ode to Beethoven, and the movements were originally entitled "Struggle," "Triumphant March," and "Starry Crown") give the clue to the emotional content. A motto, necessary for the performer and the listener to heed, stands at the beginning: the *"leiser Ton"* is otherwise easily missed. The keynote of the first movement is revolt, which persists to the very end, when there comes a change and a relaxing heavenly peace descends. Beethoven's strife is over. The second part is his art triumphant; the third, his apotheosis. It is one of the greatest pieces of the romantic renaissance in Germany, infinitely satisfying for one's self-expression.

The following "Arabesque" and "Blumenstück," especially the latter, are not very exhilarating, though tuneful and full of sentiment. The Sonata in G minor, Op. 22, is rather a favorite nowadays, possibly because it is short, goes at a rapid pace, and has very little sentiment. The adagio is a lovely moonlight scene, but this is the only part which is not bustling with energy, scurrying, cackling, and rushing to the end. It is short, compact, and vivacious. Schumann directs at the beginning: *"So schnell als möglich"*; presently he says *"schneller"*; at the coda he wants the tempo *"noch schneller."*

One should play some of the other "Novelettes" besides the first. Many of them will repay study, and some are excellent for concerts. The "Nachtstücke" on the contrary are unattractive, with the exception of the one noted.

The "Faschingsschwank aus Wien," Op. 26 ("Vienna Carnival Pranks"), would be improved by cutting, a process which in the first movement is easy, and, as a matter of fact, the only place where it would be necessary. It is the A-B-A-C-A-D form that Schumann very often employs. The other four movements are perfect both in form and content, short, and to the point, the finale splendidly brilliant. The piece has elements of grandeur, and one can conceive that some Busoni could make an adequate transcription which would carry it into the world in triumph.

What conspiracy of silence has kept two of the three Romances, Op. 28, from the public? The second Romance in F♯ is, of course, well known, but the first and third are excellent pieces and quite unplayed. The three together would make a well contrasted group and might be conceived of as "Prelude,

Romance, and Scherzo." Students should try these pieces. After Op. 28 came a long interval in which Schumann wrote songs, and it is not till Op. 54, if the two-piano piece Op. 46 is excepted, that there is piano music again. This, the immortal Concerto, is one of the high lights of the literature, a remarkable achievement in writing, for Schumann has demonstrated that intimate, nontechnical music can be effective in a concert hall. One may reckon this Concerto among the deathless things. Devotees of the Concerto also love the Introduction and Allegro, Op. 92, a lesser concerto, with its richness of melody and its strong rhythms. Unfortunately, it never makes the proper impression at a public performance. A reorchestration can be made to advantage.

There is not much else. The "Vogel als Prophet" from the "Waldscenen" is the only one of that set worth considering; and later on, Op. 99, the "Bunte Blätter," about finishes the interesting compositions. These latter, tiny pieces though they are, touch poignant emotions and are really worth playing. In their miniature way they go searchingly to the heart of things. They were composed about the time Schumann was writing his opus twenties. Brahms used two of them in his Variations, Op. 9.

The recitations with piano are little known and are not very attractive, for the horrid fate of the poor little "Haidenknabe" is too dreadful for amusement and "Die Flüchtlinge" is a trifle pallid. The second Introduction and Allegro which Schumann made for Brahms was done at a time when his mind was clouding and does not compare with Op. 92. The "Albumblätter" will yield a few charming short sketches, among them the noted "Schlummerlied."

CYRIL SCOTT
(1879—)

An English Waltz.
Asphodel.
Autumn Idyll.
Ballad.
Barcarolle.
Berceuse.
Britain's War March.
British Melodies.
    All Through the Night.
    The Wild Hills of Clare.
    Sumer is Icumen in.

Caprice chinois.
Carillon.
Cavatina.
Chansonette.
*Chimes.
Columbine.
Concerto, with orchestra (Schott).
Consolation.
Dagobah.
*Danse nègre.

Danse romantique.

*Egypt: Five Impressions.

Études.
    Allegro.
    Allegro con brio.

First Bagatelle.

*Handelian Rhapsody.

*Impressions from the Jungle Book.
    The Jungle.
    Dawn.
    Rikky-Tikky-Tavy.
    Morning Song.
    Dance of the Elephant.

Impromptu.

Intermezzo.

Irish Reel.

*Little Russian Suite.
    Russian Air.
    Siberian Waltz.
    Dance.

*Lotusland.

Mazurka.

Modern Finger Exercises (based on the whole-tone scale; easy).

Notturno.

Ode héroïque.

Over the Prairie, Two Impressions.
    Andante.
    Allegretto.

Pastoral Suite.
    Courante.
    Pastorale.
    Rigaudon.
    Rondo.
    Passacaglia.

Pierette.

*Poems.
    Poppies.
    The Garden of Soul Sympathy.
    Bells.
    The Twilight of the Years.
    Paradise Birds.

Prélude solennelle.

Russian Dance.

Scherzo.

Sea Marge.

Serenata.

Second Suite.
    Prelude.
    Air varié.
    Solemn Dance.
    Caprice.
    Introduction and Fugue.

Soirée japonaise.

Solitude.

Sonata.

Souvenir de Vienne.

Sphinx.

Suite in the Old Style.
    Prelude.
    Sarabande.
    Minuet.

Summer Land.
    Play-time.
    A Song from the East.
    Evening Idyll.
    Fairy Folk.

Three Frivolous Pieces.

Three Little Waltzes.
    Allegretto poco scherzando.
    Andante languido.
    Allegretto.

*Three Pastorales.
    Allegretto.
    Con delicatezza.
    Pensoso.

Twilight Tide.

*Two Alpine Sketches (easy).

Two Sketches.
    Cuckoo Call.
    Twilight Bells.

Valse caprice.

Vesperale.

Vistas, Three Pieces.
    A Lonely Dell.
    In the Forest.
    A Jocund Dance.

Waterwagtail (Bergeronette).

Young Hearts, two series of five pieces each.

Zoo Animals for Piano.

Publishers: Ric., Schott, Schirm., Elkins.

A complete list of his piano works may be had from Elkins and Co., London.

The mood evoked in France by Debussy found an echo in England in Cyril Scott, a writer of taste, who has experimented interestingly with the newer harmonies. The rather formidable list of his works includes already about seventy-five piano pieces, nearly one hundred songs, and some chamber music. It makes one wonder whither he is tending and whether or not one may expect some day a new manner. A closer inspection reveals a quality of fragility and unsubstantiality not altogether reassuring in respect to its permanence. Meanwhile, however, many of his compositions have attained widespread popularity. The "Danse nègre," "Lotusland," and "Garden of Soul Sympathy," are frequently played. The Concerto, scored in a novel manner with all sorts of percussion instruments, achieves curious effects.

The revival of ancient British melodies with advanced harmonies cannot be called successful, though it is an effort to see tunes in a new light. The "Handelian Rhapsody" and the "Jungle Book Impressions" are counted by British critics among his best inspirations. With "Modern Finger Exercises" he makes a beginning along a new path, but the exercises are so extremely easy that they are only for beginners. Anyone finding augmented chords and the whole-tone scale strange might be helped by these exercises.

ALEXANDER SCRIABIN

(1872-1915)

Op. 1. Valse, Fm (Jurgenson).
Op. 2. Étude, Prélude, Impromptu à la Mazur.
Op. 3. Ten Mazurkas (Jurgenson).
Op. 4. Allegro appassionato.
Op. 5. Two Nocturnes (Jurgenson).
Op. 6. Sonata No. 1, Fm.
Op. 7. Two Impromptus à la Mazur (Jurgenson).
Op. 8. Twelve Études.
Op. 9. Prelude and Nocturne for the Left Hand Alone.
Op. 10. Two Impromptus.
Op. 11. Twenty-four Preludes (in all keys).
Op. 12. Two Impromptus.

Op. 13. Six Preludes.
Op. 14. Two Impromptus.
Op. 15. Five Preludes.
Op. 16. Five Preludes.
Op. 17. Seven Preludes.
Op. 18. Allegro de Concert, Bbm.
Op. 19. No. 2, G♯m, Sonate-Fantaisie.
Op. 20. Concerto, F♯m.
Op. 21. Polonaise.
Op. 22. Four Preludes.
Op. 23. Sonata No. 3, F♯m.
Op. 25. Nine Mazurkas.
Op. 27. Two Preludes.
Op. 28. Fantasia, F♯m.
Op. 30. Sonata No. 4, F♯.

Op. 31. Four Preludes.

Op. 32. Two Poems.

Op. 33. Four Preludes.

Op. 34. Tragedy.

Op. 35. Three Preludes.

Op. 36. Satanic Poem.

Op. 37. Four Preludes.

Op. 38. Waltz, A♭.

Op. 39. Four Preludes.

Op. 40. Two Mazurkas.

Op. 41. Poem, D♭.

Op. 42. Eight Études.

Op. 44. Two Poems.

Op. 45. Three Pieces.
Feuille d'album.
Poème fantasque.
Prélude.

Op. 46. Scherzo, C.

Op. 47. Quasi-valse.

Op. 48. Four Preludes.

Op. 49. Étude, Prélude, Rêverie.

Op. 51. Fragility, Prélude, Poème ailé, Danse languide.

Op. 52. Poème, Enigma, Poème languide (E.M.R.).

Op. 53. Sonata No. 5, F♯ (E.M.R.).

Op. 56. Prélude, Ironies, Nuances, Étude.

Op. 57. Désir, Caresse dansée.

Op. 58. Feuillet d'album (E.M.R.).

Op. 60. An important piano part in the "Prometheus," for orchestra.

Op. 61. Poème nocturne (E.M.R.).

Op. 62. Sonata No. 6 (E.M.R.).

Op. 63. Masques, Étrangeté (E.M.R.).

Op. 64. Sonata No. 7 (E.M.R.).

Op. 65. Three Études. (Jurgenson).
In ninths.
In augmented sevenths.
In fifths.

Op. 66. Sonata No. 8.

Op. 67. Two Preludes.

Op. 68. Sonata No. 9.

Op. 69. Two Poems.

Op. 70. Sonata No. 10.

Op. 71. Two Poems.

Op. 72. Vers la flamme.

Op. 73. Guirlandes, Flammes sombres.

Op. 74. Five Preludes.

Posthumously published Fantasia.

Poem in Form of a Sonata.
(Both edited by Sabaneff. Breit.)

Jurgenson publishes everything from Op. 65 on.

Publishers: Belaiev (except where noted), Jurgenson, E.M.R., U.E.

More than with any other composer of recent times the pianist has to concern himself with Scriabin. His figure looms too large and he is still too close to be a subject for ripe judgment, but a man who wrote exclusively for the piano (his symphonies are regarded by orchestral conductors as orchestrated piano idiom), who wrote ten great sonatas, and who imagined a new harmony and a new emotional outlook deserves profound study from the pianist who is deeply concerned with his art. Scriabin has two roles: he was an experimentalist who occupied himself with new harmonies and new rhythms, and an emotionalist, sometimes almost a sentimentalist, who strove to have every phrase come from the heart and who never lost himself in imitation of some older model—at least not after he had renounced the Chopin pattern of his early works. In some of the pieces one finds a disconcerting sweetness which may carry in itself the seeds of decay, but he wrote singularly little that is either commonplace or stupid. Although one may not compare him favorably with Chopin for invention on technical pianistic lines, one may say with truth that no man since Chopin has added more richly or entertainingly to the repertory of pianists.

Scriabin was a great pianist himself, but he was interested primarily in musical rather than in keyboard goals, and thus his compositions are first of all music. He produced in his soaring ecstatic way a new type of technique which embraced the entire range of the keyboard. It was apparently an unstudied type of technique, unlike that of previous writers, for it abjured scales, arpeggios, and all stereotyped forms. Trills occur more and more frequently as one approaches the end of his work until they become almost a mannerism, but they lose the older effect of the trill and become curious nervous things, vibrant with emotion. The technique is born of emotion and is not a dress put on the music to produce a more striking concert-hall effect.

Rhythm interested Scriabin more and more as he progressed. In some of his later works it becomes so complicated and subtle as to be almost inexpressible. He endeavored at times, witness the opening pages of the fifth Sonata, to write out the *tempo rubato* for the player by constantly changing the time signature, so that the performer has only to play strictly in time to appear to be playing freely. His demands on the player from this standpoint are severe, for he is not always so helpful as in this Sonata. Several rhythms proceed at the same time and are tossed from hand to hand, in a sort of jugglery.

His first departure from general usage in harmony was his development of chords of the seventh on the second step, for example in the first movement of the "Sonate-Fantaisie." His next change was in the development of dominant seventh and ninth chords with either augmented or diminished fifths (worked out in Op. 30 to 40). In Op. 53, the fifth Sonata, and thereafter, he makes another departure, more radical than these, by arbitrarily choosing certain notes, frequently a fourth apart, building them up four and five stories high and treating them as a consonance. His harmony becomes more and more obscure toward the end until in Op. 74 it casts off all bonds.

These chords built up on fourths were formerly called "mystic" chords. They are indeed mysterious as to their meaning, and it is uncertain as to how listeners eventually will react to them. With these chords Scriabin begins his

explorations in new harmonic fields. He has been called a composer of program music, but this is clearly wrong. His titles designate exclusively emotional states and nothing more. Such titles as "Prelude," "Étude," "Sonata,"
"Impromptu," "Concerto," "Valse," and "Nocturne"—some of them repeated too often—recall Chopin, under whose influence Scriabin grew up.
Other titles—"Poem," "Caresse dansée," "Désir," "Vers la flamme," "Enigma," "Ironies," "Flammes sombres,"—obviously indicate emotional states
rather than things. In his instructions he requests one to play, for example,
with *"une douceur de plus en plus empoissonée."* Scriabin endeavored to get
away from the traditional Italian markings, such as *"allegro agitato,"* and
"andante espressivo," and he substituted markings like "proudly," "bellicose,"
"like a cry," "with veiled joy," "with ravishment," "with false sweetness,"
"winged," "enigmatically," "fragile," "lugubriously," "with sudden strangeness," and "menacingly."

The idea that Scriabin's music is atonal lingers in the minds of many.
Those who cling exclusively to the older beauty need not fear to approach
any composition up to Op. 53. After that he begins to experiment with chords
that seem to the layman artificially created. Atonality is an elastic term, and
perhaps it has never been accurately defined. In the conception of many it
includes any chord not easily recognized, or any unusual harmonic progressions. For those unacquainted with Scriabin's music a progressive scheme is
appended with the hope that it may be of assistance to those for whom advanced harmonies are incomprehensible. No indication of the difficulty of the
composition is indicated in this list:

> Group 1. Op. 8, 11, 15, 16, 19, 20.
> Group 2. Op. 30, 32, 36, 42, 51, 52, 53,
> 57.
> Group 3. Op. 58, 62, 65, 68, 69, 70.
> Group 4. Op. 64, 66, 71, 72, 73, 74.

Group 1 contains nothing which could offend the most conservative taste;
Group 2 takes one gently to the door of the "unknown"; Group 3 opens wide
the door; and Group 4 discloses the paradise or the inferno, according to one's
temperament. It may be remarked here that from Op. 53 on the compositions
are generally rather dissonant. Op. 11 is a delightful collection—Chopin style
with Russian sauce, to begin with. It consists of twenty-four preludes in all

keys, and all are very pleasing. Josef Lhevinne told me that, on playing the études for him, Scriabin himself laughed at the ambitious markings he had so exuberantly placed there and said they were ridiculous. It is pleasant to know that one need not forego the études for lack of sufficient velocity.

The study of the sonatas gives enormous pleasure. They represent various phases of Scriabin's development and are important in his artistic life. The group may be compared with the *Well-tempered Clavichord* and with the sonatas of Beethoven or the works of Chopin, for it represents another peak of the literature. The first Sonata is Brahmsian, with an added Russian coloring; the second, third, and fourth are similar in character, but become more personally Scriabinesque; the fifth represents the turning point in his harmonic freedom and therefore occupies an important place; the sixth, seventh, and eighth are very difficult and frankly in the new harmony; the ninth is less strange harmonically, but is of an introspective character; the tenth, also generally less unfamiliar harmonically, is rather open and beautiful. Analyses of the second, fifth, and ninth sonatas are appended for assistance to those unaccustomed to Scriabin's style. These analyses, from the different periods, may aid in the study of the other sonatas.

SONATE-FANTAISIE, OP. 19

This romantically beautiful composition represents Scriabin at the height of his first period, when memories of the vanishing romantic German period still haunt him. It is in two movements, of 136 and 110 measures and stands in the key of G♯ minor, though the first movement closes in E major. The first movement was written in 1892, the second in 1897. In mood they are contrasting and complementary, and the first retains the old sonata form. Scriabin's sonatas have one to four movements, but they usually follow the classic form and frequently, strange to say, the four or eight-measure group or phrase.

Three themes are developed in the first movement of this work. A very striking and beautiful theme is rhythmically animated in a way that evidently pleased the composer so well that it is found also in the following Sonata, in the Concerto, and in some of the shorter pieces. This is succeeded by a long melodious passage into which the first theme often breaks, and from it emerges a theme dealt with in the development; an unforgettable and eloquent expressive theme of only three and one-half measures follows. The development is short, only twenty-nine measures, but remarkably skillful, vigorous, and terse. It contains, aside from a few harmonic notes, nothing whatever but the three themes united most happily. Chords of the seventh on the second step give the movement its peculiar essence. These soft harmonies are in contrast to the simple tonics and dominants of the close and to the vigorous dramatic rhythms of the opening. The end of the movement recalls vaguely the "Magic Fire" scene in mood, though not in any other way.

The second movement is a sort of perpetual motion, though the motion is not always in the same hand. It suggests somewhat the finale of Chopin's Sonata in Bb minor, the "wind-over-the-graves" movement. The emotional difference might be expressed in this way: The human element in the Chopin piece has had its say and has gone, leaving nature alone; in the Scriabin work there still remains a tragic mourning human figure depicted by a noble melody.

SONATA, OP. 53, F♯ MAJOR

This work marks the turning point in Scriabin's style. It consists of 455 measures played without pause. The introduction, in forty-six measures, has two distinct parts; the first is a short, extravagantly impetuous allegro of twelve measures, like the rude tearing away of an obstruction to the vision. The passage which rips across the keyboard and sounds exceedingly unorthodox, harmonically speaking, is found to be on closer inspection nothing in the world but the E major scale with its D♯, A, and E stressed. This probably should be classed as a "mystic" chord. The second part of the introduction brings a theme destined to considerable importance. The languid quality is admirably expressed by a constantly changing time signature. Its thirty-four measures occur three times in the course of the Sonata, the second time transposed up a tone, and, finally, in the coda, where, immensely broadened and abridged, it shrieks out its curious message in the highest register of the piano. It is a strange, formless, embryonic tune, curiously harmonized; it probably serves to characterize those hidden forces alluded to in the verse from the "Poem of Ecstasy" placed at the head of the work. In the development, strange to say, it is used but sparingly.

The main body of the work now appears and progresses without let or hindrance for three pages in a steady flow of music. There is a principal theme and two trumpet-like motifs, both used again later. The true second subject, of twenty measures, is a sensuous melody supported by strange harmonies. The development is ushered in by a new and strongly rhythmical motif, which after seventeen measures is interrupted by the motif of the opening. Again the veil is torn away, and the languid theme of the hidden forces revealed, this time reduced to nineteen measures. Then, suddenly, the development begins again and proceeds for seven pages that close in a gorgeous and passionate climax. The twenty measures of the second subject are heard again, and the Sonata is brought to a close with one of Scriabin's cyclonic codas of fifty-five measures. Scriabin uses the words "vertiginous," "furious," "fantastic," and even "inebriated" to indicate the meaning. The player who does not become ecstatic in the course of the performance must indeed be emotion proof, or else too much occupied by hosts of enormous and curious chords to be able to allow himself the luxury of becoming "inebriated."

Some further account of the Sonata should perhaps be given, for it represents the turning point in the composer's career, and one can well imagine his excitement at having discovered a new path. Like many of his pieces which had their genesis as studies or offshoots of important and larger things he was writing, it is said to be an offshoot of his fourth Symphony, *The Poem of Ecstasy*. It was dashed off at white heat in five days at Lausanne in 1908. With this work he turns away from his old style and remains faithful to the new discovery to the end. At the beginning of this Sonata stands a verse from the "Poem of Ecstasy" in Russian and French:

> I call to you, O mysterious forces,
> Submerged in depths obscure
> Of the creator spirit, timid embryons of life;
> To you I now bring courage.

He still retains the key signature, which he soon abandons as unnecessary, and the Sonata is curiously formal in the old sense. It has the statement-development-recapitulation formula as well as the four-bar phrase idea. The technical demands of this work are not of the bravura type; the difficulties arise rather from the inner complexity, the unusual harmonies, and the intensity of emotion. His ever-increasing power over the entire keyboard at once serves to complicate matters. The task set is severe, but of fascinating aspect. From the opening threatening rumors in the bass to the last shriek at the close, the tension is constant. Scriabin, in his harmonization of the second subject, here first gives a glimpse of those chords described as "mystic," built up in fourths or according to some new formula of his invention.

SONATA, OP. 68

This sonata was begun in 1911 and finished in 1913 in Moscow. It is a work in one movement and cannot strictly be called a sonata, since it lacks a recapitulation and joins its vertiginous coda to the development. This interesting change may be regarded as the only original suggestion as to the future development of the sonata offered by Scriabin.

An atmospheric, chromatic passage opens the work, after which the first theme appears in the bass. It is short, rhythmically impressive, and interesting. Supporting this motif is a harmony very similar to one in the fifth sonata, of a diminished fifth superimposed on a perfect fifth. This harmony dominates the entire sonata and gives it its intrinsic character. The trills which Scriabin uses to excess in his later sonatas appear in this one. No one ever used them just as he does. Their effect is bizarre. After they cease the second theme enters, very tentatively at first, as if trying out its opening measure before proceeding. It is marked *avec langueur naissante* and is a rather fragmentary affair of three phrases in as many measures. The development begins presently with a résumé of the opening measures. This is the longest section of the piece and necessarily so, since there is no recapitulation. It is a trifle rambling, but of real interest.

It is difficult to determine just where the coda begins, one might even say that there is no coda. The second theme, now grown bolder through its various metamorphoses, appears in various rhythms accompanied by peculiar changing harmonies, though chiefly by the harmony described above. This theme is the last heard, although a section of one of the others supplies rhythmical life to the rest. At the end the ethereal harmonies of the beginning again resound, and the work dies away pianissimo.

The ultimate impression is one of darkness. Scriabin called it a "Black Mass" and probably intended an effect of diabolism. The effect is undoubtedly weird and to many people repulsive. To those who see beauty only in pleasant things there is little to admire in it, but there is something of the poisonous beauty of the snake, especially toward the end when the second theme stands out in insistent dissonances against the curious basic chord mentioned. There is a brilliant glitter that is almost evil. The close, before the somber atmosphere settles down, is a triumph of satanic power; it might be compared to a nightmare. It is much more of a "satanic poem" than the one so named (Op. 36), for Scriabin had penetrated far more deeply into the expression of the darker emotions by this time.

CONCERTO, OP. 20

Attention is called to the Concerto, a lovely lyrical work of no great difficulty, and most satisfying to play. There is only one weak spot, the first part of the finale, which is a rather dull rondo; but that spot passed, the rest is effective and melodious.

CHRISTIAN SINDING

(1856—)

Op. 2. Variations, for two pianos, E♭ (Hansen).

Op. 3. Suite.
Prélude.
Courante.
Sarabande.
Gavotte.
Presto.

Op. 6. Concerto, D♭.

Op. 7. Studies.
(All Hansen)

Op. 24. Five Piano Pieces.

Op. 31. Seven Piano Pieces.

Op. 32. Six Piano Pieces (No. 3, "Frühlingsrauschen").

Op. 33. Six Character Pieces.

Op. 34. Six Character Pieces.

Op. 35. Suite (four hands).
(All Peters)

Op. 44. Fifteen Capriccios.

Op. 48. Six Burlesques.
Burlesque.
Plaisanterie.
Bagatelle.
Coquetterie.
Étude melodique.
Arlequinade.

Op. 49. Six Character Pieces.
Prélude.
Minuetto.
Concert étude.
Humoresque.
Arabesque.
Pittoresque.

Op. 52. Mélodies mignonnes.

Op. 53. Character Pieces.

Op. 54. Four Morceaux de salon.

Op. 58. Five Études.
(All Hansen)

Op. 59. Waltzes (four hands).

Op. 65. Intermezzi.

Op. 74. Six Pieces.

Op. 76. Ten Pieces.

Op. 82. Ten Pieces.

Op. 84. Four Pieces.
Aube.
Rivage.
Decision.
Joie.

Op. 88. Three Pieces (Schott).
In the Spring.
Nocturne.
Humoresque.

Op. 91. Fatum Variations (Breit.).

Op. 97. Five Pieces (Schott).
Le Matin.
Sur l'eau.
Intermezzo.
L'Orage.
Aquarelle.

Op. 103. Tone Pictures.
Frühlingswetter.
Reigen.
Scherzando.

Silhouette.
Stimmung.

Op. 110. Pieces of Medium Difficulty.

Op. 113. Five Pieces.
Alla burla.
Canzonetta.
Humoresque.
Mélodie.
Scherzino.

Op. 115. Six Pieces.

Op. 116. Three Intermezzi.

Op. 118. Five Fantasias.
Décision.
Meditation.
Caprice.
Nocturne.
Conte.

(All Breit.)

This list is not complete.

Publishers: Hansen, Peters, Breit., Schirm., Schott, Simrock.

The nomenclature of Sinding's piano pieces is depressing. What sort of individualized reactions can one get from "Six Piano Pieces," "Ten Piano Pieces," "Seven Piano Pieces," or "Fifteen Capriccios?" It reads like an auction list. To be fair, however, one should say that several of these opus numbers have titles, and after all, Bach called most of his pieces "Prelude and Fugue," Beethoven called many of his "Sonata," and Brahms used the terms "Intermezzo" or "Capriccio." A fecund composer should keep a person to name his pieces. It might have been a full-time job with Sinding, whose pieces are as standardized as Fords equipped with interchangeable parts.

Sinding's Scandinavianism brought promise of a new Grieg, but his paucity of invention as regards passage work, the chief glory of the keyboard, is obvious to the most casual observer, and, after Grieg, his melodies are lacking in charm. It seems, on looking deeper into this music, as if it were obvious even to the composer that it was impossible for him to escape from the nightmare grip in which the arpeggios and scales held him, for he tried to distract attention from his difficulties by an agile jumping from key to key. This is intended to appear daring, but it achieves only a restless, undignified, and futile result.

The long "Fatum Variations" are probably intended to present a summing up of his entire art after the manner of Bach, Beethoven, and Brahms; but the moments of grandeur, not to mention interest, are too few to carry player and listener through thirty-eight large and finely printed pages. So, too, some of the other works though they have moments of charm, end by boring one. Sinding possessed a fatal fluency.

Aside from the chamber music which is his best work—the quintet is really striking—the Concerto is probably his best piece. It possesses considerable style. It is a pleasure to find Wagner's elemental idiom peeping out at us. The slow movement is especially attractive in its folklore style.

FRIEDRICH SMETANA
(1824-1884)

Op. 1. Six morceaux caractéristiques.

Op. 2. Feuillets d'album, six pieces (2 vols.).

Op. 4. Sketches, four pieces.

Op. 5. Sketches, four pieces.

Op. 7. Trois polkas de salon.

Op. 8. Trois polkas poétiques.

Op. 12. Souvenirs de Bohème (polkas).

Op. 13. Souvenirs de Bohème (polkas).

Op. 17. Étude de concert, "Na brehu morskem" ("By the Seashore").

WITHOUT OPUS NUMBER

À Nos jeunes filles.

À Robert Schumann.

Rêves, six pieces.
Lost Happiness.
Consolation.
In Bohemia.
In the Salon.
At the Castle.
Kermess in Bohemia.

Danses tchèques (2 vols.).
Vol. 1. Polkas.
Vol. 2. Furiant, Slepicka, Oves, Medved, Cibulka, Dupak, Hulan, Obkrocak, Skocna, Sousedska.

Fantaisie de concert, on Czech national airs.

POSTHUMOUS WORKS

Feuillets d'album.

Caprice in C.

Bagatelles.

Impromptus.

Allegro capriccioso, and Romance.

Three Études, C, A, C.

COLLECTIONS

The Polkas (3 vols.), ed. by Roman Vesely.

Smetana Album, twelve pieces (Schirm).

Choix de Compositions (3 vols.: Vol. I, easy; Vol. II, difficult; Vol. III, very difficult, ed. by H. de Kaan).

A *Collection of thirty excellent pieces is also published by U.E. It has 125 pages and is probably the best way of buying Smetana, for it gives one his most important compositions.

Publishers: Forberg, Urbanek, U.E., Hudebni Matice. Everything is now published by the last named and available through U.E.

The piano works of this minor poet have been neglected by the public at large. What Chopin did for the mazurka, Smetana did for his national dance, the polka, in which field he achieved charming results. The only piece which has attained widespread fame is the étude "By the Seashore." Certain of the second volume of "Danses tchèques" might well be added to the lighter side of one's repertory. Though all Smetana's pieces are strongly, one might say unashamedly, national in character, he is the least provincial Czech composer and the one who best rewards the explorer.

Those interested in the polka as a dance and as an art form may find interesting material in "Souvenirs du temps jadis," a collection of old Czech polkas (Hudebni Matice) by Jaraslav Bradac.

MISCELLANEOUS SPANISH COMPOSERS

P. J. ANTONIO

Preludios vascos ("Basque Preludes"),
    four books containing twenty-one
    pieces (Casa Erviti).

JOAQUÍN CASSADÓ
(1867-1926)

Hispania, with orchestra (Mathot).

OSCAR ESPLÁ
(1886—)

Romanza antiqua.

MANUEL DE FALLA
(1876—)

Valse caprice.
Serenata andaluza.
Nocturne.
    (All Orfeo Tracio, S. A. Madrid)
*Noches en los jardines de España, with
    orchestra (Eschig).
*Pièces espagnoles (Durand).
    Aragonese.
    Cubaña.
    Montañesa.
    Andaluza.

*Fantasia Baetica (Chest.).
Homenaje por "Le Tombeau de Claude
    Debussy" (Chest.).
Concerto, for clavicembalo and small or-
    chestra (Eschig).

MANUEL INFANTE
(1904—)

Sevillana (Impressions des fêtes à Seville).

*El Vito (variations on a popular theme and original dance. A simplified edition also exists).

Gitanerias.
(All Mathot)

*Danses andalouses, for two pianos.
Ritmo.
Sentimiento.
Gracia.

FEDERICO MOMPOU
(1895—)

Suburbia, five pieces.
Fêtes lointaines, six pieces.

Scènes d'enfants.
(All Senart)

JOAQUÍN NIN Y CASTELLANO
(1883—)

Sixteen Sonatas by Old Spanish Composers (2 vols. Eschig).
Vol. I. Soler, Albéniz, Cantallos, Serrano, Ferrer.

Vol. II. Rodriguez, Soler, Freixanet, Casanovas, Angles, Galles.
Canço i dança populare (U.M.E.).
Danza ibérica (Eschig).

ADOLFO SALAZAR
(1890—)

Tres preludios (Chest.).

JOAQUÍN TURINA
(1882—)

Trois danses andalouses (R.L.).
Petenera.
Tango.
Zapateado.
Femmes d'Espagne (R.L.).
La Madrileña classique.
L'Andalouse sentimentale.
La Brune coquette.
Contes d'Espagne, Histoires en sept tableaux (*Nos. 3, 4. R.L.).
Coins de Seville, suite of four pieces (Eschig).
Soir d'été.
Ronde d'enfants.
Danses de "Seises" dans la cathédral.
A los toros.

Danzas fantásticas (Chest.; U.M.E.).
Exaltación.
Ensueño.
Orgia.
Recuerdos de mi rincón, Tragedia cómica (U.M.E.).
Album de viaje (U.M.E.).
Jardins d'Andalouse, three pieces (R.L.).
Sonate romantique sur un thème espagnol (Eschig).
*Sanlucar de Barrameda, sonata pintoresca (U.M.E.).
Ocean Voyage, three pieces.
Circus, suite of six pieces.

191

ROGELIO VILLAR
(1873—)

Canción española.

Paginas líricas.

Serenata andaluza.

Canciones leonesas, twenty-five pieces.
  (All Orfeo Tracio)

Danzas montanesas (2 vols. U.M.E.).

Pièces espagnoles, three pieces (Matamala).

Other writers include Pedrell, the pioneer Spanish composer who wrote five pieces for piano, Bacarisse, Font y de Anta, Beobide, Burges, Arregui, and Pahissa.

Since the death of Granados, De Falla has been the premier Spanish composer. He is primarily occupied with orchestral writing, but has given the piano a few pieces of value. First among them is the beautifully orchestrated and well-written *Noches en los jardines de España* ("Nights in the Gardens of Spain"), in which the piano is treated as an orchestral instrument. This piece is not "effective" for the piano, but it is so lovely and so full of entrancing atmosphere that it gives great pleasure to the student. Much is lost, of course, if one plays it with a second piano (when the piece is played as a duet), for the thrills of harp, celeste, and strings *sul ponticello,* are then very much subdued. The "Pièces espagnoles" and the "Fantasia Baetica" (Baetica is the Latin name for Andalusia) are recommended. These pieces get away from the inferior type of Spanish dance, but retain the Spanish essence.

Infante offers lovers of two-piano playing the best opportunity of exploring Spanish rhythms and harmonies, for his "Danses andalouses" are genuinely entertaining. Although they are not easy and need careful study, they are rewarding. "Garcia" is a version for two pianos of the "El Vito," a most engaging though very light-minded set of variations.

Turina is next in importance. He is an excellent salon writer and, for those who like that style, offers good material. "Sanlucar de Barrameda" rises considerably above the rest of his piano works in point of seriousness and is not only musically interesting but effective as a concert sonata, though it is somewhat long. It can, however, be cut. This is a good piece for one who would like a Spanish sonata which gets away from the more or less commonplace Spanish dance type.

Mompou has a phobia. He fears bar signs, and at first glance his pages look novel and amusing, but they turn out to be simple, and one finds the music singularly rhythmical and four-square.

Villar is inadequately educated as a composer, but shows talent. He uses folk melodies as a basis for some of his collections of pieces.

Antonio is also unimportant as a composer. He is listed here only for those who would like to become acquainted with the music of the Basques. The preludes are only sketchily done, and the composer seems content to reproduce the song rather literally without trying to get it into piano idiom.

Salazar and Cassadó are likewise unimportant.

Spanish composers have been so obsessed by their national music that it has been a positive drawback to them. They have been standardized, but at present there is some improvement. Albéniz, Granados, De Falla, and Turina have written music which, although still recognizable as Spanish, attains a broad and firm musical basis.

KAROL SZYMANOWSKI

(1883-1937)

Op. 1. Nine Preludes (1900-02).

Op. 4. Four Études, Ebm, Gb, Bbm, C (1903).

Op. 8. Sonata No. 1 (1905, later awarded a prize).

Op. 10. Variations on a Polish Folk Song (ten variations; 22 pages).

Op. 21. Sonata No. 2, Am.

Op. 29. Metopes.
  The Isle of the Sirens.
  Calypso.
  Nausicaä.

Op. 33. Twelve Études (22 pages, intended to be played without pause).

Op. 34. Masques: Three Pieces.
  Scheherazade.
  Don Juan.
  Tantris.

Op. 36. Sonata No. 3.

Op. 50. Mazurkas (5 vols.).

WITHOUT OPUS NUMBERS

Symphonie concertante, with orchestra.
Four Mazurkas.
Preludes and Fugues.

Variations.
Publisher: U.E.

Undoubtedly the most important composer of the day, Karol Szymanowski has written music so rich in ideas, so exuberant in harmony, and so lively in rhythm that one may assign him a high place in art. His first manner, unlike that of most composers who patterned at first on older models, was entirely his own, uninfluenced by other writers and more strictly personal even than that of Scriabin. Harmonically one may draw the line between Op. 21 and Op. 29, where his second manner begins. Sonata Op. 21 is the climax of his first period and is a work of such magnitude and intricacy that many will turn from it discouraged, but it is full of interest. It is in two movements, the first in regular sonata form, the second slow movement and finale in one. The form of this second part is particularly interesting. It begins with a theme of sixteen measures and several variations and slips into a saraband of thirty-six measures followed by a cadenza, a minuet of fifty-nine bars, a return to the beginning, and a development of eighty-four measures, succeeded by a closing section consisting of a fugue of eighty-five more measures. It is, of course, merely a highly sophisticated form of theme-and-variation style, but the appearance of a sarabande, a minuet, and a cadenza gives the pages a strange look. They are black with notes from the conclusion of the minuet on, and the massive chordal progressions are intricate and difficult, but the music is of an unusually high quality and is worth the trouble, even if merely to struggle through it once. The close is jubilant and ecstatic. As introductory studies to this music Op. 1, 4, and 10 are recommended; all of these are within the grasp of a good pianist. Op. 1 is the simplest, but harmonically even this will be found not easy to master.

It is difficult to comment on the works of Szymanowski's second manner, for they drift into a region remote from tradition. They offer to the eye most extraordinary pictures, drawn by a mind rich in the power to invent harmonic and rhythmic intricacies. The effects are never duplicated, and something new greets one on every page. The third Sonata is to be played without pause. A grotesque and gnomelike fugue forms a finale to the work. It is almost clownish in its tumblings and is amusingly harmonized, sometimes with minor seconds. The first movement (presto) and the second (adagio) are fairly well articulated. "Masques," "Metopes," and the "Twelve Études" are only for virtuosi who have the modern harmonic sense, but they all give the impression of intellectual power of a new order and present technical novelties of great interest as well as a harmonic scheme of a personal nature. This type of composition, dependent as it is on contrasting sonorities to clarify its advanced harmony to the listener, is not at its best on the piano, whose colder and more monotonous tone quality ill reflects the shimmering, finely nuanced timbres obviously desired by the composer.

CARL TAUSIG
(1841-1871)

ORIGINAL WORKS

Op. 1. Das Geisterschiff (Schuberth).

Op. 1. Études de concert: F♯, A♭ (Senff).

(Duplication of Op. 1 was caused by mis-understanding between publishers.)

Op. 2. Reminiscences of "Halka" by Moniuszko (Schuberth).

Valse caprices (Peters).
*Nachtfalter, E♭.
*Man lebt nur einmal, C.
Wahlstimmen, A.

*Hungarian Gipsy Melodies (Senff).

L'Espérance, Nocturne varié (Schirm.).

TRANSCRIPTIONS

Scarlatti, D......*Sonata, Gm.
*Sonata, Fm.
*Sonata, Gm.
*Sonata, ("Pastorale"), Em.
*Sonata ("Capriccio"), E.
(Steingr., Peters, Ric., and others)

Schubert ......*Op. 51. Military March, D♭.
*Op. 75. No. 3, Polonaise, C♯m.
*Andantino varié.
Op. 84, No. 2. Rondo, on French motifs.

Bach..........*Toccata and Fugue, Dm.

Berlioz .... Chorus of Gnomes and Dance of the Sylphs.

Schumann .....*Der Contrabandista (Schlesinger and Roszavölgyi).

Wagner .... Three Paraphrases from *Tristan*.
Siegmund's Love Song.
Ride of the Valkyries.
(Last three, Schott)

Weber ....*Op. 65. Invitation to the Dance.

ÉTUDE WORKS

Clementi ......*A Condensation of the "Gradus ad Parnassum."

Tausig-Ehrlich . Daily Studies.

Publishers: Steingr. (the chief), Schuberth, Senff, Schott, Schirm.

Steingräber publishes three volumes which contain practically everything.

Tausig is known chiefly for his transcriptions of Bach, Schubert, and Scarlatti, which were at the time epoch-making and still stand unchallenged. Some of his original things, however, are also worth reviving now and then. The two waltzes, "Nachtfalter" and "Man lebt nur einmal," are not very difficult (unlike Godowsky's more recent efforts in this field), and the "Hungarian Gipsy Melodies," though somewhat long (but may be cut), is musically so excellent and differs so radically from Liszt's rhapsodies that one should make an effort to acquaint oneself with it. The piece is in two sections, with a dizzy but logical, splendid, and playable coda. It does not suffer from the lack of cohesion which mars some of Liszt's rhapsodies.

"Das Geisterschiff" is a not too successful kind of ballade with a spooky program. It is better adapted to the orchestra. The "Halka" Fantasia, a once immensely popular piece, appears no more. Who knows it now except by reputation? The two études are good salon music, smooth and fluent; they are better than many published since. The reduction of the Clementi "Gradus ad Parnassum" to reasonable size was an excellent inspiration of Tausig's. He eliminated all the polyphonic parts—Bach is available for that sort of practice.

It is to the transcriptions that one turns, after all, to appreciate the great and lasting contributions Tausig made to the literature. First and foremost is the superb arrangement of the organ Toccata and Fugue in D minor. It achieved instant and wide popularity, which it has retained for at least sixty years. It is doubtful if any pianist with any claim to distinction has not studied it. Almost equal fame attends the "Pastorale" and "Capriccio" sonatas of Scarlatti, for they have also become permanent additions to the literature. Why do not pianists play the other three of this group? They are all three as good and in some ways better than the two celebrated ones. The "Military March" of Schubert was also one of the favorites of pianists of bygone days. If played with spirit it is still worth hearing. Less known though very beautiful are the "Andantino varié" and the "Polonaise," also by Schubert. That rakish song by Schumann, "Der Contrabandista," is a vigorous dashing piece that is good fun to play, as are, for one's own delectation, the Wagner transcriptions. Pianists are deeply indebted to this musician.

PETR TCHAIKOVSKY

(1840-1893)

*Op. 1. Scherzo à la russe, Impromptu.

*Op. 2. Ruines d'un château, Scherzo, Chant sans paroles.

Op. 4. Valse.

*Op. 5. Romance, Fm.

Op. 7. Valse scherzo.

Op. 9. Rêverie, Polka de salon, *Mazurka.

Op. 10. Nocturne, *Humoresque.

Op. 19. Six Pieces.

Rêverie du soir.
Scherzo humoristique.
Feuillet d'album.
Nocturne.
Capriccio.
*Theme and Variations.

Op. 21. Six Pieces on One Theme.
Prelude.
Fugue, G♯m.
Impromptu, C♯m.
Marche funèbre.
*Mazurka, G♯m.
*Scherzo, A.

*Op. 23. Concerto No. 1, B♭m.

Op. 26. Sérénade mélancholique.

*Op. 37a. Sonata, G (Jurgenson).

Op. 37b. The Months.
Jan. At the Fireside.
Feb. Carnaval.
Mar. *Song of the Lark.
Apr. Snowdrops.
May Bright Nights.
June *Barcarolle.
July Song of the Reaper.
Aug. The Harvest.
Sept. Hunting Song.
Oct. Autumn Song.
Nov. *Troika.
Dec. Christmas.

Op. 39. Children's Album, twenty-four Pieces (Schott; Breit.).

Op. 40. Twelve Pieces (easy. Schott).
Étude.
Chanson triste.
Marche funèbre.
Mazurka.
Mazurka.
Chant sans paroles.
Au village.

Valse, A♭.
Valse, F♯.
Danse russe.
Scherzo.
Rêverie interrompu.

Op. 42. Souvenir d'un lieu cher.
Méditation.
Scherzo.
Mélodie.

Op. 44. Concerto No. 2, G (Jurgenson).

Op. 51. Valse, Polka, Menuet, Natha Valse, Romance, Valse.

Op. 56. Fantasie, with orchestra, Gm (Rahter).

*Op. 59. Doumka, Scène rustique russe (Jurgenson).

Op. 72. Eighteen Pieces (Schirm.).
Impromptu.
*Berceuse.
Tendres reproches.
*Danse caractéristique.
Méditation.
Mazourka pour danser.
Polacca de concert.
Dialogue.
Un Poco di Schumann.
Scherzo-Fantaisie.
Valse bluette.
L'Espiègle.
Echo rustique.
Chant élégiaque.
Un Poco de Chopin.
Valse à cinq temps.
Passé lointain.
*Invitation à la Trepak.

Op. 75. Concerto No. 3, E♭ (Rahter).

Op. 79. Andante and Finale, with orchestra (Belaiev).

WITHOUT OPUS NUMBER
(posthumous)

Impromptu-Caprice.
Impromptu, A♭.
Momento lirico.

Sonata, C♯m (sometimes listed as Op. 80).

TRANSCRIPTIONS
(also posthumous)

Mouvement perpétuel, after Weber (for the left hand alone).

Fifty Folk Songs (four hands).

TRANSCRIPTIONS OF TCHAIKOVSKY'S
MUSIC BY OTHER WRITERS

Pabst......Paraphrase on *Eugène One-gin*.

Pabst......Paraphrase on the *Sleeping Beauty*.

Grainger...Paraphrase on the "Flower Waltz."

Publishers: Bessel up to and including Op. 21, with reprints by other houses; then Jurgenson, Rahter, B. and B., Belaiev, Schott, and Schirm.

To the piano Tchaikovsky confided in the main his lighter ideas, and for this reason his hundred odd pieces are somewhat disappointing. Some half dozen works loom above the monotonous mass of salon music, a few of them unknown; these will repay the effort of acquaintance.

Op. 1 is an incredibly gaunt, rugged, massive, and elemental composition. What a start for all the tame waltzes, mazurkas, and *chansons sans paroles* that follow! It is interesting, not for content alone but also for its form, which is used in several of the other piano works and might be thought of as an adaptation of the passacaglia idea. A theme of eight measures endlessly repeated with ever changing variants grows ever wilder until, like the dancing dervishes, it drops from sheer dizziness. The effect is tragically intense, Oriental in its cumulative fatalism—a dance under the sword of Damocles—a pursuit by the Furies. Op. 1, the "Scherzo à la russe," has this demonic, ecstatic quality to a marked degree and is an important piece. It is not easy to play with the necessary reserve and power.

The "Doumka," Op. 59, is another important piece differing from most of the other pieces. For some reason no one plays it although it is a delight. It is a Slavic ballade—a Russian peasant scene. Its rather somber opening gives way presently to a rising vivacity that grows madder and madder until it collapses and one returns to sad reality.

The "Invitation à la Trepak," Op. 72, No. 18, is the third and last piece of this type; it is built on the already described plan, but its manner is more reserved. It is neither so long nor so wild nor so rugged as the first two, but none the less it is desirable as a concert number or for one's own pleasure.

In the Sonata in G, Op. 37*a*, a greater Tchaikovsky produced a long work of magnificent proportions, fine ideas, and great variety. It is national without being provincial, and when properly played gives an effect of overwhelming grandeur. It is the last great sonata of the romantic period, and as such it should be cherished. Its chief fault is that the opening section of the first movement occurs too often and is a trifle noisy; but if care be taken not to expend oneself on this part, if the climaxes are approached with discretion, and if the *pp* passages are treated with extra tenderness, the piano will be found capable of the task set. The adagio with its endearing second theme and its climaxes is superb; the scherzo, *ppp* throughout, elfin and fragile, is a welcome contrast; and the finale, a sort of rondo made of two strongly contrasting Slavic themes (one rather regal in its swing), more than adequately closes this dramatic and unusual work. It is really a symphony for piano. With regard to the dynamic marking of the coda, a modulated *ff* through to the end is far preferable to the anti-climactic *p* suggested by the composer. Cuts can be made in the rather uninteresting and repetitive opening section, but they are not satisfactory. The only way to play it is not to let down on the speed of performance each time this theme recurs.

The Concerto in B♭ minor is a notable favorite and has completely eclipsed "the other one," as Op. 44 is usually called, though there is a third. The melodies of Op. 44 are less inspiring, and there is a certain sobriety which acts depressingly on the spirits of those wanting a repetition of the thrill of Op. 23.

The posthumous sonata has moments of beauty, but is really not usable in its present form. Tchaikovsky knew it was not good and left it unpublished, but he used its scherzo, or rather, adapted it, to one of the symphonies. Some of the shorter pieces have moments of exquisite inspiration: the "Ruines d'un château" with its shadowy hunt; the languorous, dreamy "Berceuse"; the dramatic "Romance," Op. 5; the tuneful though sentimental "Méditation," Op. 72, No. 5; the sultry June "Barcarolle"; the wholesome "Theme and Variations," Op. 19, No. 6; and the romping "Danse caractéristique."

CARL MARIA VON WEBER

(1786-1826)

Op. 1. Six Fughettas (four hands).
Op. 2. Variations on an Original Theme.
Op. 5. Variations on "Castor and Pollux."

Op. 6. Variations on "Samori" (also with violin and cello).
Op. 7. Variations on "Vien quà, Dorina bella."

Op. 9. Variations on an Original Theme.

Op. 11. Grand Concerto in C, with orchestra.

Op. 12. Momento capriccioso (see Godowsky).

Op. 21. Grand Polonaise.

*Op. 24. Sonata No. 1, C (the finale is the celebrated "Perpetuum mobile"—see under Godowsky, Brahms, and Henselt).

Op. 28. Variations on "Joseph."

Op. 32. Grand Concerto, Eb, with orchestra.

*Op. 39. Sonata No. 2, Ab.

Op. 40. Variations on "Schöne Minka."

Op. 49. Sonata No. 3, Dm.

Op. 55. Variations on a Gipsy Song.

*Op. 62. Rondo brillant, Eb ("La Gaieté").

*Op. 65. Invitation to the Dance (see under Tausig, Henselt, and Godowsky).

Op. 70. Sonata No. 4, Em.

Op. 72. Polacca brillant (*transcribed by Liszt for piano and orchestra).

*Op. 79. Concertstück, Fm, with orchestra.

Six Ecossaises (Chest.).

Henselt has edited, adapted, partially transcribed, and rearranged Weber's compositions in the happiest manner. This edition is recommended as the best for the student of Weber. It is published by Schlesinger. The following pieces have been worked over: Op. 12, 21, 24, 39, 62, 72, 79, and the "Perpetuum mobile" as a separate piece, as already noted above.

The florid variation sets of Weber no longer thrill the nerves, and it is not to these that one turns to seek his nowadays much subdued voice, but rather to the sonatas (especially the first two), the perennial "Invitation to the Dance," the "Rondo brillant" (Op. 62), the "Concertstück," and the "Polacca brillant" in Liszt's transcription. These few pieces contain Weber's best and most enduring work for the piano. The rest may be left on the shelf until the taste of that day recurs.

Pianists who want to enjoy Weber must be in the mood to welcome gaiety, even frivolity, and willing to be amused with obsolete elegancies and polished manners, for even in his sonatas he does not don cap and gown. In a serious mood one turns to some other composer for solace. But in this frivolity and light-heartedness much real beauty resides which is easily overlooked by the seeker after the "big" things. The present is so sophisticated and difficult in its amusements that nothing short of Brahms or Bach will feed its fastidious musical intelligences. Often even Mozart is too light. Weber challenges one. If a pianist is too "high-brow" to be amused by him, let him take Franck or Brahms and leave Weber to the less self-conscious.

The attention of Weber students is directed to the first two sonatas, both of them romantic, *Freischütz*-like compositions, brilliant, smooth, and polished, but not dull or commonplace, even though the harmonies are not particularly striking. The slow movements are Weber's weakest side, the defect of his quality, but at least the one in the second sonata is effective and pianistic and flows along untroubled by deep feeling, for which technical devices are substituted—combined staccato and legato, melodic passage-work, octaves, and imitation of orchestral effects. The "Concertstück," grand old stand-by that it is, still occasionally makes a brave showing. It is interesting to recall that it was the first piece of its type, and that Mendelssohn was so entranced by it that he copied its form fairly literally in his "Capriccio brillant," Op. 22. The legato-staccato chords and melody as well as the march movements of both are obviously related. Op. 72 in the Liszt transcription is another brilliant piece. The Henselt arrangements should be used.

COMPOSITIONS FOR PIANO AND ORCHESTRA

The publishing houses are not listed here. If necessary, refer to a work as listed under the individual composer.

Albéniz, I. . . . . . Concerto.

Albert, E. d' . . . . Concerto, Op. 2 and Op. 15.

Alkan, C. . . . . . . Concerto da camera, Am.

Antheil, G. . . . . Concerto.

Arensky, A. . . . . Concerto, Op. 2, F.
Fantaisie russe, Op. 48.

Bach, C. P. E. . . Concertos for one and two pianos. (Also for three pianos.)

Bach, J. C. . . . . . Concertos in G, E, D, Bb, Eb.

Bach, J. S. . . . . . Concertos for one, two, and three pianos.
Concertos for piano, in connection with other solo instruments and quartet.

Bach, W. F. . . . . Concertos in Eb, Em, D, Am, F.

Bartók, B. . . . . . Rhapsody, Op. 1.
Concerto.

Becker, J. J. . . . . Concerto arabesque.

Beethoven, L. van . . . . Concertos in C, Bb, Cm, G, Eb.
Fantasia, with chorus.
Rondo, Bb (posthumous).

Bloch, E. . . . . . . Concerto grosso, with strings.

Blumenfeld, F. . Allegro de concert.

Bordes, C. . . . . . Rhapsodie basque.

Bortkiewicz, S. . Concerto, Bbm.

Brahms, J. . . . . . Concertos in Dm, Op. 15, and Bb, Op. 83.

Busoni, F. . . . . . Concerto, Op. 39, C, with chorus.
Concertino, Op. 31b, with additional movements published as Op. 54.
Indian Fantasia, Op. 44, based on American Indian themes.

Carpenter, J. A. . Concertino.

Casella, A. . . . . . A notte alta.

Catoire, G. . . . . Concerto.

Chausson, E. . . . "Concerto" for piano, violin, and quartet.

Chopin, F. . . . . Concertos, Em, Fm.
Andante spianato, and Polonaise.
Variations on "La ci darem la mano."
Fantasia on Polish Airs.
Krakoviak.

Copland, A. . . . Concerto.

Cowell, H. . . . . Concerto.

Debussy, C. . . . . Fantaisie.
Danse sacrée et danse profane, with strings.

Delius, F. . . . . . Concerto, Cm.

Dohnányi, E. . . Concerto, Op. 5.
Variations on a Children's Song.

Dussek, J. . . . . . Concerto, Gm, Op. 50 first movement only).

Falla, M. de . . . . Nights in the Gardens of Spain.
Concerto, for clavicembalo or piano, flute, oboe, clarinet, violin, and violon cello.

Fauré, G. . . . . . Ballade.
Fantaisie.

203

Field, J........Concerto, A♭ (first movement only).

Franck, C......Symphonic Variations. The Djinns.

Gershwin, G....Rhapsody in Blue. Concerto, F.

Glazunov, A....Concertos, Fm, Bm.

Godard, B......Concertos, Op. 31, 49, and 145.

Grieg, E. ......Concerto, Am.

Haba, A.......Concert symphonique, Op. 8.

Handel, G. F...Concertos for organ or harpsichord.

Harris, R. .....Concerto for piano, clarinet, and quartet.

Haydn, J.......Concertos, F, G, D.

Heerman, H....Concerto for cembalo and small orchestra.

Henselt, A. ....Concerto, Fm.

Hindemith, P...Concerto with a small group, Op. 36, No. 1.
Concerted music for piano, brass, and harp (Concerto No. 2).

Hinton, A......Concerto, Op. 24.

Holbrooke, J. ..Poem-Concerto, "Gwym-ap-nudd."

Honegger, A....Concertino.

Howells, H.....Concerto.

Hummel, J. N..Concertos, Am, Bm, A♭, etc.

Huss, H. H.....Concerto.

Indy, V. d' ....Piano part in the *Mountain Symphony.*

Ireland, J. ....Concerto, E♭.

Jacob, G.......Concerto, with strings.

Juon, P........Triple Concerto, for piano, violin, cello.

Kaun, H.......Concerto, Op. 50.

Křenek, E......Concerto, Op. 18.

Kronke, E......Symphonic Variations on a Northern Theme, for two pianos.

Liapounov, S...Concertos, Op. 4 and 38.
Ukrainian Rhapsody, Op. 28.

Liszt-Busoni ...Spanish Rhapsody.

Liszt, F........Concertos, E♭, A.
Concerto pathétique, in various forms.
Dance of Death ("Dies irae").
Fantasia on Themes from Beethoven's *Ruins of Athens.*
Malediction, for piano and strings.

Loeffler, C. M..Pagan Poem, with obbligato English horn and three trumpets.

MacDowell, E..Concertos, Dm, Am.

Mackenzie, A...Scottish Concerto.

Malipiero, G...Variazioni senza tema.

Markevitsch, I..Concerto.
Partita.

Martucci, G....Concerto.

Mason, D. G...Prelude and Fugue.

Medtner, N....Concerto No. 1, Cm.
Concerto No. 2.

Mendelssohn, F.Concertos, Gm, Dm.
Capriccio brillant, Op. 22.
Serenade, and Allegro giojoso, Op. 43.

Migot, G. .....Suite.

Milhaud, D....Suite.

Moscheles, I....Concertos Op. 58, 87, 90, etc.
Gesellschaftskoncert, Op. 45, with small orchestra.

Moszkowski, M.Concerto, E, Op. 59.

204

Mozart, W. A... Concertos (28) for one, two, and three pianos.

Napravnik, E... Concerto symphonique.
Fantaisie russe.

Novaček, O. ... Concerto eroico.

Oldberg, A. ... Concerto.

Ornstein, L. ... Concerto.

Paderewsky, I. J. Concerto, Am.
Fantaisie Polonaise.

Pick-Mangia-
galli, R. ... Sortilegi.

Pierné, G. ... Concerto.

Pirani, E. ... Scene veneziane.

Poulenc, F. ... Concert champêtre.

Powell, J. ... Rhapsodie nègre.

Prokofiev, S. ... Concertos (5).

Rachmaninoff, S. Concertos (4).

Raff, J. ... Concerto.

Ravel, M. ... Concerto for the Left Hand. (Unpublished, performed 1933.)

Reger, M. ... Variations and Fugue on a Theme of Bach (arranged by Pillney).
Concerto, Fm.

Reinecke, C. ... Concertos, F♯m, Em.

Respighi, O. ... Concerto in the Mixolydian Mode.

Rhené-Baton ... Variations on a Theme in the Aeolian Mode.

Rieti, V. ... Concerto.

Rimski-
Korsakov, N. Concerto, C♯m.

Rózycki, L. ... Concerto.
Ballade.

Rubinstein, A... Concertos (5).
Caprice russe.
Concertstück.

Saint-Saëns, C.. Concertos (5).
Africa.
Wedding Cake.
Rhapsodie d'Auvergne.
Carnival of Animals, with small orchestra.

Sauer, E. ... Concertos (2).

Schelling, E. ... Suite fantastique.
Episodes de la vie d'un artiste.

Schubert-Liszt . Wanderer Fantasia.

Schumann, R... Concerto, Am.
Introduction and Allegro, Op. 92.
Introduction and Allegro, Op. 134.

Scott, C. ... Concerto.

Scriabin, A. ... Concerto, Op. 20.
A piano part in the "Prometheus."

Sinding, C. ... Concerto, D♭.

Sorabji, K. ... Concertos (2).

Sowerby, L. ... Ballade, for two pianos, "King Esthmere."

Stanford, C. ... Variations on "Down Among the Dead Men."

Sterndale-Ben-
nett, W. ... Concertos (4).

Strauss, R. ... Burleske.

Tansman, A. ... Concertos (2).
Concertino.
Symphonie Concertante, for piano, quartet, and orchestra.
Suite, for two pianos.

Tchaikovsky, P.. Concertos (3).
Fantaisie, Gm.
Andante and Finale.

Tcherepnin, A.. Concerto, F.

Weber, C. M... Concertos (2).
Concertstück, Fm.

205

Weber-Liszt ... Polacca, Op. 72.
Wessel, M. .... Concerto, for piano, horn, and orchestra.
Widor, C. ..... Concerto.
Fantaisie.

Zanella, A. .... Concerto.
Fantasia e fugato sinfonico.
See also I. Philipp, Favorite Movements of Piano Concertos Arranged for Piano Solo.

SONATAS
(The clavichordists are not included here.)

Albéniz, I. .... Sonatas (5).
Alkan, C. ..... Sonata.
Balakirev, M. .. Sonata.
Bax, A. .... Sonatas (3).
Beethoven, L. van Sonatas (31, and 1 for four hands).
Bowen, Y. .... Sonata.
Brahms, J. .... Sonatas (3).
Bréville, P. de .. Sonata.
Bridge, F. ..... Sonata.
Busoni, F. ..... Sonatinas (6).
Cadman, C. ... Sonata.
Campbell-
  Tipton, L. .. Sonata.
Chavez, C. .... Sonata.
Chopin, F. .... Sonatas (3).
Citkowitz, I. ... Sonatina.
Clementi, M. .. Sonatas (64).
Dobroven, I. ... Sonata.
Dussek, J. L. ... Sonatas (especially Op. 61, 70, 77).
Elwell, H. ..... Sonata.
Glazunov, A. .. Sonatas (2).
Godard, B. .... Sonatas.
Godowsky, L. .. Sonata.
Griffes, C. .... Sonata.
Griffis, E. ..... Sonata.
Harris, R. ..... Sonata.
Haydn, J. ..... Sonatas (34).
Hummel, J. N.. Sonata Op. 81.
Indy, V. d' .... Sonata.
Ireland, J. .... Sonata.
Ives, C. .... Concord Sonata.
Jensen, A. ..... Sonata.
Korngold, E. .. Sonatas (3).
Lekeu, G. ..... Sonata.

Liapounov, S... Sonata.
Liszt, F. ...... Sonata, Bm.
Longo, A. ..... Sonata.
MacDowell, E.. Sonatas (4).
MacFayden, A.. Sonata.
Medtner, N. .. Sonatas (9).
Miessner, O. .. Sonata.
Mozart, W. A.. Sonatas (18, 4 for four hands, 1 for two pianos).
Niemann, W. .. Sonatas (3).
Prokofiev, S. .. Sonatas (5).
Rachmaninoff, S. Sonatas (2).
Ravel, M. ..... Sonatina.
Reger, M. .... Sonatinas, Op. 23.
Röntgen, J. ... Sonata.
Roussel, A. .... Sonata.
Rubinstein, A.. Sonatas (4, 1 for four hands).
Schubert, F. ... Sonatas (10).
Schumann, R.. Sonatas (3).
Scott, C. ...... Sonata.
Scriabin, A. ... Sonatas (10).
Sessions, R. ... Sonata.
Shepherd, A. .. Sonatas (2).
Sinding, C. .... Sonata.
Sorabji, K. .... Sonatas (2).
Sterndale-
  Bennett, W.. Sonatas.
Stockhoff, W. .. Sonata.
Strauss, R. .... Sonata.
Stravinski, I. ... Sonata.
Szymanowski, K. Sonatas (3).
Tchaikovsky, P.. Sonatas (2).
Tcherepnin, A.. Sonata.
Weber, C. von. Sonatas (4).
Weiss, A. ..... Sonata.

PIECES FOR TWO PIANOS

Arensky, A.   Suites Op. 15, 23, 33, 62, 65.

Bach, C. P. E...Concertos.

Bach, J. S.....Concerto.

Bax, A. ....The Devil Tempted St. Anthony.
The Poisoned Fountain.
Moy Mell.

Beach, H. .....Suite Founded on Irish Melodies

Beecher, C. ....The Jester.

Brahms, J. ....Variations on a Theme of Haydn, Op. 56b.
Sonata, after the quintet.
Waltzes, Op. 39 (originally for four hands, but may be had for two pianos).

Brahms-Maier...Six Liebeslieder Walzer, two sets from Op. 52.

Busoni, F. .....Duettino concertante.
Improvisation on a Chorallied.
Rondo concertante, on a Mozart concerto.

Chabrier, E. ...España Rhapsody.

Chopin, F. ....Rondo, C, posthumous.

Chopin-Maier .Two Études, Gb.
Étude, Fm.

Clementi, M. ..Sonatas.

Friedman, I. ..Suite, in three parts, Op. 70.

Glière, R. .....Six Pieces, Op. 26.

Godowsky, L. ..Invitation to the Dance, Weber, with an obbligato third piano.

Gouvy, T. ....."Lilliburlero" Variations.
Fantaisie, Op. 69.

Grainger, P. ...."Blithe Bells," Ramble on an Aria of Bach, "Sheep May Graze in Safety."

Grieg, E. .....Romance and Variations, Op. 51.
A second piano part to four of the sonatas of Mozart.

Handel, G. F...Four Concerti grossi.

Hill, E. B......Jazz Study.

Hodge, H. ....Omens.

Infante, M. ....Danses andalouses.

Liszt, F. ......Concerto pathétique.
Reminiscences of "Don Giovanni" (published simultaneously with the two-hand version).

Mason, D. G...Divertimento.

Moscheles, I. ..Hommage à Handel.

Mozart, W. A...Concerto, Eb.
Sonata, D.
Fugue.

O'Neill, N. ....Variations and Fugue on an Irish Tune (Schott).

Rachmaninoff, S.Suites Op. 7, 17.

Raff, J. ....Chaconne, Am, Op. 150.

Reger, M. ....Variations and Fugue on a Beethoven Theme, Op. 86.
Introduction, Passacaglia, and Fugue, Op. 96.
Transcription from Wagner's *Walküre* and *Tristan*.

Reger-Rheinberger ......Goldberg Variations of Bach (selected by Reger), arranged for two pianos by Rheinberger.

Reinecke, C. . . La Belle Griselidis, Impromptu on a Seventeenth Century French Melody.

Bilder aus dem Süden.

Impromptu on a Theme from Schumann's "Manfred."

Röntgen, J. . . . Ballade on a Norwegian Melody.

Rubinstein, A. . Fantasia, Fm, Op. 73.

Rudorff, E. . . . Variations, Op. 1.

Saint-Saëns, C. . Polonaise, Op. 77.

Scherzo, Op. 87.

Variations on a Beethoven Theme, Op. 35.

Schmid, H. K. . . Paraphrase on a Theme of Liszt.

Schmitt, F. . . . . Three Rhapsodies, French, Polish, Viennese.

Schumann, R. . . Andante and Variations, Op. 46.

Sinding, C. . . . Variations, Op. 2.

Strauss-Schulz-Evler . . . . . Arabesques on the "Blue Danube" Waltzes, arranged for two pianos by A. Chasins.

Strong, G. . . . . An der Nixenquelle, and In der Hexenhölle.

Vuillemin, L. . . Quatre Danses: Bourrée, Gigue, Pavane, Passepied.

It may be added that both Breitkopf and Schott publish a "Bibliothek für zwei Klaviere," consisting of transcriptions. Schott's contains forty-three pieces, each piece may also be had separately.

There is a good selection of arrangements of fifty compositions for two pianos, four and eight hands, issued by F. Hofmeister. Some of the études of Chopin have been arranged for two pianos by E. Hesselberg (published by Clayton F. Summy).

CONCERT ÉTUDES

Alkan, C. . . . . . Twelve études in the major keys, Op. 35.

Twelve études in the minor keys, Op. 39.

Three études, Op. 76.

Arensky, A. . . . Four études, Op. 41.

Bartók, B. . . . . . Three études, Op. 18.

Brahms, J. . . . . Étude after Chopin's Op. 25, No. 2.

Busoni, F. . . . . . Six études, Op. 16.

Six Paganini-Liszt études transcribed.

Chopin, F. F. . . . Twenty-four études, Op. 10 and 25.

Three Nouvelle études.

Debussy, C. . . . Twelve études.

Delafosse, L. . . . Twelve Études de concert.

Dohnányi, E. . . Six études, Op. 28.

Godard, B. . . . . Twelve Études artistiques, Op. 42.

Twelve Nouvelles études, Op. 107.

Godowsky, L. . . Transcriptions of the études of Chopin, chiefly for the left hand.

Goossens, E. . . . Concert Study, Op. 10.

Two études.

Grovlez, G. . . . . Two études — Naiades; Kobolds.

Henselt, A. . . . . Twelve Characteristic Études, Op. 2.

Twelve Études de salon, Op. 5.

Holbrooke, J. . . Ten Rhapsody-études.

Huber, H. . . . . . Études.

Jensen, A. . . . . . Twenty-five études, Op. 32.

Liadov, A. . . . . . Études, Op. 5, 12, 37, 40, 48.

Liapounov, S. . . . Twelve études d' exécution transcendante, Op. 11.

Liszt, F. . . . . Twelve études d' exécution transcendante.

Six études after Paganini.

Waldesrauschen, and Gnomenreigen.

Three concert études.

Ab-Irato.

MacDowell, E. . Étude de concert, F♯, Op. 36.

Twelve études for technique and style, Op. 39.

Twelve virtuoso études, Op. 46.

Moszkowsky, M. Three concert études, Op. 24.

Two concert études, Op. 48.

Prokofiev, S. . . . Four études, Op. 2.

Rachmaninoff, S.Nine Études-Tableaux, Op. 35.

Nine Études-Tableaux, Op. 39.

Roslavetz, N. . . Three Études.

Rubinstein, A. . Six Études, Op. 23.

Six Études, Op. 81.

Étude on "wrong notes."

Saint-Saëns, C. . Six Études, Op. 52.

Six Études, Op. 111.

Six Études for the Left Hand Alone, Op. 135.

Schloezer, B. de. Étude, A♭.

Schumann, R. . . Études after Paganini, Op. 3 and 10.

Études symphoniques, Op. 13.

Scott, C. . . . . . . Two études.

Scriabin, A. . . . . Twelve études, Op. 8.

Eight études, Op. 42.

Three études, Op. 65.

Seeling, H. . . . . Twelve concert études.

Séverac, D. de . . Cerdaña, five études pittoresques.

Sinding, C. . . . . Five Études, Op. 58.

Stravinski, I. . . . Four concert études.

Szymanowski, K.Four Études, Op. 4.

Twelve Études, Op. 33.

Tansman, A. . . . Three Études transcendantes.

Tausig, C. . . . . . Two Études de concert, Op. 1.

Tcherepnin, A. . Six études.

Toch, E. . . . . . . Études, Op. 55, 56, 57, 58, 59.

PIECES FOR CHILDREN AND YOUNG PEOPLE

Achron, J. . . . . . Children's Suite, Op. 57, twenty pieces (U.E.).

Akimenko, F. . . Six pieces, "Ukrainiennes" (R.L.).

Albéniz, I. . . . . . Yvonne en visite (R.L.).

Album for the
Young . . . . . Four volumes (Steingr.).

Album pour enfants, petits et grands . . . A collection written for the purpose of introducing modern music to young people, by twenty-two French writers (Chest.).

At the Court of Queen Anne, twenty pieces (Chest.).

Arensky, A. . . . . Six Pieces (four hands. *The Cuckoo).

Bartók, B. . . . . Eighty-five Little Pieces Without Octaves (U.E.).
Ten easy pieces (U.E.).
A Gyermekeknek, forty-two pieces for children (U.E.).

Bossi, M. E. . . . Iridescenza (Ric.).
Album pour la jeunesse (Carisch).
Juvenilia (Ric.).
Miniatures (Carisch).

Bréville, P. de . . Album pour enfants (R.L.).

Bridge, F. . . . . . Three Miniatures pastorales.

Casella, A. . . . . Eleven Pieces for Children (U.E.).

Franck, C. . . . . . Lament for the Doll (Schirm.).

Glière, R. . . . . . Twelve Children's Pieces, Op. 31.
Twenty-four Characteristic Pieces for Young People, Op. 34.

Goossens, E. . . . Kaleidoscope, Album of twelve pieces (Chest.).

Gretchaninov, A. Das Kinderbuch, Op. 92.

Grovlez, G. . . . . A Child's Garden, six easy pieces (Chest.).

Handel, G. F. . . Fourteen Easy Original Pieces (Schott).

Haydn, J. . . . . . Album, Thirty-three Pieces for Small Hands (Aug.).

Holbrooke, J. . . . Three Bagatelles (W. Rogers).
Piano Album (W.R.).

Indy, V. d' . . . . Pour les enfants de tout age, twenty-four pieces selected from various composers, from Couperin to Debussy, and also including German writers (R.L.).

Inghelbrecht, D. Le Nursery (Mathot).

Ireland, J. . . . . . Leaves from a Child's Sketchbook (W. Rogers).

Jensen, A. . . . . . Wanderbilder, Op. 17 (* "The Mill." Peters).

Křicka, J. . . . . . Suite of Puppet Dances, Op. 45 (Hudebni Matice, Prague).

Liadov, A. . . . . . Petite valse, Op. 26 (Belaiev).

Library for the Young . . . . . Leichte Stücke (easy pieces), by Bach, Beethoven, Handel, Mendelssohn, Reinecke, Schubert, Wagner (each composer a volume. Breit.).

MacDowell, E. . Twelve Études, Op. 39 (Breit.).

Master Series for the Young . . Twelve volumes (Schirm.).

Mendelssohn, F. Children's Pieces, Op. 72.

Niemann, W. . . Was den Kindern Freude macht, Op. 58 (Kahnt).

Novák, V. . . . . . Jeunesse, Op. 55 (2 vols. of ten and twelve pieces respectively. Chest.).

Ornstein, L. . . . Seeing Russia with Teacher (Schirm.).

Ravel, M. .....Ma Mère l'oie ("Mother Goose"), five pieces (four hands. Durand).
Les Étrennes de Noël.

Rebikov, W. ...Sredinikh ("Among Themselves"), five pieces in the whole-tone scales. Les Démons s'amusent, etc.

Reinecke, C. ...Hausmusik, Op. 77.
Three Sonatinas, Op. 98 (also for four hands).
Ein neues Notenbuch, Op. 107.
Six Very Easy Sonatinas, Op. 127a.
Fairy Tales, Op. 147.
Musical Kindergarten, Op. 206 (9 vols.).
Unsere Lieblinge (a collection of popular melodies arranged very simply. Senff; Siegel; Breit.).

Ropartz, G. ....Ten Petites pièces (four hands. R.L.).

Samazeuilh, G..Chanson à ma poupée.

Schumann, R. ..Scenes from Childhood, Op. 15.
Album for the Young, Op. 68.
Twelve Pieces, Op. 85. (four hands).
The Christmas Ball, Op. 130 (four hands).

Scott, C. ......Modern Finger Exercises, very easy exercises based on the whole-tone scale (Ric.).

Sévérac, D. de..En vacances, ten pieces (2 vols. R.L.).

Siloti, A. ......Nineteen Easy Transcriptions for the Young (Gutheil).

Šín, O. ....Les Vacances, ten pieces.
De l'aube au crépuscule.

Smetana, F. ...Trésor des mélodies.

Stravinski, I. ...Five-finger Exercises.
Three Pieces with an Easy Bass Part.
Three Pieces with an Easy Treble Part.
(All Chest.)

Tarenghi, M. Pages intimes, ten pieces (2 vols.).
Nuovo album per la gioventù, twelve pieces (2 vols.).
Piccole scene d'infanzia, six pieces.
Impressions et sentiments.
(All Carisch)
Bozzetti dal vero, Op. 71 (four hands).
Album de petits morceaux, Op. 41.
Suite of Three Pieces.
(All Ric.).

Tchaikovsky, P..Children's Album, Op. 39, twenty-four easy pieces.
Twelve Pieces, Op. 40.

Two Collections edited by
Rehberg ....Six Viennese Sonatinas of Mozart (Schott).
From Bach to Beethoven, a collection of eighteen easy pieces (2 vols. Schott).

Voormolen, A. ..Le Livre des enfants, twelve little pieces.

Appendix to the List for Young People

A list of volumes published by Breitkopf containing collections of more or less easy compositions, not all of them originally written for piano.

Abendmusik ("Evening
Music") . . . . A collection of eight old dances, easy.

Alte Meister . . . . A collection of valuable pieces of the seventeenth and eight-eenth centuries. Sixty pieces (3 vols.).

Cesi, B. . . . . Musica antica italiana. A collection of six pieces of medium difficulty.

FitzWilliam Virginal
Book . . . . A selection of twenty-one pieces (2 vols.) of medium difficulty.

Handel, G. F. . . . . Easy Pieces.

Israel, K. . . . . A collection of German, Swedish, Breton, Portugese, Hungarian, and other national melodies, easy.

Klassiker, Der junge . . . . . A collection of pieces of easy and somewhat more advanced grades of difficulty in chronological order (4 vols.), arranged by E. Pauer.

March Album . . . . Forty celebrated marches, German, French, and Italian, from Lully to Beethoven, medium difficulty.

Mazurka Album . . . . A collection of thirty-six mazurkas, of medium difficulty.

Neue Meister . . . . A collection of pieces chosen from the works of the less-known composers of the nineteenth century, of medium difficulty.

Riemann, H. . . . . Rococo, a collection of old dances by contemporaries of J. S. Bach (easy).

Sonntags-Musik . . . . A collection in three volumes of one hundred pieces selected from celebrated church music and other serious music, partly arranged by E. Pauer.

Unsere Lieblinge, ("Our
Favorites") . . . . "The Most Beautiful Melodies of Former Times and Today," arranged by Carl Reinecke (4 vols.), very easy.

Unsere Meister . . . . A gigantic collection in two series of celebrated German composers. The two series (49 vols.) devote a volume to each single composer. Medium difficulty.

FIRST SERIES

1. J. S. Bach	7. F. Schubert
2. G. F. Handel	8. F. Mendelssohn
3. J. Haydn	9. F. Chopin
4. W. A. Mozart	10. R. Schumann
5. L. van Beethoven	11. J. S. Bach
6. C. M. von Weber	12. G. F. Handel

13. J. Haydn	29. F. Liszt
14. W. A. Mozart	30. A. Corelli
15. L. van Beethoven	31. M. Haydn
16. C. M. von Weber	32. L. Cherubini
17. F. Schubert	33. R. Wagner
18. F. Mendelssohn	34. F. Couperin
19. F. Chopin	35. S. Thalberg
20. R. Schumann	36. C. Reinecke
21. C. W. Gluck	37. R. Wagner
22. S. Heller	38. C. Loewe
23. N. W. Gade	39. S. Jadassohn
24. J. B. Cramer	40. J. Raff
25. A. Henselt	41. A. Lortzing
26. A. Rubinstein	42. H. Marschner
27. S. Heller	43. H. Hofmann
28. G. Meyerbeer	

SECOND SERIES

1. G. Bizet	4. T. Kirchner
2. P. Tchaikovsky	5. A. Jensen
3. J. Sibelius	6. J. Offenbach

Alte Tänze . . . . A collection of German, French, and Italian gavottes.

Bibliothek für den musi-
calischen Unterricht

("Library of Teaching
Pieces") . . . . A collection for four hands (3 vols. and an elementary volume, medium difficulty).

Classical and modern
pianoforte music . . . . . A collection (6 vols.).

Deutsche Tänze . . . . A collection of twenty-five pieces, Landlers and Valses, thirty-eight pieces (2 vols.).

Jugendbibliothek
("Library for Young
People") . . . . A collection (8 vols.). Vols. 1, 3, 5, and 6, classics; Vols. 2, 4, 7, and 8, romantics (all fairly easy; four hands).

Music at the
Prussian Court . . . . A collection of the music played at a fancy dress ball in Berlin, Feb. 27, 1897 (7 vols.).

Music at the
Saxon Court . . . . A collection, some of which was written by members of the royal house (10 vols.).

213

Perles musicales ....A collection of short pieces of all times (4 vols.).

Piano Music, classic and
    modern ....A good collection (4 vols.), ed. by Carl Reinecke (for four hands, medium difficulty).

Polish Dances ....A collection of fifty mazurkas.

Salon Music ....Twenty-five pieces each (2 vols.).

Scandinavian Folk Tunes A collection by Hartmann containing fifty pieces (2 vols.).

Tarentella Album ....A collection of ten pieces, ed. by E. Pauer (difficult).

Tuma, F. ....Album of ten arrangements of ancient music by O. Schmid.

Vortrags-Album ("Pieces
    to Play") ....A collection (12 vols.), graded in difficulty from easy to medium difficulty, ed. by E. Pauer.

THE PROGRAMS GIVEN BY ANTON RUBINSTEIN IN 1885-1886, DESIGNED TO EXHIBIT THE SCOPE OF THE LITERATURE OF THE PIANO

(These were probably the first historical recitals ever given.)

PROGRAM 1

William Byrd .. The Carman's Whistle.

John Bull ...... The King's Hunting Jig.

François
    Couperin ... La Ténebreuse.
        Le Réveil-matin.
        La Favorite.
        Le Bavolet flottante.
        La Bandoline.

Jean P.
    Rameau .... Le Rappel des oiseaux.
        La Poule.
        Gavotte and Variations.

Domenico
    Scarlatti .... Cat's Fugue, Sonata, A.

J. S. Bach ..... Preludes and Fugues in Cm and D (*Well-tempered Clavichord*).
        Chromatic Fantasia and Fugue.
        Gigue in B♭.
        Sarabande.
        Gavotte.

Georg F.
    Handel ..... Fugue, Em.
        The Harmonious Blacksmith.
        Sarabande and Passacaglia, from Gm Suite.
        Gigue, from Suite in A.
        Lied with Variations.

Carl P. E. Bach. Rondo, Bm.
        La Xenophon.
        Sybille.
        Les Langueurs tendres.
        La Complaisante.

Joseph Haydn .. Theme and Variations, Fm.

Wolfgang A.
    Mozart ..... Fantasia in Cm.
        Gigue in G.
        Rondo.

PROGRAM 2

Ludwig van
    Beethoven .. Eight Sonatas:
        Op. 27, No. 2.
        Op. 31, No. 2.
        Op. 53.

        Op. 57.
        Op. 90.
        Op. 101.
        Op. 111.

PROGRAM 3

Franz Schubert. Fantasia in C ("Wanderer").
        Moments musicales, Nos. 1-6.
        Minuet, Bm.
        Impromptus, Cm and E♭.

Carl Maria
    von Weber .. Sonata, A♭.
        Momento capriccioso.
        Invitation to the Dance.
        Polacca brillant, E.

Felix
  Mendelssohn. Variations sérieuses.
          Capriccio in E♭m.

Ten Songs Without
    Words.
Presto and Capriccio.

PROGRAM 4

Robert
  Schumann .. Fantasia, Op. 17.
          Kreisleriana, Nos. 1-8.
          Études symphoniques.
          Sonata, F♯m.
          Fantasiestücke, Op. 12.
          Des Abends.

In der Nacht.
Traumeswirren.
Warum?
Vogel als Prophet.
Romanza, B♭m.
Carnaval, Op. 9.

PROGRAM 5

Muzio Clementi. Sonata, B♭, with the
          Toccata for closing
          movement.
John Field .... Three Nocturnes, E♭, A,
          and B♭.
Ignaz
  Moscheles .. Études caractéristiques.
          Reconciliation.
          Juno.
          Conte d'enfant.
Adolf Henselt .. Poème d'amour.
          Berceuse.
          Liebeslied.
          La Fontaine.
          "If I Were a Bird."
Sigismund
  Thalberg ... Étude, Am.
          Fantasia on "Don
          Juan."

Franz Liszt .... Étude, D♭.
          Valse caprice.
          Consolations in E and
          D♭.
          Au bords d'une source.
          Rhapsodies hongroises,
          Nos. 6 and 12.
          Soirées musicales (after
          Rossini).
          La Gita in gondola.
          La Danza.
          La Regatta.
          Transcriptions of Schu-
          bert's Songs:
          Auf dem Wasser zu
          singen.
          Ständchen.
          The Erlking.
          Soirée de Vienne in A.
          Fantasia on "Robert,
          the Devil."

PROGRAM 6

Frédéric Chopin Fantasia, Fm.
          Preludes: Em, A, A♭,
          B♭m, D♭, Dm.
          Barcarolle.
          Waltzes: A♭ (the small
          one), Am, A♭ (the
          large one).

Impromptus: F♯, G♭.
Scherzo, Bm.
Nocturnes: D♭, G, Cm.
Mazurkas: Bm, F♯m,
    A♭, B♭m.
Ballades: Gm, F, A♭,
    Fm.

216

Sonata, B♭m.
Berceuse.

Polonaises: F♯m, Cm, A♭.

PROGRAM 7

Frédéric Chopin. Études: A♭, Fm, Cm, E♭m, E♭, Bm, A♭, C♯m, Cm.

Anton Rubin-
stein ...... Sonata in F.
Theme and Variations from Sonata in Cm.
Scherzo from sonata in Am.

Michael Glinka. Tarentella.
Barcarolle.
Souvenir de Mazurka.

Mili Balakirev.. Scherzo.
Mazurka.
Islamey.

Petr Tchaikov-
sky .... Chant sans paroles.
Valse.
Romance.
Scherzo à la russe.

César Cui ..... Scherzo-Polonaise.

Nikolai Rimski-
Korsakov ... Étude.
Novelette.
Valse.

Anatol Liadov . Étude.
Intermezzo.

Nicolas Rubin-
stein ...... Feuillet d'album.
Valse.

REFERENCES

I have divided the references into four lists. Almost the only books to concern themselves with the piano literature as a whole are those by Weitzmann, Bie, Westerby, and Niemann. The work of Prosniz, though all-inclusive up to the early years of the century, has more the nature of a catalogue, and Bonaventura is superficial and generalized. The first list therefore is short. In the second list are books dealing with details of the subject. The third has the chief dictionaries, which, it is true, deal with much more than piano literature, but offer much that is apposite. I conclude with a list of articles from music periodicals of various nations.

The periodical list is obviously open to criticism, but it will be found sufficient for most students. It deals chiefly with living people. The magazines are full of articles by composers about other composers. There is much diligent searching for "meaning" and "trends" and other subtleties. It may safely be here assumed that in his heart no composer knows whither he is trending; and this should not be construed as a reproach, for it is reasonably certain that none of the great composers of the past was consciously aware of any particularly distinct goal. New men are often feverishly written up before they have really shown their mettle, and one is bidden to worship some new god whose feet subsequently turn out to be of clay. To learn of new men one turns to the periodicals, which publish reviews of their work. To the American who wishes to keep abreast of the times the following may be recommended: *The Musical Quarterly* (New York: Schirmer), *The Chesterian* (London: Chester), *La Revue musicale* (ed. by Henri Prunière, Paris), and *Acta musicologica* (Bâle). The reader will run across the Italian periodicals during his reading of the list, but they are not given here because few people cultivate a knowledge of Italian. The first two named above will probably suffice for most students.

BOOKS DEALING WITH PIANO LITERATURE AS A WHOLE

Bie, Oskar
   Das Klavier und seine Meister. Munich: Bruckmann, 1901.
      This book has many interesting illustrations and is a classic. An edition has been translated: History of the Pianoforte and Pianoforte Players (New York: Dutton, 1899).

Bonaventura, Arnaldo
  Storia e letteratura del pianoforte. Livorno: Giusti, 1925.

Fillmore, John C.
  Pianoforte Music. Philadelphia: Presser.

Hamilton, Clarence
  Piano Music, Its Composers and Characteristics. Boston: Ditson, 1925.

Hofmeister, Friedrich
  Handbuch der musikalischen Literatur. Leipzig: Hofmeister, 1844—.

Krehbiel, Henry E.
  The Pianoforte and Its Music. New York: Scribners, 1911.

Niemann, Walter
  Das Klavierbuch, Geschichte der Klaviermusik und ihre Meister, des Klavierbaues, und der Klavierliteratur. Leipzig: Kahnt, 1907.

Perry, Edward B.
  Descriptive Analyses of Piano Works. Philadelphia: Presser, 1902.

Prosniz, Adolf
  Handbuch der Klavierliteratur. Wien: L. Doblinger, 1904. 2 vols.

Ruthardt, Adolf
  Wegweiser durch die Klavierliteratur. Zürich: Geb. Hug, 1914.

Schneider, K. E.
  Musik, Klavier und Klavierspiel. Leipzig: Leuckart, 1872.

Villani, Luigi
  L'Arte del clavicembalo. Torino: Fratelli Bocca, 1901.

Weitzmann, Karl F.
  A History of Pianoforte Playing and Pianoforte Literature. New York: Schirmer, 1893.

BOOKS DEALING WITH COMPOSERS AND COMPOSITIONS

Ceillier, Laurent
  Roger-Ducasse, le musicien—l'oeuvre. Paris: Durand, 1920.

Corder, H.
  Liszt. New York: Harpers, 1925.

Cortot, Alfred
  The Piano Music of Claude Debussy. London: Chester, 1922.
  French Piano Music. London: Oxford Univ. Press, 1932.

Cowell, Henry (Ed.)
  American Composers on American Music. Stanford University, Calif.: Stanford Univ. Press, 1933.
    This book is not confined to piano music.

Fellowes, Edmund H.
  Orlando Gibbons, a Short Account of His Work. London: Oxford Univ. Press, 1925.
  William Byrd, a Short Account of His Life. London: Oxford Univ. Press, 1923.

Finck, Henry T.
    Edvard Grieg. London: Lane, 1909.

Gilman, Lawrence
    Phases of Modern Music. New York: Harper, 1904.

Glyn, Margaret H.
    About Elizabethan Virginal Music and Its Composers. London: Reeves, 1924.

Hull, Arthur E.
    Alexander Scriabin, Russian Tone Poet. New York: Dutton, 1920.
    Cyril Scott. Boston Music Co., 1918.

Huneker, James G.
    Chopin, the Man and His Music. New York: Scribner, 1900.
        This is a model of what writing about music should be. Every piece of the com-
        poser is intelligently and interestingly discussed.
    Liszt. New York: Scribner, 1911.
    Mezzotints, Studies of Chopin, Brahms, Liszt. New York: Scribner, 1900.

Kleczyński, Jan
    Chopin's Greater Works. London: Reeves, 1896.

Leichtentritt, Hugo
    Analyse der Chopinschen Werke. Berlin, 1921.
    Busoni. Leipzig, 1916.

Manuel, Roland
    Maurice Ravel et son oeuvre. Paris, 1914.

Mason, Daniel G.
    Beethoven and His Forerunners. New York: Macmillan, 1930.
    The Romantic Composers. New York: Macmillan, 1906.
        Essays on Schubert, Schumann, Mendelssohn, Chopin, Berlioz, and Liszt.
    From Grieg to Brahms. New York: Outlook Co., 1902.
        This book includes essays on Grieg, Dvořák, Saint-Saëns, Franck, Tchaikovsky,
        and Brahms.

May, Florence
    The Life of Johannes Brahms. London: E. Arnold, 1905. 2 vols.
        This book is mentioned here because it was written by a piano pupil of Brahms
        and is interesting to pianists. The first volume is delightful.

Paribeni, Giulio C.
    Muzio Clementi nella vita e nell'arte. Milan: Podrecca, 1921.
        Contains a Clementi bibliography.

Perrachio, Luigi
    L'Opera pianistica de Claude Debussy. Milan: Bottega di poesia, 1924.

Pourtalès, Guy de
    Franz Liszt. New York: Henry Holt, 1926.
        This book gives little space to the piano pieces, but it interprets Liszt in a way
        to make his value clear to the student.

Riemann, Hugo
    Analysis of J. S. Bach's the Wohltemperirtes Clavier. London: Augener, 1900—.

Rosenfeld, Paul
    Musical Chronicle. New York: Harcourt Brace, 1923.
        Contains articles on the "Six," Satie, Cyril Scott, Franck, Casella, Szymanowski, Carpenter, Pizzetti, Malipiero, etc.

Samazeuilh, Gustav
    Paul Dukas. Paris, 1913.

Schumann, Robert
    Music and Musicians. London: Reeves, 1880.
        In this book there are many interesting first notices of music that is famous today.

Selden-Goth, G.
    Ferrucio Busoni. Vienna: E. P. Thal, 1922.

Sérieyx, Auguste
    Vincent d'Indy. Paris: Meissein, 1914.

Vuillemin, Louis
    Albert Roussel et son oeuvre. Paris, 1924.
    Gabriel Fauré et son oeuvre. Paris, 1914.

Westerby, Herbert
    How to Study the Pianoforte Works of the Great Composers. London: Reeves.

Miniature Essays. London: Chester.

The footnotes to the Beethoven sonatas in the various editions.

DICTIONARIES OF MUSIC

Grove's Dictionary of Music and Musicians. 3rd ed. by H. C. Colles. New York: Macmillan, 1927.
Cyclopedic Dictionary of Music. Dunstan's 4th ed. London: Curwen, 1925.
A Dictionary of Modern Music and Musicians. Ed. by A. E. Hull. London, 1924.
Biographical Dictionary of Musicians. 3rd ed. by A. Remy. New York, 1919.
Musik-Lexicon. Ed. by Hugo Riemann, 9th ed. by Einstein. Berlin, 1919.
Dizionario dei musicisti. Ed. by A. de Angelis. Rome, 1922.
Encyclopédie de la musique et dictionnaire du conservatoire. Ed. by Albert Lavignac. Paris.

ARTICLES

Subject

Albéniz, Isaac . . . . Grew, Sidney. The Music for Pianoforte of Albéniz. Chest., 6 (Nov., 1924), 43-48.

Alkan, C. V. . . . . Bellamann, H. H. The Works of C. V. Alkan. Mus. Quart., 10 (1924), No. 2, 251-62.

Auric, Georges ....Roussel, Albert. Young French Composers. Chest., 1 (Oct., 1919), 34-35.

Schloezer, Boris de. Georges Auric. Rev. Musicale, 7 (Jan., 1926), No. 3, 1-21.

Bantock, G. ....Antcliffe, Herbert. A Brief Survey of the Works of Granville Bantock. Mus. Quart., 4 (1918), No. 3, 117-27.

Bartók, Bela ....Henry, Leigh. Bela Bartok. Chest., 3 (Apr., 1922), 161-67.

Calvocoressi. Bela Bartok. Il Pianoforte, Apr., 1922.

Bax, A. ....Blom, Eric. Arnold Bax. Chest., 1 (Feb., 1920), 136-39.

Evans, Edwin. Arnold Bax. Mus. Quart., 9 (1923), No. 2, 167-80.

Belaiev, V. M. ....Nathan, M. Montagu. Belaiev—Maecenas of Russian Music. Mus. Quart., 4 (1918), No. 3, 450-65.

Berners, Lord ....Goossens, Eugène. Lord Berners. Chest., 1 (Dec., 1919), 65-68.

Bliss, A. ....Goossens, Eugène. Arthur Bliss. Chest., 2 (June, 1921), 481-86.

Bloch, E. ....Gatti, Guido. Ernest Bloch. La Critica musicale, Jan., 1920.

Bridge, F. ....Antcliffe, Herbert. Frank Bridge. The Sackbut, 5 (May, 1925), 286-88.

Busoni, F. ....Leichtentritt, Hugo. Ferrucio Busoni as a Composer. Mus. Quart., 3 (1917), No. 1, 69-79.

Prunières, Henri. Ferrucio Busoni. Il Pianoforte, June, 1921.

Liuzzi, Fernando. Ferrucio Busoni. L'Esame, 3 (July-Aug., 1924), 484-92.

Gatti, Guido. In memoria di Ferrucio Busoni. Revista musicale italiana, 31 (Dec., 1924), Fasc. 4, 565-80.

Cadman, C. W. ......Porte, John F. Charles Wakefield Cadman, An American Nationalist. Chest., 5 (May, 1924), 223-26.

Casella, A. ....Gatti, Guido. Alfredo Casella. Mus. Quart., 6 (1920), No. 1, 171-91.

Castelnuovo-
    Tedesco, M. ....Rossi-Doria, Gastone. Mario Castelnuovo-Tedesco. Chest., 7 (Jan.-Feb., 1926), 114-19.

Gatti, Guido. Castelnuovo-Tedesco. La Critica italiana, July, 1919.

Chausson, E. ....Lavauden, Thérèse. Ernest Chausson. Chest., 8 (June, 1927), 231-34.

Various writers. Ernest Chausson. Rev. musicale, 7 (Dec., 1925), numero special, 99-219.

Chopin, F. ....Huneker, James. The Classic Chopin. Mus. Quart., 1 (1915), No. 4, 519-25.

Clementi, M. . . . . .Saint-Fox, Georges de. Muzio Clementi. Mus. Quart., 9 (1923), No. 3, 350-82.

Concertos . . . . .Bellamann, H. H. Of Notable Piano Concertos, Neglected and Otherwise. Mus. Quart., 7 (1921), No. 3, 399-407.

Cosyn, B. . . . . .Fuller-Maitland, J. A. Cosyn's Virginal Book. Chest., 4 (Feb., 1923), 129-32.

Debussy, C. . . . . .Gatti, Guido. The Piano Works of Claude Debussy. Mus. Quart., 7 (1921), No. 3, 418-60.

Dukas, P. . . . . .Fraser, Andrew A. Paul Dukas. Chest., 7 (July-Aug., 1926), 253-58.

Dvořák, A. . . . . .Newmarch, Rosa. Anton Dvořák. Chest., 4 (Jan., 1923), 97-100.

Falla, M. de . . . . .Thomas, Juan M. Manuel de Falla's Concerto. Chest., 8 (Dec., 1926), 92-93.

Castelnuovo-Tedesco, M. Manuel de Falla. Il Pianoforte, Jan., 1923.

Fauré, G. . . . . .Schmitt, Florent. Gabriel Fauré. Chest., 6 (Dec., 1924), 73-78.

Copland, Aaron. Gabriel Fauré, A Neglected Master. Mus. Quart., 10 (1924), No. 4, 573-86.

Various writers. Gabriel Fauré. Rev. musicale, 4 (Oct., 1922), numero special, 3-116.

Feinberg, S. . . . . .Belaiev, V. Contemporary Russian Composers. The Sackbut, 5 (June, 1925), 326-29. (Comments on Feinberg are found in this article.)

Franck, C. . . . . .Cortot, Alfred. The Piano Music of César Franck. Rev. musicale, 7 (Jan., 1926), No. 3, 22-33.

Gibbons, O. . . . . .Fuller-Maitland, J. A. Orlando Gibbons. Chest., 6 (May, 1925), 177-80.

Goossens, E. . . . . .Scott, Cyril. Eugene Goossens. Chest., 1 (Sept., 1919), 13-16.

Griffes, C. T. . . . . . . .Peterkin, Norman. Charles T. Griffes. Chest., 4 (Mar., 1923), 161-66.

Honegger, A. . . . . . . .Douël, Martial. Arthur Honegger. Chest., 8 (Nov., 1926), 37-40.

Ibert, J. . . . . .George, André. Jacques Ibert. Chest., 8 (Dec., 1926), 73-78.

Indy, V. d' . . . . .Landormy, Paul. Vincent d'Indy. Chest., 6 (July-Aug., 1925), 249-54.

Ireland, J. . . . . .Evans, Edwin. John Ireland. Mus. Quart., 5 (1919), No. 2, 213-20.

Jongen, J. . . . . .Closson, Ernest. Joseph Jongen. Chest., 5 (Dec., 1923), 69-72.

Keyboard Music . . . . .Fuller-Maitland, J. A. English Keyboard Music. Chest., 3 (Sept., 1921), 4-8.

Kodály, Z. . . . . .Bartók, Bela. Z. Kodaly. Il Pianoforte, Apr., 1922.

Korngold, E. . . . . .Fleischmann, Hugo. Erich Wolfgang Korngold. Chest., 8 (Apr., 1927), 181-84.

Lekeu, G. . . . . .Blom, Eric. If They Had Lived. Chest., 7 (Mar., 1926), 154-60.

Liadov, A. . . . . .Swan, Alfred. Liadov, the Wizard of the Russian Fairy-Tale and Folk-Song. Chest., 3 (Oct., 1921), 45-48.

Liapounov, S. . . . . . . .Newmarch, Rosa. Serge Liapounov. Chest., 6 (Jan., 1925), 116-18.

Liszt, F. . . . . .Jean-Aubry, G. The Glory of Liszt. Chest., 1 (Feb., 1920), 129-35.

Malipiero, G. F. . . . . .Prunières, Henri. G. F. Malipiero. Mus. Quart., 6 (1920), No. 3, 326-41.

Gatti, Guido. G. F. Malipiero. L'Esame, 2 (Oct., 1923), 823-31.

Medtner, N. . . . . .Swan, Alfred. Nicholas Medtner. Chest., 10 (Dec., 1928), 77-81.

Gerstlé, Henry S. The Piano Music of Nikolai Medtner. Mus. Quart., 10 (1924), No. 4, 500-510.

Riesemann, Oskar von. N. Medtner. The Sackbut, 5 (May, 1925), 302-4.

Miaskowsky, N. . . . . . .Belaiev, V. Contemporary Russian Composers. The Sackbut, 5 (May, 1925), 296-99.

Milhaud, D. . . . . .Roussel, Albert. Young French Composers. Chest., 1 (Oct., 1919), 36.

Ornstein, L. . . . . .Buchanan, Charles L. Ornstein and Modern Music. Mus. Quart., 4 (1918), No. 2, 174-83.

Pianoforte . . . . .Dent, Edward J. The Pianoforte and Its Influence on Modern Music. Mus. Quart., 2 (1916), No. 2, 271-94.

Piano Music in U.S.A.. Kramer, A. Walter. Piano Composition in the United States. Chest., 9 (Sept., 1927), 13-15.

Pizzetti, I. . . . . .Gatti Guido. I Pizzetti. L'Esame, 2 (Jan., 1923), 25-33. I Pizzetti. Il Pianoforte, Aug., 1921.

Poulenc, F. . . . . .Durey, Louis. Francis Poulenc. Chest., 4 (Sept., 1922), 1-4.

George, André. Francis Poulenc. Chest., 6 (Mar., 1925), 141-46.

Prokofiev, S. . . . . .Fraser, Andrew A. Serge Prokofiev. Chest., 10 (Apr.-May, 1929), 181-86.

Ravel, M. . . . . .Durey, Louis. Maurice Ravel. Chest., 2 (Apr., 1921), 422-26.

Roger-Ducasse, J. . . . .Swan, Alfred. Roger-Ducasse. Chest., 5 (Jan., 1924), 105-110.

Roussel, A. . . . . .Evans, Edwin. Albert Roussel. Chest., 7 (Dec., 1925), 73-78.

Russian Sonatas . . . . .Martens, Frederick H. The Modern Russian Piano Sonata. Mus. Quart., 5 (1919), No. 3, 357-63.

Saint-Saëns, C. . . . . . .Jean-Aubry, G. Camille Saint-Saëns. Chest., 3 (Jan., 1922), 97-100.

Satie, E. . . . . Chennevière, Rudhyat D. Erik Satie. Mus. Quart., 5 (1919), No. 4, 469-78.

Jean-Aubry, G. The End of a Legend. Chest., 6 (May, 1925), 191-93.

Schönberg, A. . . . . Wellesz, Egon. Schönberg and Beyond. Mus. Quart., 2 (1916), No. 1, 76-95.

Schubert, F. . . . . Green, L. Dunton. Franz Schubert's Piano Music. Chest., 10 (Nov., 1928), 60-65.

Scriabin, A. . . . . Hull, A. Eaglefield. A Survey of the Pianoforte Works of Scriabin. Mus. Quart., 2 (1916), No. 4, 601-14.

Schloezer, Boris de. Scriabin. Rev. musicale, 2 (July, 1921), No. 9, 28-46.

Antcliffe, Herbert. The Significance of Scriabin. Mus. Quart., 10 (1924), No. 3, 333-45.

Sévérac, D. . . . . Jean-Aubry, G. Déodat de Sévérac. Chest., 2 (May, 1921), 449-52.

Smetana, F. . . . . Löwenbach, Jan. Fedrich Smetana. Chest., 5 (Feb., 1924), 137-43.

Stravinski, I. . . . . Henry, Leigh. Igor Stravinsky and the Objective Direction in Contemporary Music. Chest., 1 (Jan., 1920), 97-102.

Ansermet, Ernest. Stravinsky. Rev. musicale, 2 (July, 1921), No. 9, 1-27.

Cimbro, A. Stravinsky. Il Pianoforte, Mar., 1922 (with a bibliography).

Tibi, O. Stravinsky. Il Pianoforte, Aug., 1924.

Tibi, O. Stravinsky. Ibid., Sept., 1924.

Szymanowski, K. . . . . . Jachimecki, Zlzislaw. Karol Szymanowski. Mus. Quart., 8 (1922), No. 1, 23-37.

Collins, Adrian. The Later Style of Szymanowski. Chest., 9 (Nov., 1927), 33-38.

Tailleferre, G. . . . . Roussel, A. Young French Composers. Chest., 1 (Oct., 1919), 37.

Weber, C. M. von . . . . Roussel, Albert. Weber. Chest., 3 (Feb., 1922), 135-40.

Goossens, Eugène. Weber. Chest., 7 (June, 1926), 214-19.

"Six Ecossaises," published in music supplement, Chest., 7 (June, 1926), no paging.

Beethoven, Schumann, Berlioz, Liszt, Wagner, and Debussy . . . Opinions on Weber. Chest., 7 (June, 1926), 235-38.

INDEX OF COMPOSERS